DATE DUE

AP 5'01			
MY 10'01			
NO 28 01			
AP 2'02			
MY 12 04			
JE 2 04			
DE 17 07			

the wide world of **JOHN STEINBECK**

the wide world of

BY PETER LISCA

RUTGERS UNIVERSITY PRESS

JOHN STEINBECK

NEW BRUNSWICK, NEW JERSEY, 1958

Portions of this book in progress have appeared under various titles as follows: "Motif and Pattern in *Of Mice and Men*," in *Modern Fiction Studies* (Winter, 1956–57); "*The Grapes of Wrath* as Fiction," in *PMLA* (March, 1957); "*The Wayward Bus*—A Modern Pilgrimage," "Steinbeck's Fable of the Pearl," and "John Steinbeck: A Literary Biography," in *Steinbeck and His Critics*, edited by E. W. Tedlock, Jr., and C. V. Wicker. For permission to use this material here in somewhat different form, the author is grateful to the Purdue Research Foundation, the Modern Language Association, and the University of New Mexico Press.

Permission to quote at length from two of Steinbeck's articles, "Critics, Critics Burning Bright" (*Saturday Review of Literature*, November 11, 1950) and "the novel might benefit by the discipline . . ." (*Stage*, January, 1938), has been granted by the editors of *Saturday Review* and *Theatre Arts*, respectively. The first paragraph of Ernest Hemingway's *A Farewell to Arms* is quoted through the permission of Charles Scribner's Sons. Material from Harry Slochower, *No Voice Is Wholly Lost*, copyright 1945 by Creative Age Press, is quoted by permission of the publishers, Farrar, Straus and Cudahy, Inc. The lines from Pare Lorentz, *The River*, copyright 1938 by Stackpole Sons, are quoted by permission of The Stackpole Company. Substantial quotations from Steinbeck's books are made possible through the kind permission of The Viking Press, Inc.

Quotations from letters are included here by special permission of John Steinbeck and his publishers. All rights reserved. For any reprinting or other use of the letters previously quoted by Lewis Gannett in his Introduction to *The Portable Steinbeck* (1946), as cited in the Notes, formal authorization must be obtained from The Viking Press, Inc., 625 Madison Avenue, New York 22; for use of other letters, from Mr. Steinbeck's representatives, McIntosh & Otis, Inc., 18 East 41st Street, New York 17.

for Dorothy
and for Pat

PREFACE

Although John Steinbeck has over a period of almost thirty years written sixteen volumes of fiction, and although he is generally recognized as one of America's major living novelists, there has not yet appeared a full-length study of his work. In an age of criticism such as ours this is a curious situation, and the reasons for this situation are explored in detail in the first chapter of this book.

Because Steinbeck has been subject to so little critical attention, and because that attention has usually focused on the "social message" of his fiction (two facts intimately related), this book attends particularly to the relatively unexplored aspect of his craftsmanship. Steinbeck's novels and short stories are taken up in their chronological order and examined for techniques employed, as well as for the content achieved by those techniques. Concurrently, an attempt is made to relate these two aspects of the work under discussion to those of preceding and subsequent works. Thus the analysis of individual works provides also a history of Steinbeck's artistic development. No attempt is made to force his work into chapters having preconceived "themes," and the particular critical strategy or strategies used are dictated by the nature of the individual work itself. As much pertinent material from Steinbeck's letters and manuscripts and as much biographical information as feasible have been included so that where errors in their interpretation are made these may be corrected by others.

Because of the frequency with which Steinbeck's books are quoted, it has been found impractical to provide each of these references with a footnote. When the source is the book which is the main subject of the chapter in which the reference appears, the source is made clear in the context. In other cases, an abbreviated identification is provided. *In Dubious Battle*, for example, is represented by IDB; *Sea of Cortez* by SC; *The Log from the Sea of Cortez* by LSC; *Bombs Away* by BA; *The Pastures of Heaven* by PH; *A Russian Journal* by RJ. All page references to Steinbeck's books are to first editions, complete data on which are given in the working checklist.

A method of abbreviation is also followed for references to Steinbeck's correspondence. Steinbeck's letters to his agents, McIntosh & Otis, are indicated by JS-MO; to his editor at Viking Press, Pascal Covici, by JS-PC; to his early publisher, Robert O. Ballou, by JS-RB; to Ben Abramson by JS-BA; to C. V. Wicker by JS-CVW. Steinbeck's letters to another of his early publishers, Covici-Friede, are now in the possession of his agents, who made them available to me, and are indicated by JS-CF. References to all other letters used are clear in the text. The reversal of initials in these abbreviations, such as PC-JS or MO-JS, of course signifies that Steinbeck was the recipient of the letter. I have indicated the date of each letter when known, have added the approximate date when verifiable by internal evidence, and have used a question mark to indicate uncertainty of date. Those letters previously quoted by Lewis Gannett in his Introduction to *The Portable Steinbeck* (1946) and which I could not locate when examining the agents' files in February of 1954 are cited in the Notes.

I cannot overemphasize my great indebtedness to Miss Elizabeth Otis of McIntosh & Otis, Steinbeck's agents, and to Mr. Pascal Covici of the Viking Press. Both Miss Otis and Mr. Covici made available to me their files of correspondence with Mr. Steinbeck and volunteered certain pertinent biographical information. Mr. Covici also made available to me those Steinbeck manuscripts in his possession. Mr. Steinbeck's cooperation in these matters was, of course, invaluable. In addition, he took time from his work to talk with me about this study and to answer some questions in writing.

For his kindness and consideration in making available to me the private correspondence, notebooks, and journals of Edward F. Ricketts, I am indebted to Mr. D. P. Abbott of the Hopkins Marine Station. I am also grateful to Mr. James Bloom of New York, who made available to me his fine collection of Steinbeck items, including some letters; to the late Ben Abramson of the Argus Book Shop in Chicago, who talked to me at length about Steinbeck's early career; and to Mr. C. V. Wicker for some lively exchanges of opinion and for making available to me those letters in his possession.

To the University of Wisconsin I am indebted for a financial grant permitting me to travel to New York for the purpose of examining the above Steinbeck materials, and to the University of Washington for defraying most of the expenses of preparing the manuscript for publication.

For stimulating encouragement and for acute criticism of my first manuscript version, I am most of all indebted to Mr. Frederick J. Hoffman, whose patience and wisdom have contributed more than I can express. For reading the manuscript in its various stages and making many constructive suggestions, I wish to thank Mr. O. B. Hardison, Mr. Otto Reinert, Mr. Jerome Beaty, Mr. Jordan Kurland, and, particularly, my wife. For generous assistance with preparing the manuscript for the press, I am indebted to Mrs. Barbra Prong.

I must also here acknowledge my great debt to Mr. Robert Humphrey, who had the misfortune to share an office with me during part of the time that this book was in progress and who was always willing to discuss my problems, making many valuable suggestions—"and gladly wolde he lerne and gladly teche."

Contents

Preface *vii*

1 Introduction: The Failure of Criticism *3*
2 *Cup of Gold* *21*
3 *To a God Unknown* *39*
4 *The Pastures of Heaven* *56*
5 *Tortilla Flat* *72*
6 *The Long Valley* *92*
7 *In Dubious Battle* *108*
8 *Of Mice and Men* *130*
9 *The Grapes of Wrath* *144*
10 *Sea of Cortez*, War Writings, *The Moon Is Down* *178*
11 *Cannery Row* *197*
12 *The Pearl* *218*
13 *The Wayward Bus* *231*
14 *Burning Bright* *248*
15 *East of Eden* *261*
16 *Sweet Thursday, The Short Reign of Pippin IV,*
    Some Conclusions *276*

Notes *297*
Checklist of Steinbeck's published work *310*
Index *315*

John Steinbeck's literary reputation continues to suffer from a body of criticism whose assumptions were established on the first three of his novels to receive serious attention and whose prejudices have obscured the very considerable accomplishment of his fiction. Coming as they did near the end of the Great Depression and dealing with proletarian materials, it was inevitable that *In Dubious Battle* (1936), *Of Mice and Men* (1937), and *The Grapes of Wrath* (1939), should have been both accepted and rejected on sociological rather than aesthetic terms.

This basic inadequacy was compounded by the extension of these terms to cover earlier as well as subsequent fiction. Claude E. Jones, for example, although specifically denying that Steinbeck was in the technical sense of the word a "proletarian" writer, nevertheless found that even his first novel, the romantic *Cup of Gold* (1929), reflected a social consciousness—an "unsympathetic, in some places excoriating, treatment of middle-class morality and ideals." [1] Similarly, Barker Fairley, whose social sympathies were obvious, discovered that this novel was "an allegory of materialism defeated." [2] In this critical reconstruction of Steinbeck's early career *Tortilla Flat* (1935) received rough treatment because it did not fit the critical pigeonhole being carved for his works. "If the author's social sympathies had been awake all of the time," wrote Mr. Fairley, "there are parts that might not have been written." [3] *To a God Unknown* (1933) was generally treated as another deviation, an early attempt to escape his social responsibilities as writer by resorting to myth and symbolism. Ten years after *Of Mice and Men,* the persistence of this sociological bias was evident in a review of *The Wayward Bus* (1947) which expressed the conviction that "each of Steinbeck's principal characters may be dimly identified with a stock role in a leftist parable." [4]

Although often based on this kind of sociological evaluation, Steinbeck's reputation has never been so high as it was between 1936, when he first came to critical attention, and 1941. Contrasting Steinbeck with John Dos Passos, Harry Slochower found that whereas in Dos Passos estrangement from society "is broken through by spectacular single acts that peter out in futile gestures," in Steinbeck's novels "a new hero is arising together with the rise of a new order, a personality who combines leadership with democratic representation of those he leads: the *communal* personality." [5] Lawrence Clark Powell, an early bibliographer of Steinbeck, saw in him "the potential 'great American novelist.' " [6] Wilbur L. Schramm proclaimed, "There is no sign that Steinbeck is at the height of his powers. . . . The only question is: How high can Steinbeck go?" [7] On the last page of *The Patterns of English and American Fiction,* Gordon Hall Gerould concluded that "there is no young English writer, one can safely assert, from whom so much may be hoped as from the Californian, John Steinbeck." [8]

There were, however, a few dissenting voices. In an essay defining Steinbeck's style as a means of creating aesthetic distance, T. K. Whipple cautioned that although this was Steinbeck's greatest asset, it might become a serious fault if applied improperly as in *In Dubious Battle,* where it effected too great a distance between the reader and the materials. [9] In 1939 Margaret Marshall began her long feud with Steinbeck's books by remarking on their "puerile symbolism" and their lack of real characters. "It remains to be seen," she warned, "whether Steinbeck's weakness in characterization is the result of incapacity or a lack of maturity." [10] Summing up the literature of the 1930's, James T. Farrell lumped Steinbeck with those realists and naturalists who had mistakenly relied on "experience *qua* experience." As a consequence, he said, their work revealed "no drive, no struggle . . . to attain a way of seeing life." [11] The three books Steinbeck published in this period—*In Dubious Battle, Of Mice and Men, The Grapes of Wrath*—received some unfavorable reviews, but these, along with the essays of Miss Marshall and Mr. Farrell, had little effect on current criticism.

In 1939 there appeared the first study of John Steinbeck in book form—Harry Thornton Moore's *The Novels of John Steinbeck,* a slim volume containing only sixty-one pages of commentary on the works themselves. Mr. Moore's approach was analytic, taking up each novel in chronological order and examining it for form and content. His analysis of the symbolism in *Cup of Gold,* the ironic structure of *The Pastures of Heaven,* and the "phalanx" theory in *In Dubious*

Battle was illuminating. Because Moore's book was so descriptively factual and because it did not hesitate to point out certain weaknesses as well as virtues of Steinbeck's novels, it is still, sixteen years later, a very useful and informative work, though limited to the prewar novels and early biography.

Lacking an easy hypothesis for subsequent reviewers and critics to follow, Mr. Moore's sober study had very little if any effect on subsequent criticism. Rather, the most influential work on Steinbeck to come out of this early period was a casual essay by Edmund Wilson called "The Californians: Storm and Steinbeck" (1940). This essay, reprinted in *The Boys in the Back Room* and *Classics and Commercials,* did have a hypothesis to offer, indeed several, and its subsequent influence can be traced through the body of Steinbeck criticism like a radioactive particle.

Candidly admitting that he had not read Steinbeck's first three books (there were only eight), Wilson saw in Steinbeck's "variability of form" not the "versatility" which others had remarked, but proof that Steinbeck was still groping toward "the right artistic medium for what he wants to say." Through some kind of remarkable special reading he concluded that "the stories in *The Long Valley* [1938] are almost entirely about animals and plants." Furthermore, he felt that this interest in plants and animal life was a pernicious influence in Steinbeck's work: "Mr. Steinbeck almost always in his fiction is dealing either with the lower animals or with human beings so rudimentary that they are almost on the animal level. . . . Mr. Steinbeck does not have the effect, as Lawrence or Kipling does, of romantically raising the animals to the stature of human beings, but rather of assimilating the human beings to animals. . . . This animalizing tendency of Mr. Steinbeck's is, I believe, at the bottom of his relative unsuccess at representing human beings." Of the Steinbeck novels he had read, Edmund Wilson liked *Tortilla Flat* best, although its characters were "not quite human beings," but "cunning little living dolls who amuse us like pet guinea-pigs or rabbits." The characters of *The Grapes of Wrath* fared no better: "It is as if human sentiments and speeches had been assigned to a flock of lemmings on their way to throw themselves into the sea." Quoting from *In Dubious Battle, Of Mice and Men,* and *The Grapes of Wrath,* Wilson tried to persuade his readers that it is only "on this primitive level that Mr. Steinbeck deals with moral questions: the virtues like the crimes for Mr. Steinbeck are still a part of these planless and almost aimless, of these almost unconscious processes of life." Though none of Steinbeck's novels (of the ones he had read) were "precisely first-rate," there being too much "theatricalism," and "tricks," Wilson did find one virtue in Steinbeck's work—an "unpanicky questioning of life." [12]

Of course, some of these ideas had been hinted at in earlier reviews and essays, but Wilson was the first influential critic to voice them and embody them in a terminology which subsequent writers could use. In her book *The Novel and Society* (1941), Elizabeth N. Monroe remarked that Steinbeck expected us to admire Casy for preaching that "all things are good because they are assumed to be natural." [13] In *On Native Grounds* (1942), Alfred Kazin quoted with approval several of Wilson's phrases and turned his "pet guinea-pigs" into "symbolic marionettes." Like Wilson, also, Kazin summed up his discussion of Steinbeck by remarking on the "stage cunning" and the "trickiness." [14] In an essay written in 1942, Stanley Edgar Hyman said of the stories in *The Long Valley* that "their general theme seems to be, as Edmund Wilson has pointed out, an identification of people with animals." [15] Actually, Wilson had said only that they were *about* plants and animals. Reviewing *The Moon Is Down* (1942), Max Eastman quoted Wilson's remarks about the characters of *Tortilla Flat* with great approval and went on to apply them to Steinbeck's characters generally. [16] In "John Steinbeck: Earth and Stars," Woodburn Ross repeated Wilson's notion that for Steinbeck whatever is "natural" is good, giving the same example of Lennie, and also assuming that this was the theme of *Tortilla Flat*.[17] Maxwell Geismar carried Wilson's idea about Steinbeck's interest in animals to an extreme in his review of *The Pearl* (1947) by saying, "And what one notices again is how much more interested Steinbeck really is in the natural scene, and in animal life, than in the people or the human emotions of his narratives." [18] Even Joseph Henry Jackson, long a supporter of Steinbeck, concluded in his review of *The Wayward Bus* (1947) that "now he seems to look at human beings almost as animals." [19] In another review of this book, Freeman Champney remarked that the characters were "animated by the simpler forms of protoplasmic irritability." [20] After quoting Wilson's essay, Frederick J. Hoffman commented in *The Modern Novel in America* (1951) that Steinbeck's failure to give a "convincing definition of his people" was caused by his having "reduced the *scale* of definition to their animal nature." [21] John S. Kennedy, in *Fifty Years of the American Novel* (1951), also acknowledged his debt to Edmund Wilson in regard to Steinbeck's animalism, saying that "habitually and characteristically Steinbeck sets human conduct and animal conduct side by side, on the same plane, not simply as commentaries one on the other but as indications of the same nature in the two apparently disparate parts of creation." [22] Reviewing *East of Eden* (1952), Harvey C. Webster mentioned Edmund

Wilson's study of Steinbeck with approval and added that "in his earlier novels, men approach the condition of animals with a uniformity that sometimes becomes monotonous." [23]

That this kind of criticism does not indicate a consensus based on independent research but an imitation (for which Mr. Wilson has no responsibility) is attested to not only by the similarity of phrasing and terminology, but also by the frequency with which Edmund Wilson is explicitly cited. Since the appearance of Wilson's article in 1940 there have been published some dozen articles and two or three chapters in histories of American literature which are much more comprehensive, analytical, and precise. But none of them has managed to excite the imagination of critics and reviewers. Fifteen years later, Wilson's casual essay, limited to his reading of five early novels, is still the greatest single influence in Steinbeck criticism, as was attested by reviews of *East of Eden* and *Sweet Thursday*.

In 1941 there began to appear a series of articles and chapters which attempted for the first time a serious survey of Steinbeck's career up to that point. In July of 1941 Frederick I. Carpenter published his "John Steinbeck: American Dreamer," in which he attempted to find unity in Steinbeck's works by relating them to American social history. "But beneath this apparent variety," Carpenter wrote, "Steinbeck has been astonishingly consistent. A single purpose has directed his experimentation, a single idea has guided his literary thought. Always his fiction has described the interplay of dream and reality; his thought has followed the development of the American dream." The death of Jody's red pony, for example, was supposed to be a symbol for the death of "the old American ideal of life—the 'genteel tradition' of the past." [24] Such a hypothesis, having for its major premise that Steinbeck was picking his plots with an eye to illustrating American history (and chronologically, too) was of course made possible only by simplifications amounting to distortion.

Stanley Edgar Hyman also attempted to relate Steinbeck's work to some social concept. For Mr. Hyman, all Steinbeck's books illustrated one basic problem—the relation of the individual to society: "In that sense all his books are social. Around this problem the books move in two marked trends, from extreme unsociality or individualism to a height of sociality, and then back to individualism with a new name, this time scientific isolation. The first pivotal point is the play-novel *Of Mice and Men* and the second . . . the play-novel *The Moon Is Down*." [25] Mr. Hyman's argument was based on two errors. One of these errors, an identification of the author with his characters, resulted in his seeing *Cup of Gold* as individualistic philosophy, *The Pastures of Heaven* as an attempt to prove that nature was good and man evil, and *In Dubious Battle* as Steinbeck's temporary acceptance of communism. Hyman also seemed to assume that Steinbeck had brought on the Great Depression in order to exploit it in his development as a writer, for only this would explain why Steinbeck did not write *Cup of Gold* (1929) after *The Grapes of Wrath* (1939), why the stock market crash did not come *after* the Depression.

Another critic who engaged in this kind of search for social values was Maxwell Geismar, who saw Steinbeck's whole career up to *The Grapes of Wrath* as a long, erratic search for values: "In the variety of his early 'solutions'—the life of egotistic adventure, and that of bloody daring, the primitive way, the natural and anti-social life, the return to the soil, the dabblings with the abnormal—Steinbeck seems almost to traverse the entire circuit of contemporary artistic

escapes. In him are reflected the evasions of his generation." [26] Mr. Geismar betrays exactly the same kind of error
as Mr. Hyman—a confusion of the author with his characters
and materials.

Many of these sociological evaluations of the 1940's centered on *The Grapes of Wrath*. One such study was Chester
E. Eisinger's examination of "Jeffersonian Agrarianism in
The Grapes of Wrath." [27] Like Carpenter's "The Philosophical Joads," [28] Eisinger's essay did much to relate *The Grapes
of Wrath* to American philosophical thought and to dis-
courage the view that Steinbeck's ideas came by direct wire
from Moscow. In his *American Idealism* (1943) Floyd Stovall
also used *The Grapes of Wrath* to place Steinbeck in the
mainstream of American thought.[29]

There were a few essays in this period (1941–1947) which
concerned themselves with aesthetic problems, but they, too,
were either fragmentary or limited in scope. The best of
these studies are Joseph Warren Beach's two chapters on
Steinbeck in *American Fiction 1920–1940* (1941). In "John
Steinbeck: Journeyman Artist," he surveyed, rather sketchily,
Steinbeck's work up to 1939, paying particular attention to
"The Chrysanthemums," *To a God Unknown*, and *Tortilla
Flat*, all of which he admired for their narrative skill and
prose style. In his chapter on *The Grapes of Wrath*, which
novel he thought "perhaps the finest example so far produced
in the United States of the proletarian novel," [30] Mr. Beach
offered several good arguments for the unity of Steinbeck's
great novel by relating the interchapters to the narrative.
He also commented on Steinbeck's characters, which, unlike most critics, he found credible and moving (except for
Doc Burton). Barker Fairley's analysis in "John Steinbeck
and the Coming Literature" (1942) was unconfused but
very limited indeed: "I submit that his performance thus

far is good in proportion as he masters and relies on the common speech. When he doesn't use it at all his books are bad, when he does use it in its place, even tritely, his books are good, when he surrenders to it his books are inspired." [31] Mr. Fairley made it clear that by "common speech" he meant the bunkhouse talk of *Of Mice and Men.*

Both Alfred Kazin (*On Native Grounds,* 1942) and W. M. Frohock ("John Steinbeck's Men of Wrath," 1946) saw as one of Steinbeck's major aesthetic failings his inability to create living characters. Kazin did comment favorably on Steinbeck's use of "a realism less terror-ridden than the depression novel, yet one consciously responsible to society . . . not submissive to the spiritual stupor of the time; a realism equal in some measure, if only in its aspiration, to the humanity, the gaiety, the wholeness, of realism in a more stable period." But despite this "humanity," this "moral advantage," and this poetry, "there is something imperfectly formed about Steinbeck's work; it has no creative character. For all his moral serenity, the sympathetic understanding of men . . . Steinbeck's people are always on the verge of becoming human, but never do." Mr. Kazin attached so much importance to this weakness that for him it vitiated all the good qualities, making Steinbeck's moral serenity "sterile" and allowing him to slip into a "calculated sentimentality" which after a dozen books still marked him as a "distinguished apprentice." [32]

After commenting on Steinbeck's ability to control violence and use it effectively, W. M. Frohock also launched into a criticism of Steinbeck's characters. All his people, said Mr. Frohock, have an "esssential identity." The variations in "race, fortune, and social level are in the surface." Mr. Frohock's concept of character was not clear. Not only did he assert that "the people of *The Grapes of Wrath* and

In Dubious Battle are essentially the people of *Tortilla Flat* and *Cannery Row*," which is a proposition difficult to agree with, but he went on to say that *The Grapes of Wrath* is a good tragedy because there "his people have the requisite human dignity." [33] This is the kind of meaningless inconsistency to which almost all critics were driven when attempting to discuss Steinbeck's characters, an inconsistency resulting from their willingness to apply ready-made formulas indiscriminately.

Another kind of dissatisfaction with Steinbeck's characters was best expressed by Norman Cousins in "Who Are the Real People?" (1945). "It should be at least possible," said Mr. Cousins, "to write about the mainstream of humanity without putting a halo on the half-wit, deifying the drunk, or canonizing the castoff." [34]

Although a great deal of Steinbeck criticism between 1941 and 1947 was unfavorable, most of it reflected a disinclination to make final judgments. The feeling was that there were bad things about Mr. Steinbeck as a writer, but there were some good ones too, and maybe he could overcome his natural handicaps. Perhaps he would learn to create living characters; perhaps he would abandon his sentimentality. The only two books of fiction published in these years were *The Moon Is Down* and *Cannery Row*. *The Moon Is Down* might be excused as a hasty bit of war effort, and *Cannery Row* was, after all, no worse than *Tortilla Flat*. Perhaps now Steinbeck would settle down to his true vein—that of *In Dubious Battle, Of Mice and Men,* and *The Grapes of Wrath,* though these, too, had many faults.

This attitude of watchful waiting gave way to one of violent reaction with Steinbeck's publication in 1947 of *The*

Wayward Bus and *The Pearl,* which seemed to confirm all the critics' suspicions. In an essay called "Steinbeck against Steinbeck" (1947), Donald Weeks chastised the author for gross sentimentality and asked, "What *is* the matter with Steinbeck?" Mr. Weeks could not take "seriously" *The Moon Is Down, Cannery Row,* and *The Wayward Bus.*[35] Ben Ray Redman called his prosecution "The Case of John Steinbeck" (1947) and accused the author of having learned his trade and now becoming a hack. He saw in *The Wayward Bus* "a failure of emotion or sentiment, which has been part of Steinbeck's genius."[36] Norman Cousins called his essay "Bankrupt Realism" (1947) and saw a general falling off of Steinbeck's powers. *The Wayward Bus,* unlike *The Grapes of Wrath,* was "realism without purpose."[37] Whereas Freeman Champney advised that Steinbeck's best field was "the sub-rational and the inarticulate,"[38] in the same year Maxwell Geismar wrote, "Of all the ranking modern writers who have gone back to primitive materials as a protest against and a solace for contemporary society, Steinbeck is, as a matter of fact, the least well-endowed. . . ."[39] In "Steinbeck: One Aspect" (1949), Blake Nevius criticized *two* aspects: Steinbeck's tolerance of illusions, as illustrated particularly in *The Pastures of Heaven* and *Cannery Row,* and his refusal to assign positive blame for evil—even in *The Grapes of Wrath.* Like Freeman Champney, Blake Nevius blamed Steinbeck's increasingly "scientific" view of things for his decline, because it prompted a "sentimental evasion."[40]

Steinbeck fared no better in those chapters devoted to him in literary histories. In *The Novel and The World's Dilemma* (1947), Edwin B. Burgum called his chapter "The Fickle Sensibility of John Steinbeck," and found that Steinbeck's books were good in proportion to the adequacy of his social views, which had declined sharply since *The Grapes of*

Wrath.[41] In *The Modern Novel in America* (1951), Frederick
J. Hoffman found that *In Dubious Battle* was a good novel,
but that "Steinbeck was not to repeat this accomplishment in
his fiction, for taken as a whole, his novels reveal the deficiencies of a homespun philosophy, in which the suggestions
made are vitiated and confused by a 'hausfrau sentimentality' and a naive mysticism." [42] In a book called *In My Opinion* (1952),Orville Prescott titled his chapter on Steinbeck,
Sinclair Lewis, and Hemingway "Squandered Talents." He
found *The Grapes of Wrath* "greatly superior to anything else
Mr. Steinbeck has done." Only three other works were good
—*Of Mice and Men, The Red Pony,* and *The Pearl.* "The
rest are a curious grab bag of literary odds and ends." [43] This
opinion was directly opposed to that of George D. Snell in
The Shapers of American Fiction (1947), who thought *The
Grapes of Wrath* "as formless a novel as could well be." Concerning *Of Mice and Men,* another of Prescott's favorites,
Mr Snell said, "This is a negligible novel, seemingly written
with a determined eye on the cash register." [44] Mr. Snell also
saw in Steinbeck many similarities to Dickens: a gift for
story telling, catholicity of sympathy, and a common touch,
love of exaggeration and humor, well-wrought plotting,
popularity, and sentimentality. It was this last quality which
Mr. Snell found to be Steinbeck's worst fault. In his *Cavalcade
of the American Novel* (1952), Mr. Wagenknecht showed
his essential incapacity to understand Steinbeck by calling
Of Mice and Men "a glorification of idiocy." [45] Like Maxwell Geismar, Claude E. Jones, and Edmund Wilson before
him, Mr. Wagenknecht saw Steinbeck's "versatility" only as
proof that he could not find himself as a writer. In a
critical anthology called *Fifty Years of the American Novel,*
and subtitled "A Christian Appraisal" (1951), there appeared
an essay by John S. Kennedy entitled "John Steinbeck: Life

Affirmed and Dissolved." Mr. Kennedy insisted at length that Steinbeck "is evermore strongly affirming that, in the last analysis, man has no individual identity, that the human person as such, separately created and distinct from all others, does not in fact exist." [46] This kind of statement represents the most ridiculous extreme to which interpretations of Steinbeck's ecological thinking and biological view have been carried.

It is interesting that although this period between *Cannery Row* (1945) and *Burning Bright* (1950) produced some of the most prejudiced attacks on Steinbeck, it also produced several pieces of criticism which must be accounted among the best done so far. Two of these were book reviews by Carlos Baker. He called his review of *The Pearl* "Steinbeck at the Top of his Form" and gave high praise to that novel's "ubiquitous associational potential" and its prose style: "And he had long trained his prose for such a task as this: that supple, unstrained, muscular power, responsive to the slightest pull on the reins. . . ." [47] Another essay by Carlos Baker was his review of *The Wayward Bus*, in which he admired its "richness of texture" and "solidity of structure." Baker believed the book achieved "even more solid unity than that which distinguished *In Dubious Battle*" and showed, in addition to its "vertical structure," "as subtle and neat a horizontal structure as Steinbeck has ever evolved." Where other critics saw the book as a complete surrender to scientific naturalism, he remarked that only a sense of humor kept Steinbeck from "savage indignation." [48] Mr. Baker's serious examination of Steinbeck had begun in 1940 with his "Steinbeck of California," [49] and was continued in 1943 with "*In Dubious Battle* Revalued," which had praised that novel's technique. [50]

In addition to these book reviews, there were published in

1948 and 1949 two long and well-informed essays which attempted a serious examination of Steinbeck's biological bias without using any of the clichés which had been plaguing Steinbeck criticism since the early 1940's. In an essay called "Steinbeck and the Biological View of Man," Frederick Bracher made clear that it was not only possible but profitable to discuss Steinbeck's "biological view of man" without succumbing to the old idea of his "animalism." Whereas John S. Kennedy, for example, asserted that this biological bias equates men with animals, Mr. Bracher demonstrated by specific reference to the novels that Steinbeck's biology goes beyond animalism to a mystic reverence for "life in all its forms." It is true that his central metaphor is the tide pool, but "to be aware of the whole thing and to accept one's part in it is, for Steinbeck, the saving grace which may lift man out of the tide pool." [51] By a perceptive and skillful use of the biological terminology in Steinbeck's works, particularly in *Sea of Cortez,* Frederick Bracher was able to give a convincing definition of Steinbeck's protagonists, of his attitude towards the middle class, of his social philosophy, and of his ethics—all of which had been obscured by critical clichés.

Mr. Bracher's excellent essay was followed by an essay which seemed a continuation of his own—Woodburn Ross's "John Steinbeck: Naturalism's Priest." Mr. Ross's theory was that Steinbeck, unlike most naturalists, had been able to meet the ethical implications of his naturalism. The author had accomplished this by adding to his naturalism some things which had not hitherto seemed "logical" to it. Mr. Ross's comments are worth quoting at length.

> He has succeeded in taking the materials which undermined the religious faith of the nineteenth century and fusing them with a religious attitude in the twentieth, though a religious attitude very different from what the orthodox in the nine-

teenth century would have thought possible. Nature as described by the scientist becomes not merely the foundation of a revolutionary ethic; it also supplies . . . the basis of a sense of reverence which affectively supports the new ethic, now surprisingly turned altruistic. Steinbeck is, I think, the first significant novelist to begin to build a mystical religion upon a naturalistic base. . . . It abandons all attempts to discern final purposes in life. It virtually reduces man again to animism; for, unlike Wordsworth, Steinbeck does not see through nature to a God beyond; he hears no intimations of immortality. . . . There is only nature, ultimately mysterious, to which all things belong, bound together in a unity concerning whose stupendous grandeur he can barely hint. But such a nature Steinbeck loves, and before it, like primitive man, he is reverent.

Mr. Ross concluded that the significance of Steinbeck's work may prove to be its "curious compromise." It accepts "the intuitive, non-rational method of dealing with man's relation to the universe—the method of contemporary mystics. But, unlike them, it accepts as the universe to which man must relate himself the modern, scientifically described cosmos." [52]

These two essays by Frederick Bracher and Woodburn Ross are valuable for understanding Steinbeck because they succeed in taking exactly those materials which had provided all the critical clichés about animalism, primitivism, and immorality and reinterpreting them more convincingly as the basis of Steinbeck's humanity, his mysticism, and his reverence for life. But although these two essays were penetrating, they did not have a fructifying influence on Steinbeck criticism. In fact, except for book reviews, between 1949 and 1957 there were published only two critical articles on Steinbeck, both dealing with *The Grapes of Wrath*. One of these described that novel as a piece of "literary engineering" in the genre of "Wagons West," [53] and the other made an interesting but incomplete study of that novel's Christian symbolism.[54]

Upon the publication of every one of the four books which Steinbeck has published since 1950, at least one reviewer has found it necessary to observe that Steinbeck is no longer a writer to be taken seriously, and in reviews of *Sweet Thursday* and *The Short Reign of Pippin IV* expression of this sentiment reached the proportions of a massed chorus. The irony is that he seldom *has* been taken seriously insofar as this seriousness demands formal analysis of the works themselves.

Such a task of analysis has not been undertaken in the past because there has been a tacit assumption on the part of critics that the material did not warrant it, indeed could not sustain it. When certain of Steinbeck's novels have been accounted good, the explanations offered for this phenomenon have ranged from the social attitude expressed in them to the fact that Steinbeck is a Californian. When some little aspect of good technique has been noted, it has been usually accompanied by the kind of surprised disbelief one might feel on finding the carcass of a leopard on Mount Kilimanjaro. Writing of some good passages in *The Grapes of Wrath*, Frederick J. Hoffman has remarked that they are "those parts of it in which Steinbeck has exercised (almost unwittingly, it seems) the caution and factual decorum demanded by the material." [55] Similarly, Maxwell Geismar, writing of *In Dubious Battle*: "Through what it reveals when apparently most determined to conceal (and yet we are never quite sure whether the effect is altogether unintentional), it becomes among our contemporary labor novels a powerful and uncomfortable document." [56] These are but two examples, both by influential critics, one published in 1942, the other in 1951. Similar remarks can be found in Edmund Wilson, W. M. Frohock, and others.

The notion that such complex works of art as *The Grapes of Wrath* and *In Dubious Battle* were accomplished "unwittingly" or "unintentionally" is dispelled when these works are accorded the respect of close attention. And this same close attention will reveal in Steinbeck's work as a whole those qualities of insight and discipline which are essential to the creation of great art.

2 } *Cup of Gold*

Any full consideration of John Steinbeck and his work must begin with the fact that he was born and came to maturity in the Salinas Valley. In this fertile valley of California, bounded on the north by Monterey Bay (into which the Salinas River empties), extending south to San Luis Obispo and bounded on the west and east principally by the Santa Lucia and the Gabilan Mountains, Steinbeck found the materials of his fiction. There he came to know and admire the *paisanos* and bums of *Tortilla Flat, Cannery Row,* and *Sweet Thursday;* there he first met and worked with the migrant laborers of *In Dubious Battle, Of Mice and Men,* and *The Grapes of Wrath;* there also he came to know the people of *The Long Valley, The Pastures of Heaven, The Red Pony, The Wayward Bus,* and *East of Eden.* From his California valley and its sheltering mountains, Steinbeck gained that intimate knowledge and love of nature which figures so prominently in his works. From the tide pools and littoral of Monterey Bay, he obtained that biological view of life which informs his observation of man and society.

John Ernst Steinbeck was born in the town of Salinas on February 27, 1902, the only son of John Ernst Steinbeck, Sr. His mother's maiden name was Olive Hamilton. Like John Whiteside and George Battle in *The Pastures of Heaven*, Joseph in *To a God Unknown*, and Adam Trask in *East of Eden*, Steinbeck, Sr., came to California shortly after the Civil War; like Elizabeth in *To a God Unknown*, Molly Morgan in *The Pastures of Heaven*, and Olive Hamilton in *East of Eden* (an authentic portrait), Steinbeck's mother taught in the public schools of the Salinas Valley area—Peachtree, Pleyto, Big Sur. John Steinbeck, Sr., who built a flour mill in King City, was for many years treasurer of Monterey County, and his son's early novels and stories are written in the pages of abandoned double-entry ledgers.

Steinbeck's childhood was in many ways like that of the boy Jody in *The Red Pony*, whose love for the Gabilan Mountains to the east and fear of the Santa Lucia range toward the ocean Steinbeck has acknowledged as a personal childhood experience on the opening page of *East of Eden*. Like the Jody who made a death symbol out of the black cypress trees under which the pigs were scalded and a life symbol out of the mossy tub which caught spring water, Steinbeck was a sensitive boy. Replying to a publisher's request for early biographical information, Steinbeck wrote back that the most important things in his childhood would be of no meaning to others—"the way the sparrows hopped about on the mud street early in the morning when I was little. . . . the most tremendous morning in the world when my pony had a colt." (JS-RB, 6/10/32) This sensitivity to

the experiences of childhood is also revealed in some remarks Steinbeck made just before beginning *The Red Pony*:
"I want to recreate a child's world, not of fairies and giants
but of colors more clear than they are to adults, of tastes
more sharp and of queer heart breaking feelings that over-
whelm children in a moment. I want to put down the way
'afternoon felt'—and the feeling about a bird that sang in
a tree in the evening." (JS-BA, *ca.* Feb., 1936)

Another important factor in Steinbeck's early years was
undoubtedly his mother's former position as a schoolteacher.
There were many books around the house to interest a
young boy. In *The Pastures of Heaven* Steinbeck represents
Molly Morgan as reading to her pupils from the novels of
Sir Walter Scott, Zane Grey, James Oliver Curwood, and
Jack London. Junius Maltby reads to the boys from Stevenson's *Treasure Island* and carries copies of *Kidnapped* and
Travels With a Donkey in his pockets. Commenting on his
early reading, Steinbeck once wrote that he remembered
"certain books that were realer than experience—*Crime and
Punishment* was like that and *Madame Bovary* and parts of
Paradise Lost and things of George Eliot and *The Return of
the Native*. I read all of these when I was very young and I
remember them not at all as books but as things that happened to me." [1] (JS-BA. *ca.* Feb., 1936) The most important
reading Steinbeck did in these early years, however, was in
Malory's *Morte Darthur,* of which he wrote in 1957: "The
first book that was my own—my very own—was the Caxton
Morte d' Arthur. I got it when I was nine years old. Over the
years I have been more affected by it than by anything else
except possibly the King James Version. Later it caused a
fairly intensive study of Anglo-Saxon, Old and Middle English all of which I suspect have had a profound effect on my
prose." (JS-CVW, 1/16/57) One of Steinbeck's three sisters,

Mrs. E. G. Ainsworth, recalls that her brother and another sister, Mary, used to read sections of Malory together and then act them out.

Steinbeck must have been a pretty well-read boy when he entered high school. His being president of the senior class, however, was more because of his positions on the track and basketball teams than his scholarship or literary efforts for *El Gabilan*, the school paper. During his high school years he extended his experience of the California countryside and its people by spending many of his holidays as a hired hand on nearby ranches. In the year's interval between graduation and entering Stanford he took employment as assistant chemist in a sugar-beet factory just southwest of Salinas.

Steinbeck's career at Stanford was sporadic. Although he registered as an English major and was in attendance intermittently over a period of five years, 1920–1925, he did not take a degree, earning less than half the required units.[2] During his years at Stanford he contributed two stories to *The Stanford Spectator* and three poems to the *Stanford Lit*. One story, called "Fingers of Cloud: A Satire on College Protervity," is an account of a subnormal girl who marries a migrant Filipino laborer but leaves him because he insists on keeping horse heads in the rain barrel. This odd mixture of the realistic and the fantastic is even more pronounced in the other story, "Adventures in Arcademy: A Journey into the Ridiculous," an obscure and satirical allegory of college life at Stanford. Various fruit trees seem to symbolize courses of study, and penguins, pigeons, buffaloes, and other animals seem to represent the faculty. The three poems published in the *Stanford Lit* are in the same vein of comic satire, as the titles indicate: "If Eddie Guest Had Written the Book of Job: HAPPY BIRTHDAY," "If John A. Weaver Had Written Keats' Sonnet in the American Language: ON LOOKING

AT A NEW BOOK BY HAROLD BELL WRIGHT," and "Atropos: Study of a Very Feminine Obituary Editor." Steinbeck had apparently settled on a career as a writer, and although he was not admitted into the play-writing class, he did manage to take other courses in writing, along with his many electives in science.

During those intervals when he was not in attendance at Stanford, Steinbeck worked at a variety of jobs. While working in a haberdashery store in Oakland, he lived with a fellow employee who took him to church one Sunday, where Steinbeck embarrassed his host by taking vociferous objection to the preacher's sermon, breaking out from the congregation with "Feed the body and the soul will take care of itself," and "I don't think much of preaching. . . . Go on. . . . You're getting paid for it." [3] Working on various ranches, he frequently argued socialism with his fellow laborers, though he believed that man's innate stupidity and greed made that form of government improbable. For another period, Steinbeck worked on a labor gang which was building the first road below Big Sur, the relatively unexplored country of *To a God Unknown*. Also, he returned to work as night chemist in the sugar-beet factory. That these were experiences from which he profited is evident on every page of *In Dubious Battle* and *The Grapes of Wrath*.

In 1925 Steinbeck left Stanford for good, and in November of that year he went to New York to become a writer. The unfortunate circumstances of his first stay in New York he has recorded in an amusing piece of autobiography—his jobs as laborer and reporter, his unsuccessful attempts to publish some short stories, and his ignominious retreat to California as a deck hand via the Panama Canal. The experience was so bitter that fifteen years later, even when he was a celebrity, he came to New York "as a St. Anthony to temptations," and as soon as possible he "fled the whore of Babylon with relief and virtuous satisfaction." [4]

Back in California, Steinbeck took a job as caretaker of an estate on Lake Tahoe, and later, after being fired for "allowing" a huge tree to crash through the roof, he worked in a nearby fish hatchery. It was during the two winters he spent in the High Sierras that he completed his first published novel. *Cup of Gold*, subtitled *A Life of Sir Henry Morgan, Buccaneer, with Occasional Reference to History*, appeared in August of 1929 under the imprint of Robert M. McBride & Company, who three years earlier had turned down a volume of short stories written for them at the suggestion of one of their former editors.

Cup of Gold was Steinbeck's fourth attempt at a novel and was rewritten six times from an unpublished story called "A Lady in Infra-Red," which he wrote during his days at Stanford.[5] An echo of this title may be found in the name of one of the book's characters—*La Santa Roja*, or The Red Saint. Aside from a few reviews, the only recognition accorded this first novel was Berton Braley's "thanks and acknowledgements" for Steinbeck's permission to use some of the incidents in a doggerel epic, *Morgan Sails the Caribbean* (1934).

Cup of Gold gives the surface impression that if its author had been an experienced hack purposely writing for Hollywood he could not have done a better job of it. Seven years later, Steinbeck said he was "not particularly proud" of this novel and that "outside of a certain lyric quality" there wasn't much to it. He believed *Cup of Gold* would be the only book of his that could be filmed. (JS-MO, 4/15/36) The plot seems made to order: A young boy dreams of running away to sea and becoming a pirate. In the seaport he is betrayed by a companion and sold as an indentured servant, but he never loses sight of his plans. When his term is up, he organizes a pirate troop and by imagination and daring soon becomes the most feared buccaneer on the high seas. The peak of his career is reached when he takes the city of Panama (the Cup of Gold) and captures the beautiful woman known to all men as *La Santa Roja*. After an impressive amount of carnage and pillage, he is ready to retire, is forgiven by the king, is knighted for his efforts against the enemy Spain, is married to a beautiful young woman of high society, and lives out his life as the wealthy governor of Jamaica—Sir Henry Morgan. Here are all the requirements of a Hollywood historical extravaganza.

Steinbeck, however, was no experienced hack; rather, he was an inexperienced but very ambitious writer, and he took for the theme of his first novel nothing less than the Faust legend, especially as adapted in some form or other by Hawthorne for almost every one of his works.[6] Like Faust, Morgan is obsessed with one overpowering ambition; like Faust, Morgan finds that his pleasures fade. And, like such Hawthorne characters as Roger Chillingworth, Dr. Rappaccini, Septimius Felton, and Ethan Brand, Morgan finds that his exclusive attention to a single purpose separates him from humanity—the unforgivable sin. However, where Hawthorne's characters usually become aware of their own evil through some catastrophic event (the death of Beatrice in "Rappaccini's Daughter," the death of Georgiana in "The Birthmark"), Morgan grows gradually more and more aware of the consequences of isolation, this very awarenes, like that of Faust, leading to greater excesses as forms of escape. This parallel to the Faust theme even includes a last scene in which Morgan is confronted by personifications of his sins and the fate of his soul is decided.

In Steinbeck's novel the Faustian theme is carried by two

symbols: the cup of gold and the name Elizabeth or its Spanish equivalent of Ysobel. These two symbols are developed, alternately and together, throughout the novel.

The cup of gold symbol is first introduced and partially defined by Merlin, an old Welsh bard to whom young Morgan is sent by his father for advice concerning his dreams of sailing to the Indies and becoming a buccaneer: "Merlin searched the boy's face closely. Sadly he looked up at his harps. 'I think I understand,' he said softly. 'You are a little boy. You want the moon to drink from as a golden cup; and so, it is very likely that you will become a great man—if only you remain a little child. All the world's great have been little boys who wanted the moon. . . .'" From this point in the novel, images of gold, concavity, and roundness become frequent, pointing in the direction of the two main symbols and often fusing them. Thus when Henry Morgan gets his first ship, he names her the *Elizabeth*, and as he stands on her deck, "the wind, blowing out of a black, dreadful sky, was a cup of wine to him, and a challenge, and a passionate caress." His beautiful "golden skinned" slave girl with limbs that "twinkled like golden flames" jealously sees him "fondle the wheel" of the *Elizabeth* with "the strong dear touch of lover's fingers." During Morgan's drive on the Cup of Gold (Panama), his pirates are described in these terms: "Their cheeks were shallow cups under their cheek bones." When Morgan becomes aware that his only friend, Coeur de Gris, has beaten him to *La Santa Roja*, the chapter ends with, "there was a clash of golden service thrown on the pile." After he has collected the ransom on *La Santa Roja*, for whose love he had consciously (Ysobel) and unconsciously (Elizabeth) taken Panama, he sits musing with the money in front of him: "It could have been cut in no more charming shape, either. A square would not answer, nor an ellipse.

And money was really worth more than money. He tumbled a tower and built it up again." These are only a few of the images which help sustain the tenor of the symbols between the more important stages of their development.

As she actually appears in the beginning of the novel, Elizabeth is merely the daughter of a very poor cottager, with whom the adolescent hero is in love and whom he leaves without a farewell because he has guilt feelings about his dreams concerning her. By the time Morgan has met Tim, the sailor who sells him to the ship captain, he has elaborated on his original relationship to this Elizabeth by adding a tender scene of farewell. When he tells his golden-skinned slave girl about Elizabeth, she becomes the daughter of a wealthy squire; he himself had been taken away from her by a "gang of bastard sailors," and it is "a bitter thing to lose Elizabeth." In telling Coeur de Gris about Elizabeth, she becomes the "daughter of an earl" and they had "loved too perfectly—too passionately," she spending all of one night in his arms. By now the instrument of separation was the Earl himself, who seized young Henry and sold him into slavery. Near the end of the book, Morgan tells the King that Elizabeth had been a "princess of France," that he had come upon her bathing in a river, naked, and that within an hour she had lain passionately in his arms. In this version, the princess had been imprisoned in a tower by her father, who also had her whipped. Unable to endure this separation, the princess had taken poison and died: These incremental changes in the Elizabeth symbol carry one of the novel's dominant themes. It is significant that all the variations are given by Morgan when he has been drinking, which suggests these fabrications are not the altogether conscious exaggerations of a romantic liar, but to some extent the manifestations of a deep need for self-aggrandizement. This need becomes more demanding as Morgan realizes that despite his gold, his governorship, and his knighthood, he has failed. As Merlin had warned, ". . . he who shields a firefly in his hands, caught in reaching for the moon, is doubly alone; he only can realize his true failure, can realize his meanness and fears and evasions."

Despite his successes, therefore, Morgan becomes more and more obsessed with the Elizabeth symbol. His irrational desire to capture Panama (the Cup of Gold) is symbolic, because he identifies *La Santa Roja* with the Elizabeth of his imagination, saying of her, "This woman is the harbor of all my questing." He indulges in orgies of pillage. The sacking of Maracaibo is given in short, impressionistic scenes reminiscent of motion-picture techniques, and each is bracketed by such statements as "(There is a woman in the Cup of Gold, and they worship her for unnamable beauties)," "(There is a woman in the Cup of Gold, and she is lovely as the sun)," "(There is a woman in Panama—)."

With Morgan's capture of Panama, the symbols of Elizabeth, the Cup of Gold, and *La Santa Roja* merge. After the city has fallen, a young woman comes to him.

"My name is Ysobel," she announces. "It was said that you sought me."

"Sought you?" asks Morgan.

"Yes," she replies. "I have been called La Santa Roja by certain young idiots."

Morgan is disappointed, for his mind's image had far surpassed the woman before him. He had imagined her as a pure saint, an unreal thing, not a married woman who rode horses like a man, fenced very well, and was full of frankly sensual passion. But, in faithfulness to that figment created by his imagination, he proposes marriage: "You must marry me Elizabeth—Ysobel." (This Freudian slip in name is another important indication of his subconscious drives.) *La Santa Roja* scorns him, however, because she realizes that he is in love with a dream. In an action which is symbolic of his essential failure, Morgan yields Ysobel for a ransom, just as he had left Elizabeth for buccaneering. Ysobel prophesies that he will "take no more cups of gold . . . will turn no more dreams into unsatisfactory conquests." It is one of the book's ironies that Morgan does marry an Elizabeth, but neither the Elizabeth of his childhood nor this Elizabeth of the Cup of Gold. He is trapped into marriage by his cousin Elizabeth, the orphan daughter of Sir Edward Morgan, a very ordinary woman who drowns his life in social engagements and who shows her love by "hectoring, badgering and brow beating."

This fusing of symbols is illustrated by another incident. After his disappointment with Ysobel, Morgan finds among the loot taken in Panama an actual cup of gold, very curiously inscribed. Around the outside is a frieze of "four grotesque lambs." Inside, however, on the bottom, "a naked girl lifted her arms in sensual ecstasy." Captain Morgan perceives that the contrast between the exterior and interior of the cup symbolizes precisely the contrast between his own naïve dreams and the reality which he has been made to face. He violently throws the cup across the room.

The ubiquity of this cup imagery, combined with the quest motif, suggests a subsidiary theme to the Faust legend —the quest for the Holy Grail, a theme which had fascinated Steinbeck since early childhood and with which he was to deal more explicitly in *Tortilla Flat*. But Henry Morgan is no Galahad or Percival, and all three cups of gold (Panama, Ysobel, the actual inscribed cup) prove counterfeit for him.

Earlier in this chapter it was suggested that Henry

Morgan, like many of Hawthorne's main characters, suffers an estrangement from mankind through the sin of intellectual pride. Although Morgan's isolation is implicit in his actions throughout the book, Steinbeck makes it clear at several points. When Morgan removes the gallows from public view and conducts his executions in secret, we are told that "this was not a kindness. He knew out of his own reasoning, that the unknown thing can never become the normal thing; that unseen punishments could be far more horrible . . . than those seen under the light of the sun." Similarly, Morgan never lets anyone know what he is thinking, for then they would have "a hold on him which would be difficult to shake off. He must be cold and distant and insulting to those below him." In this regard his treatment of the slaves is significant: "The slaves worked deliriously under the whips which followed them to the fields, but there was nothing personal in the whips. The old overseer had delighted in punishment, but Henry Morgan was not cruel. He was merciless. He merely speeded the wheels of his factory. One could not think of being kind to a sprocket or a flywheel. . . ." Later, Morgan is to feel the same way toward his fellow pirates. Even the devoted slave girl whom he owns while he is still an indentured servant finds no place in his heart. "Henry thought of her as a delicate machine perfectly made for pleasure, a sexual contraption." As his career progresses, even this pleasure fades, and he takes no part in the general revelry of women and wine with which his fellow pirates celebrate their successes.

Finally, Morgan's estrangement from his fellow man becomes so great that even his ambition is not enough to sustain him and he turns to Coeur de Gris for friendship: "Listen to me, Coeur de Gris! Can you not imagine that I

may need a friend? . . . For ten years I have ravaged the
seas like a silent wolf, and I have no friend anywhere." On
the march to Panama, Morgan irritates his new friend, who
is wracked with fever, by boasting of the uniqueness of his
own desires and ambitions and the impossibility that anyone
else could share them: "No, you can't understand my yearning." At this his friend loses caution:

> "I do not understand!" he cried scornfully. "Do you think I do
> not understand? I know; to your mind your feelings are new
> things, discoveries of fresh importance. Your failures are un-
> precedented. This gigantic conceit will not allow you to believe
> that this cockney behind you—yes, he who sometimes rolls on
> the ground in fits—might have the same hopes and despairs as
> yourself. You cannot believe that these men feel as deeply as
> you do. . . ."
> Captain Morgan had flushed under the lash of words. He
> did not believe it. It was monstrous to think that these men
> could feel as he did.

Although there is a great deal of carnage in the novel,
Henry Morgan is shown killing only three men. One of these
is the plantation overseer who has gone mad and whom he
shoots to prevent arson. Significantly, the other two are this
Cockney and Coeur de Gris.

There is one more important parallel to the Faustian theme
in *Cup of Gold*. If the book is read only on its superficial
level of romantic adventure, the concluding scene comes as
a shock—the same kind of shock most readers get from the
last scene in *The Grapes of Wrath*. If, however, the book's
theme and symbolic levels of meaning are kept in mind, it
will be apparent that this last scene is of a piece with the
rest of the book.

Sir Henry Morgan, now Governor of Jamaica, is lying on

his deathbed. He has refused to confess his sins to the vicar, and as the doctor begins to bleed him again, he loses consciousness and hears "a vibrant, rich organ tone, which filled him, seemed to emanate from his brain, flood his body, and from it to surge out over the world." He finds himself in a dim grotto, assailed by "strange beings, having the bodies of children, and bulbous, heavy heads, but no faces." These are his past deeds, and they surround him clamoring "Why did you do me?" "Why did you think me?" and "Me! answer me!" Their voices become "more and more strident and harsh, so that they overwhelmed the great Tone." Goethe's angelic choirs of Christian mythology here give place to "the great Tone," but the parallel to Faust's dying moment is evident. It is even more obvious when these past deeds cower and kneel before the approach of his childhood's Elizabeth—the Margaret, the Gretchen, of our Morgan. As he tells the truth about their relationship for the first time, he finds his past deeds disappearing before his stare. And once this truth is acknowledged, his memories begin to fade, and they no longer seem important. He can ask Elizabeth, "But you became a princess, did you not?" And she can answer, "Yes, perhaps I did. I hope I did. I, too, forget." As Henry Morgan dies, he hears again, but only for a moment, the "deep, mellow pulsation of the Tone."

If one comes to this first novel by way of Steinbeck's later fiction, the most striking thing, apart from historical setting, is its prose style, which often seems indebted to Elizabethan drama and particularly to Shakespeare. One cannot read "a hundred sagging mouths opened on his body and every one laughed blood" without thinking of Mark Antony's funeral oration or of some messenger describing an off-stage murder. When Coeur de Gris, Morgan's only friend and conscience, is stricken with fever and falls, in Morgan's words we hear King Lear speaking to his fool: "Lie still, boy! Lie quietly! You must not move yet. I am afraid. In a moment I thought you were dead and all the world shriveled. Lie quietly! . . . Now we will take up the Cup of Gold together, and it shall be a chalice of two handles." He then lifts Coeur de Gris and carries him to the shade of a tree.

Often the echoes are not so specific, but the tone, imagery, and accent of Renaissance drama are there. After Coeur de Gris is dead, Morgan says, "He might have been a vital half of me, which, dying, leaves me half a man." And Coeur de Gris suggests the lecherous dukes and cardinals of Jacobean drama in, "Sir, I have heard a seaman all rotten with disease whispering to himself in the night, 'If this thing were not on me, I would go adventuring for La Santa Roja.'" Of course *Cup of Gold* is a historical novel, and much of this prose, whatever its effect, represents Steinbeck's attempt to capture what he thought to be the idiom of that time. Certainly the short stories written while at Stanford indicate this was not his idea of normal speech.

A more accurate estimate of Steinbeck's early prose style can be obtained from those passages which he writes *in propria persona,* especially descriptions of nature, such as these opening paragraphs from *Cup of Gold.* (The italics are mine.)

All afternoon the wind sifted out of the black Welsh glens, *crying notice that Winter was come sliding down over the Pole.* . . . The gently moving air *seemed to be celebrating the loss of some gay thing with a soft, tender elegy.* But in the pastures great work horses nervously stamped their feet, and all through the country small brown birds, in cliques of four or five, flew twittering from tree to tree and back again, *seeking and calling in recruits for their southing.* . . .

> The afternoon passed slowly, *procession-like, with an end of evening, and on the heels of the evening an excited wind rushed out, rustled in the dry grasses, and fled whimpering across the fields. Night drew down like a black cowl, and Holy Winter sent his Nuncio to Wales.*

There is a hint of the later Steinbeck in the description of horses and birds, but in the main this is a "literary" style full of personifications and "pathetic fallacies." The clear statement and objective rendering of detail are here garbled with emotionalized interpretation. There are other such passages of nature description, for example this: "A fierce, steady wind poured out of the blue heavens and shrilled toward the valley. Upward, the strewn rocks were larger and more black and dreadful—crouched guardian things of the path."

Despite the archaic style and the historical subject of *Cup of Gold*, Steinbeck clearly expresses several ideas which become important in his later works. The biological view of man which he was to utilize so fully in his subsequent novels and which he was to explain at length in *Sea of Cortez* can be seen here in germ. Of young Morgan's yearning, Steinbeck writes, "It was a desire for a thing he could not name. Perhaps the same force moved him which collected the birds into exploring parties and made the animals sniff up-wind for the scent of winter." The terms in which Panama is described previous to its capture suggest what he would later call, in terms of biology, a "weak survival quotient." The inhabitants "had grown soft in their security," because "when there was no danger anymore, a different breed of men came to live in Panama. . . . fearful and cowardly. . . ." Rodriguez, the captain defending Panama, sees his troop of horsemen "following his orders as though they were the multi-members of one great body governed by his brain."

These are only random and scattered references. Steinbeck had not yet met Ed Ricketts, whose friendship helped him to evolve the theory in greater detail.

There are also in this first novel occasional references to religion and to the man of skill, both of which play important parts in later works, but the only topic of importance in Steinbeck's later works which is treated fully in *Cup of Gold* is the attitude toward sex and prostitution. In a conversation with Morgan, Coeur de Gris calmly states that his mother is a "free woman." When Morgan is shocked that a woman of good family should turn to prostitution, his friend asks, ". . . why should I interfere with what she considers a serious work [?] She is proud of her position, proud that her callers are the best people in the port. . . . Why should I change the gentle course of her ways, even if I could? No, she is a dear, lovely woman, and she has been a good mother to me. Her only fault is that she is filled with over-many little scruples. She nags at me when I am at home, and cries so when I leave. She is dreadfully afraid that I may find some woman who may do me harm." When Morgan asks, "That is strange, is it not?—considering her life," Coeur de Gris replies, "Why is it strange? Must they have a different brain in that ancient profession?" He assures Morgan that "her life is immaculate—prayers thrice a day. . . ."

This unconventional attitude toward sex is carried further in the story told by "The Other Burgundian." It sounds like something out of Maupassant. Four friends (three artists and "one who had possessions") love the same girl. She marries the one with possessions, but continues to be mistress to the other three. "And Emil, the husband, did not mind. He loved his friends. Why not? They were his true friends, but poor." This happy group is broken up by a "blind," "idiotic" force called "Public Opinion," which compels Emil to challenge the other three to a duel. Emil kills two and maims the other (the teller of the story, now Emil's inseparable companion). Then again comes "this Public Opinion, like a blundering, powerful ox," and, having forced the duel, forces the duelist to leave France. With the exception of a few refinements, such as those in *Cannery Row, Burning Bright,* and *East of Eden,* Steinbeck's first novel pretty well expresses an attitude toward sex which is reflected in almost all his mature works. *The Pastures of Heaven,* his next published book, was to devote an entire section to this same topic, again making society the villain.

In addition to stating, tentatively, several preoccupations of his mature work, *Cup of Gold* also seems to have purged Steinbeck of certain tendencies which might have harmed him as a writer. Hereafter, with few exceptions, he avoided "literary" prose; he also avoided heroic protagonists and historical settings. He turned instead to a simple but balanced prose, to the kind of people he had known since his childhood, and to that particular area of California where he had been born and had lived all his life—the Salinas Valley.

3 To a God Unknown

Although *To a God Unknown* was published late in 1933, a year after *The Pastures of Heaven*, Steinbeck wrote in that year that he "had been making notes for it for about five years." (JS-RB, 2/11/33) His agents, McIntosh & Otis, were trying to find a publisher for one version, called "To an Unknown God," before he started work on *The Pastures of Heaven* early in 1931. (JS-MO, 5/8/31) An even earlier version, called "The Green Lady," had been rejected by several publishers. This version had for its protagonist a character who fell in love with a forest, somehow identified with his daughter, and who killed himself by walking sacrificially into that forest while it was ablaze.[1] "To an Unknown God" failed to find a publisher, and in May of 1931 Steinbeck wrote to his agents: "To an Unknown God should have been a play. It was conceived as a play and thought of and talked of as such for several years. . . . It is out of proportion because it was thought of as two books. I should like to write it again."[2] (JS-MO, 5/8/31) Three months later he wrote to say that because the imperfections in the book had bothered him since he first submitted it, their failure to find a publisher for it was "neither unwelcome nor unpleasant. . . . I know, though, that the story is good. I shall re-write it immediately. . . . Certainly I shall make no effort to 'popularize' the story." (JS-MO, 8/18/31)

Steinbeck was still working on *The Pastures of Heaven,* which he expected to finish by Christmas, and did not find time for reworking "To an Unknown God" until January of 1932. At this time he wrote a long letter explaining his plans for the book.

> I have no intention of trying to patch it up. It would surely show such surgery, especially since it was finished nearly two years ago. I shall cut it in two at the break and work only at the first half. . . . With the material in the first half I shall make a new story, one suggested by recent, and to me, tremendous events.
>
> Do you remember the drought in Jolon that came every thirty-five years? We have been going through one identical with the one of 1880. . . . the description of the effect on the people was correct but inadequate for when it was written the thing had not reached its height. . . . rain came in December. I've seen decorous people dancing in the mud. They have laughed with a kind of crazy joy when their land was washing away. . . . The new novel will be closely knit and I can use much of the material from the Unknown God, but the result will be no rewritten version. (JS-MO, 1/25/32)

Four months later Steinbeck was still working on the book and thought it would not be ready for at least another six months. The book was "growing too fast," not in length but "in implication." He had by now destroyed the first part and was doing it over; it had "a good many characters scraped off." He thought the book was worth taking time with and that it wouldn't be worth anything if time were not taken. Also, he was trying to find another title for it. (JS-MO, 5/17/32)

Work proceeded slowly, however, and it was interrupted by Steinbeck's unsuccessful plan to take a four-hundred-mile horseback trip through Mexico. (JS-MO, 10/2/32) Another time he wrote that "the necessity for making a living suspended work on the new novel." (JS-MO, 11/2/32) In January of 1933 he was planning one more draft, and finally in February he sent off the manuscript of *To a God Unknown,* saying, "I think its structure is pretty good. . . . It is *not* a revision of the other mss." (JS-MO, 2/11/33) No other Steinbeck novel except *East of Eden* has been in progress so long or undergone such extensive re-working.

To a God Unknown took for its epigraph a poem from the Rigveda celebrating the Creator of all things, the "God over Gods." Each stanza ends with the refrain, "Who is He to whom we shall offer our sacrifice?" It is worth noting that Steinbeck's version differs in several respects from the standard translations. The original hymn (Rigveda, Book X, No. 121) has ten stanzas, not six. Steinbeck combines five and six, seven and eight, as well as omitting the first and last stanzas. The omissions are significant, for the first stanza invokes Hiranyagarba, the "golden seed," and the last stanza is a prayer for fertility and increase. There are other minor omissions and differences in translation. The rhythm is made more regular, obviously patterned on the Psalms. The most important change is that where other versions follow the original in giving the lines "May He not injure us, Who is the begetter of earth, the true and faithful one who begat the sky, who begat the great and shining waters" as a prayer, a request, Steinbeck makes them interrogative: "May He not hurt us, He who made earth,/Who made the sky and the shining sea?"

This change from prayer to question, like Steinbeck's juggling with the "timshel" symbol in *East of Eden*, is basic to the novel. For *To a God Unknown* is concerned not only with the problem of "Who is He to whom we shall offer our sacrifice?" (as the poem's refrain indicates), but also with the nature of man's proper relationship to that God. This relationship is explored through various perspectives and reaches its climax of revelation in the great drought and final sacrifice.

In addition to this poem from the Rigveda, usually known as the "Hymn to the Unknown God," there is another source for the novel's title:

Then Paul stood in the midst of Mars' hill, and said, Ye men of Athens, I perceive that in all things ye are too superstitious.

For as I passed by, and beheld your devotions, I found an altar with this inscription, TO THE UNKNOWN GOD. Whom therefore ye ignorantly worship, him declare I unto you.

God that made the world and all things therein, seeing that he is Lord of heaven and earth, dwelleth not in temples made with hands;

Neither is worshipped with men's hands, as though he needed any thing, seeing he giveth to all life, and breath, and all things. . . .

For in him we live, and move, and have our being; as certain also of your own poets have said, For we are also his offspring.

Forasmuch then as we are the offspring of God, we ought not to think that the Godhead is like unto gold, or silver, or stone, graven by art and man's device.

(Acts, XVII, 22–25, 28–29)

It will be remembered that at one stage Steinbeck's novel was called "To an Unknown God," which differs from the Biblical words only in the use of the indefinite article, and that in the letters he often refers to the book as "The Unknown God."

Knowledge of these two sources for Steinbeck's title is important, because the tensions between them (pagan and Christian, pantheistic and anthropomorphic) are reflected in the novel's characters and plot. The four Wayne brothers (Joseph, Thomas, Burton, Benjy), Father Angelo, and the old man who lives by the sea: each has a different conception of man's relationship to "The Unknown God." The meaning of the novel is the pattern woven by these different approaches, that of Joseph providing the thread of plot.

Before coming to the valley of Nuestra Senora (probably the Jolon Valley, according to early versions of the book), the four Wayne brothers, two of whom are married, live with their father on a stony Vermont farm. Fearful that the meager land will not suffice the growing families, and hungry for a farm of his own, Joseph wishes to seek new land in the West. The father, a bearded patriarch, refuses to leave his farm but gives Joseph permission to do so and promises to follow him westward after death. Although he is not the eldest son, it is Joseph who receives the patriarchal blessing, and in the old manner—placing his hand between his father's thighs. A month later, he leaves for California. On arriving, he records his homestead and builds his house, and on hearing of his father's death, he writes his brothers, urging them to join him. They arrive with their families, take up the adjoining lands, and live together in abundance, Joseph, now married, presiding over the family like an Abraham. As the older Mexican settlers predicted, however, there returns to the valley a great drought. Before it is over, the rich land is reduced to a desert and the families are forced to leave.

The main action of the novel concerns Joseph's growing mystic and ritualistic relationship to the land. Before he leaves for California, his hunger for land of his own is such as any farmer might feel. As soon, however, as he arrives in the lush valley, his feeling for the land begins to take on a symbolic meaning. "There was a curious femaleness about the interlacing boughs and twigs, about the long green cavern cut by the river. . . . The endless green aisles and alcoves seemed to have meanings as obscure and promising as the symbols of an ancient religion." Joseph mistrusts his feelings, and as he tries to combat them by thinking of home and his father he feels that his father is dead and then "knew that there was no quarrel, for his father and this new land were one." As he enters his valley a shower of rain falls, and Joseph is overcome by his passion for making the land his own. "He flung himself face downward on the grass and pressed his cheek against the wet stems. His fingers gripped the wet grass and tore it out and gripped again. His thighs beat heavily on the earth." That evening another symbolic copulation takes place as a silhouetted pine tree pierces the rising moon and then withdraws.

For reasons he cannot explain, Joseph builds his house under the protecting limb of an oak tree. Later, when his brothers write of their father's death, he feels that the tree now harbors his father's spirit and he speaks to it. From this point on, the tree plays an increasingly important role in Joseph's life. At first Joseph merely confides to it, but soon he makes it the object of his druidic practices. On the pretext of protecting the barnyard fowls, he hangs dead hawks on the tree; but no such practical reason can explain his nailing to it the earclippings from his cattle. During the *fiesta* he pours a cup of wine on the bark and places meat on its limbs. When his son is born he places the child in the "arms" of the tree, which he believes "wouldn't let him fall." When the tree dies, Joseph convinces himself that his father's spirit has gone to reside in the great moss-covered rock in the middle of a pine grove, and to this rock he now performs his oblations and his ultimate sacrifice. At no point is he able to rationalize his mystic attitude. "Joseph did not think these things in his mind, but in his chest and in the corded muscles of his legs. It was the heritage of a race which for a million years had sucked at the breasts of the soil and cohabited with the earth."

The druidic practices and ancestor worship accompany Joseph's increasing sense of responsibility for his land's fertility and his eventual identification with it. Once he identifies himself with a mounting bull. When the drought begins he says, "I'm failing to protect the land. . . . The duty of keeping life in my land is beyond my power." Joseph's assumed role as the Fisher King is perceived by his brother Thomas, who says jeeringly to Joseph, "And you'll get another wife, and there won't ever be another drought," to which Joseph answers, "It might be so." When the drought is in its final stage and the families are forced to leave the valley, Joseph thinks, "I was appointed to care for the land, and I have failed." When all his oblations prove ineffectual, including the live sacrifice of a calf, Joseph climbs up onto the great moss-covered rock, lies down, and cuts his wrists. "Then his body grow huge and light. It rose into the sky, and out of it came the streaking rain. 'I should have known,' he whispered. 'I am the rain.' And yet he looked dully down the mountains of his body where the hills fell to an abyss. . . . He saw his hills grow dark with moisture. Then a lancing pain shot through the heart of the world. 'I am the land,' he said, 'and I am the rain. The grass will grow out of me in a little while.' "

Joseph's primitive, pagan development is given further ramifications by his parallel development as a Christ figure. During her marriage ceremony, Elizabeth looks around the Protestant church for a Christ image, and "when she drew a picture of the Christ in her mind, He had the face, the youthful beard, the piercing puzzled eyes of Joseph, who stood beside her." Outside the church afterward, she "peered up at him in wonder, for her vision had not changed; the Christ's face was still the face of Joseph. She laughed uneasily and confessed to herself, 'I'm praying to my own husband.' " Near the end of the novel, Juanito also sees in Joseph's face the Christ image: "He saw the crucified Christ hanging on his cross, dead and stained with blood." When Joseph brings home his bride, Thomas's wife, Rama, tells her, ". . . this man is not a man, unless he is all men, the strength, the resistance, the long and stumbling thinking of all men, and all the joy and suffering, too. . . . He is all these, a repository for a little piece of each man's soul, and more than that, a symbol of the earth's soul." Once, while Joseph is working in the barn, he "moved into a shaft of light and spread his arms for a moment." This Christ posture is accentuated by the crowing of a cock. Thus Joseph's death is developed not only as the sacrifice of the impotent king for his land's fertility, but also as Christ's sacrifice for mankind, the families of the Nuestra Senora Valley.

This double theme, obviously related to that of *The Wasteland,* is complicated and qualified by two strategies: a pattern of coincidences, and an arrangement of perspectives. It is true that the drought begins with the death of the oak tree and is intensified by the death of Joseph's (the Fisher King's) wife. It is also true that earlier when a pig is slaugh-

tered on the tree it begins to rain and that rain falls again
during a mass primitive dance performed at the fiesta. It is
evident that the region in which the old man lives and sacrifices animals is always green and moist. Joseph's self-
sacrifice is followed by a saving rain for the valley. Taken
in isolation, these events seem contrived to support Joseph's
pagan religion, and he becomes not only the protagonist but
the hero as well.

The context of these events, however, throws a different
light on them. From the very beginning of the novel we are
made aware, through Romas and other old natives of the
region, that the drought is a periodic phenomenon which has
come to the valley "twice in the memory of old men," and
may come again. The summer preceding the killing of the
oak and the death of Elizabeth is described as an abnormally
hot one, drying up the land more than usual. Willie's night-
mares of a moon landscape, the "bright place that is dry
and dead," are prophetic visions. When Elizabeth falls from
the rock and breaks her neck, it actually rains for a while.
The rain which falls during the height of the fiesta could be
the result of Burton's frantic praying for God to break up
the pagan devil-worship, as he himself believes. It could
also be the result of Father Angelo's mass, or the libation
Joseph pours on the tree, or the pagan dance, or it could be
simply a normal rain, since it comes during the usual season
for rain in that valley. The land where lives the old man
who makes live sacrifices is always wet and green, but it is
on the western slope of the coastal range, where all night lie
the heavy ocean fogs. Likewise, there are many possible
causes for the rain which follows Joseph's self-sacrifice.
There had been signs of rain in the weather; he had killed
a calf; Father Angelo had prayed for rain; and Juanito had
burned a candle. The novelist's skill and intention are

evident in the fact that these "coincidences" never obtrude or become obvious to the extent of casting ridicule on Joseph's obsession.

The perspectives provided by Joseph's three brothers, Father Angelo, the old man, and the natives, function in a similar manner and to a similar purpose. Burton, a strict Protestant, abhors both the Roman Church and such pagan rites as mass dancing: "It's devil-worship, I tell you! It's horrible! On our own place! First the devil-worshiping priest and his wooden idols, and then this!" Burton lives almost completely in the spirit. He "had embraced his wife four times. He had two children. Celibacy was a natural state for him. Burton was never well. His cheeks were drawn and lean, and his eyes hungry for a pleasure he did not expect this side of heaven." He observes Joseph's libations to the tree several times and expresses disapproval. After seeing Joseph place his first-born in the oak, he leaves the valley for an evangelist camp at Pacific Grove. Before leaving, however, he girdles Joseph's tree so that it will die.

The youngest brother, Benjy, is a ne'er-do-well drunkard, who spends his time serenading and seducing women. He is completely irresponsible and incapable of providing for himself. Where Joseph seeks his relation to life through pagan rituals and Burton through his ascetic Christ, Benjy seeks nothing more profound than the oracle of the bottle. He meets death early in the novel, stabbed in the back while making love to Juanito's wife.

Thomas differs markedly from all three. Although like Joseph he is close to nature, his relationship to it is that of a healthy animal. And it is with animals that he has the closest rapport. They follow him around; he seems to know what pleases or displeases them. He knows to the minute when a mare or cow will drop its young. Although he is no kinder to animals than they are to each other, he is not brutish. Rather, "he was too much of an animal himself to be sentimental." His wife, Rama, "understood Thomas, treated him as though he were an animal, kept him clean and fed and warm, and didn't often frighten him." Thomas suspects any kind of ritual: "It seems a trap, a kind of little trap."

Like each of Joseph's brothers, the old man and Father Angelo also illustrate approaches to "The Unknown God." The old man is Joseph carried to the extreme. When asked why he performs his daily sacrifices to the sun, he replies, "I don't know. I have made up reasons, but they aren't true. I have said to myself, 'The sun is life. I give life to life'—'I make a symbol of the sun's death.' When I made these reasons I knew they weren't true." And Joseph breaks in, "These were words to clothe a naked thing, and the thing is ridiculous in clothes." The old man agrees, and adds, "I do it for myself. I can't tell that it doesn't help the sun. But it is for me. In the moment I am the sun. Do you see? I, through the beast, am the sun. I burn in his death." He hopes to end his life by sacrificing himself on the stone altar in the same manner he has been sacrificing the animals.

Thomas, the old man and Joseph, Burton, Benjy: if the characters are placed in this order it will be seen that together they present a scheme embracing man as animal, man as pantheist, man as anthropomorphist, and finally modern man (Benjy), who rejects all these birthrights.

In this scheme Father Angelo occupies an important position. "Father Angelo was a stern man where the church was concerned, but once out of the church, and with the matters of the church out of the way, he was a tender and a humorous man. Let him get a mouthful of meat, and a cup of wine in his hand, and there were no eyes that could twinkle more brightly than his." Before the fiesta, Father Angelo sings a mass, but he does not later interfere with the people when they hold their primitive dance. When Joseph starts the *fiesta* by sacrificially pouring a cup of wine on the earth, Father Angelo "nodded his head and smiled at the fine way in which the thing was done"; but when Joseph pours a libation on his tree, Father Angelo reproves him: " 'Be careful of the groves, my son. Jesus is a better saviour than a hamadryad.' And his smile became tender, for Father Angelo was a wise as well as a learned man."

At the height of the drought, Father Angelo is approached by Joseph, who, under the persuasion of Juanito, wants the priest to pray for the land. Father Angelo insists that they pray instead for Joseph's soul: "the land does not die." Joseph refuses, and after he leaves, the priest does pray for rain, but first prays for Joseph's soul. After the rains come, Father Angelo is aware that the people are celebrating ancient pagan rites. "The priest could see in his mind how the people were dancing, beating the soft earth to slush with their bare feet. He knew how they would be wearing the skins of animals, although they didn't know why they wore them. The pounding rhythm grew louder and more insistent, and the chanting voices shrill and more hysterical. 'They'll be taking off their clothes,' the priest whispered, 'and they'll roll in the mud. They'll be rutting like pigs in the mud.' " He starts to go out to stop them, but reconsiders. " 'I couldn't see them in the dark,' he said. They'd all get away in the dark.' And then he confessed to himself: 'They wanted the rain so, poor children. I'll preach against them on Sunday. I'll give everybody a little penance.' " Father Angelo is undoubtedly Steinbeck's most sympathetically portrayed man of religion. He represents what is best in both Burton and Joseph. In him the Vedic hymn and Paul's sermon are brought together.

Steinbeck takes care to provide his archetypal plot with

a continuum of psychological, mythical, and ritualistic allusions. Almost every action and description has its symbolic suggestions. The scene in which Joseph takes his bride through the narrow, steep pass in the mountains is so obviously symbolic of sexual intercourse and the loss of virginity that it needs no comment—the monolith, the stream, the naked white rock, the valley beyond. In another scene, a rain-bearing cloud coming over the mountains from the ocean has the shape of a goat. When Joseph discovers the pine grove which contains the altar-like rock, he finds there a strange bull, which is singled out by "the long, black swinging scrotum, which hung nearly to the knees. . . ." Even Father Angelo engages in unconscious symbolic rituals. Steinbeck takes much care to describe the altar statues which can be taken apart for packing. A few pages later we have this paragraph:

"As soon as the mass was done, people gathered close to watch Father Angelo fold up the Christ and Mary. He did it well, genuflecting before each one before he took it down and unscrewed its head."

In the aggregate these symbols and symbolic actions not only provide an appropriate, rich background for the novel's plot, they also facilitate the willing suspension of disbelief which is demanded by that plot.

To a God Unknown is an important novel for purposes of understanding Steinbeck's development as a writer. For one thing, it shows a considerable advance in prose style. The descriptive opening paragraphs of chapters 2, 14, 17, 18, and 24 cannot be matched by anything in *Cup of Gold.* Steinbeck has at various times admitted his early admiration for Thackeray, James Branch Cabell, Don Byrne, the nineteenth-century Russian novelists, Willa Cather, and others.[3] If, however, the above-mentioned paragraphs seem influenced by anyone, it is by Hemingway, of whom Steinbeck once wrote, "I'm convinced that in many ways he is the finest writer of our time." (JS-PC, *ca.* Feb., 1939) It is instructive to read again the description of early winter from *Cup of Gold* (quoted above) and compare it with this from *To a God Unknown:*

> The winter came in early that year. Three weeks before Thanksgiving the evenings were red on the mountain tops toward the sea, and the bristling, officious wind raked the valley and sang around the house corners at night and flapped the window shades, and the little whirlwinds took columns of dust and leaves down the road like reeling soldiers. The blackbirds swarmed and flew away in twinkling clouds and doves sat mourning on the fences for a while and then disappeared during a night. All day the flocks of ducks and geese were in the sky, aiming their arrows unerringly at the south, and in the dusk they cried tiredly, and looked for the shine of water where they could rest the night. The frost came into the valley of Our Lady one night and burned the willows yellow and the dogwood red.

To demonstrate that Hemingway is partially responsible for this improvement, it is only necessary to quote the well-known opening of *A Farewell to Arms:*

> In the late summer of that year we lived in a house in a village that looked across the river and the plain to the mountains. In the bed of the river there were pebbles and boulders, dry and white in the sun, and the water was clear and swiftly moving and blue in the channels. Troops went by the house and down the road and the dust they raised powdered the leaves of the trees. The trunks of the trees too were dusty and the leaves fell early that year and we saw the troops marching along the road and the dust rising and leaves, stirred by the breeze, falling and the soldiers marching and afterward the road bare and white except for the leaves.

The two paragraphs are strikingly similar not only in their use of *and* to impose a balanced, continuous rhythm, but also in their combination of such words as *trees, dust, soldiers, leaves, mountains, down the road, water,* and *that year,* as well as echoes of *breeze* and *columns.*[4]

Another reason why *To a God Unknown* is of value in understanding Steinbeck's development lies in the importance this novel places on man's unconscious heritage of the experiences of his race. This heritage is reflected in the characters' strange compulsions to engage in irrational rituals, and their susceptibility to symbols of whose significance they are not consciously aware. In later novels, this Jungian "race-memory" is given a new dimension by Steinbeck's insights into marine biology: "And we have thought how the human fetus has, at one stage of its development, vestigial gill-slits. If the gills are a component of the developing human, it is not unreasonable to suppose a parallel or concurrent mind or psyche development. If there be a life-memory strong enough to leave its symbol in vestigial gill-slits, the preponderantly aquatic symbols in the individual unconscious might well be indications of a group psyche-memory which is the foundation of the whole unconscious." (SC, 32) This passage from *Sea of Cortez* (eight years later) also indicates the source of Steinbeck's group-man theory, which, though present in *Cup of Gold* and *To a God Unknown,* does not assume critical importance until *In Dubious Battle* and *The Grapes of Wrath.*

It is this kind of orientation which is responsible for a stylistic device that makes its first appearance in *To a God Unknown.* Frequently in his works Steinbeck interrupts the flow of his narrative to insert a descriptive passage, often set off as a paragraph, depicting some predatory incident in nature. An owl may be seen pouncing on a rodent, a hawk

striking a rabbit, a weasel killing a squirrel, or big fish feed-
ing on a school of little fish. These passages are always
strategically placed in relation to some action and serve either
the author or the observing characters. They serve the author
as interpretation of or comment on that action, and the
characters as "lessons." Always, they throw light on the
moral structure of that ultimate reality with which man is
consanguineous—Nature.

When Joseph first comes to his valley, he sees a great boar
sitting on its haunches eating a little pig which is still squeal-
ing.

> Joseph jerked up his horse. His face contracted with anger
> and his eyes paled until they were almost white. "Damn you,"
> he cried. "Eat other creatures. Don't eat your own people."
> He pulled his rifle from its scabbard and aimed between the
> yellow eyes of the boar. And then the barrel lowered and a
> firm thumb let down the hammer. Joseph laughed shortly at
> himself. "I'm taking too great power into my hands," he said.
> "Why he's the father of fifty pigs and may be the cause of fifty
> more."

Near the end of the novel, after the death of his wife,
Joseph walks down to the river to meditate and to console
himself. There follows a whole page describing some wild
pigs wading into a shallow pool to slaughter the eels; in turn,
one of the pigs is killed by a mountain lion. Whereas early
in the novel Joseph's first impulse had been to set himself
morally above the boar, here he says to the lion, "If I could
only shoot you, there would be an end and a new beginning." There are many such passages in the novel, and none is
a gratuitous piece of realism.[5] Each serves some definite
purpose.

Although these descriptions of predatory activity always
illustrate the violence in nature, they do not suggest that

nature is evil. Neither do they fall into such clichés of literary naturalism as "fang and claw," or "survival of the fittest." They do not suggest that man should live by "the law of the jungle" and become the superior predator; but they do remind man of the great fecundity and enduring pattern of that nature of which he is a part and which is a part of him. They remind him of the undeniable biological heritage which is a factor in his most intellectual pursuits.

The full importance of man's biological heritage is made clear in *Sea of Cortez*. Steinbeck sees in man "a strange duality . . . which makes for an ethical paradox." Man's ideas of ethical good—generosity, humility—are concomitants of practical failure. The ethically bad qualities—cruelty, self-interest, rapacity—are concomitants of success, which man also admires, while condemning the qualities which make for it. In biology, the term "good," as used by men, would be translated as "weak survival quotient." "Thus, man in his thinking or reverie status admires the progression towards extinction, but in the unthinking stimulus which really drives him he tends toward survival." Steinbeck suggests that perhaps man, as a species, "is not set, has not jelled, but is still in a state of becoming, bound by his physical memories to a past of struggle and survival, limited in his futures by the uneasiness of thought and consciousness." (SC, 96)

In *To a God Unknown* Steinbeck explores the nature of these "physical memories" as they manifest themselves in man's need for ritual, his need to give meaning somehow to situations beyond empirical control. And although in later works Steinbeck becomes increasingly interested in the other aspect of the dilemma ("the uneasiness of thought and consciousness"), he never wholly abandons this "mystic" approach to The Unknown God, and the two are reconciled in the ideal figure of Doc, the marine biologist.

4 *The Pastures of Heaven*

While McIntosh & Otis were trying unsuccessfully to market "To an Unknown God," written immediately after *Cup of Gold,* Steinbeck was at work on his next published volume—*The Pastures of Heaven.* In May of 1931 he wrote his agents:

> The present work interests me and perhaps falls in the "aspects" theme you mention. There is, about twelve miles from Monterey, a valley in the hills called Corral de Tierra. Because I am using its people I have named it Las Pasturas del Cielo. The valley was for years known as the happy valley because of the unique harmony which existed among its twenty families. About ten years ago a new family moved in on one of the ranches. They were ordinary people, ill educated but honest and as kindly as any. In fact, in their whole history I cannot find that they have committed a really malicious act nor an act which was not dictated by honorable expediency or

out and out altruism. But about the M————s there was a flavor of evil. Everyone they came in contact with was injured. Every place they went dissension sprang up. There have been two murders, a suicide, many quarrels and a great deal of unhappiness in the Pastures of Heaven, and all of these things can be traced to the influence of the M————s. So much is true. I am using the following method. The manuscript is made up of stories each one complete in itself, having its rise, climax and ending. Each story deals with a family or individual. They are tied together only by the common locality and by the contact with the M————s. I am trying to show this peculiar evil cloud which follows the M————s. Some of the stories are very short and some as long as fifteen thousand words. I thought of combining them with that thirty-thousand ms called Dissonant Symphony to make one volume. . . . I think the plan at least falls very definitely in the aspects of American Life category. I have finished several and am working on others steadily. They should be done by this Fall. (JS-MO, 5/8/31)

Except for mentioning one more murder than appeared in *The Pastures of Heaven*, this letter is an accurate general sketch of the book's structure and content. Notations on the title sheet of the first draft (written in a 6 x 9 composition book) indicate, however, that earlier he had planned a slightly different scheme of organization. Steinbeck there noted that *"Pasturas"* would be "a curious story of which at least half—or one third—of the space is taken up with dramatis personae." His first plans called for a large portion of the book to deal with the various family histories *before* the Munroes arrive: "The first chapter will deal with the valley itself: and following that will be nine or ten chapters devoted to nine or ten families. Then will come the entrance of the M————s." The title page of this first draft also shows a different order for the stories; some, "Howard and the Spinach" and "Blind Frank," do not appear in the final ver-

sion. There are no titles in this first list which might suggest
the book's last three sections: the stories about Pat Humbert,
John Whiteside, and the group of bus passengers. Also absent
is the story of the Lopez sisters, which Harry Thornton
Moore says was originally part of *To a God Unknown*, although it would seem that the John Whiteside story, having
many parallels to that book, fits better into its scheme.[1]

This first draft abounds in deletions and additions. Steinbeck was having difficulties following his original plans, and
in the margin opposite the third story, which introduced the
Munroes, he wrote, "There are things so definitely wrong
with this story that I think it had better be remade. A large
part of it anyway." The eventual remaking was a great improvement because it brought together the two (pre- and
post-Munroe) parts of each story into one unit. In some
stories, for example the one about Pat Humbert and especially that about Shark Wicks (which was the first one he
wrote), this splicing is still evident.

By the middle of August Steinbeck was well along, writing
his agents that "The Pastures stories proceed rapidly. . . .
They should be ready to submit by Christmas." At that time
he sent along the manuscript of "Dissonant Symphony,"
which he still thought might be included "under one cover
with the Pastures of Heaven." (JS-MO, 8/18/31) It was *not*
included with the stories, however, and after publication of
The Pastures of Heaven in October, 1932, Steinbeck wrote,
"The manuscript called Dissonant Symphony, I wish you
would withdraw. I looked at it not long ago and I don't
want it out. I may rewrite it sometime, but I certainly do
not want that mess published under any circumstances, re-
vised or not." (JS-MO, 1/?/33)

The Pastures of Heaven is not, strictly speaking, a novel, partly because the several stories are too autonomous structurally and aesthetically. Many of the episodes were based on stories Steinbeck's mother used to tell about her adventures when she, like Molly Morgan, taught school in rural communities. With one or two exceptions, there is no reason why one story must precede or follow another. The section dealing with Molly Morgan, for example, is not made more meaningful or effective by the role she played in two preceding stories—those of Tularecito and Junius Maltby. Although most critics have perceived that *The Pastures of Heaven* is not really a novel, most have missed the importance of the Munroe family and have tried to make too much of the stories' unity by pinning them together with some other theme: the contrast between dream and reality,[2] the realization of life through illusion,[3] and the suppression of the individual by society.[4] Each of these themes may be made to apply to one or even two or three of the stories, but attempts to impose them on the book as a whole have only resulted in obscuring its real structure and distorting the emphasis of individual stories.

On the other hand, as Steinbeck indicated in his letter to his agents, the book has more unity than might be expected from a collection of short stories. In addition to the unity provided by a common locale and theme, the book is given a certain roundness by the two introductory stories about the valley's history, the penultimate story about the defeat of the valley's patriarch, John Whiteside, and the concluding story about the busload of tourists who look down on the valley and envy its apparent peace and tranquility. If it is kept in mind that although the Munroes are an "evil cloud," as Steinbeck put it, they never commit "a really malicious act nor an act . . . not dictated by honorable expediency or out and out altruism," it becomes obvious that these stories are given further unity by their common preoccupation with irony—the evil results of the Munroes' innocent actions.

This dominance of irony is established in the opening pages, which deal with the valley's history before the appearance of the Munroes on page 14. The valley called the Pastures of Heaven is discovered and named by a Spaniard who recaptures there some converted Indians who had abandoned their new religion to avoid forced labor in the clay pits of the Carmelo Mission. And this Spaniard who had "whipped brown backs to tatters" and whose "rapacious manhood was building a new race for California," stands with his steel hat in his hand and whispers, "Holy Mother! Here are the green pastures of Heaven to which our Lord leadeth us."

The brief history of the first two families to settle in the Pastures of Heaven, on what will become the Munroe farm, also contributes to this ironic play on the valley's name. After building the big, square house in which the Munroes will live, George Battle sends back to New York for his mother, who dies in passage and is buried at sea; "and she had wanted the crowded company of her home graveyard." George Battle then marries an older spinster with a small fortune who, before being confined in an asylum, tries twice to burn the house down. The Battles' only son, John, turns out to be a religious fanatic who "covered his clothes and hat with tiny cross-stitches in white thread" and has a habit of charging into the underbrush and driving the devils from cover with a heavy stick. One evening he disturbs a rattlesnake. "He fell upon his knees and prayed for a moment. Suddenly he shouted, 'This is the damned serpent. Out devil,' and sprang forward with clutching fingers. The snake struck him three times in the throat where there were no crosses to protect him. He struggled very little and died in a few minutes." The next settlers, the Mustrovics, appear to be doing very well until one day they mysteriously disappear, so suddenly that they leave the kitchen table set with silver, saucers of porridge, and a plate of fried eggs.

After the entrance of the Munroes on page 14, however, all the evils which overcome the people of the Pastures of Heaven seem to originate with some member of that family. Shark Wicks is undone, the whole tower of his hypothetical wealth crumbles, when he attempts to defend his daughter from the advances of young Jimmie Munroe. Tularecito, a strong, but usually harmless, idiot, is committed to an institution for the criminally insane after striking Bert Munroe with a shovel. When Helen Van Deventer and her mad daughter come to the Pastures of Heaven, Bert kindly tries to visit them and welcome them to the valley. He succeeds only in speaking to the mad Hilda through the bars of her prison room, and Hilda is shot by her mother when she escapes with the idea she is to marry the strange man who spoke to her. The idyllic existence of Junius Maltby and his son, Robbie, is ended when Mrs. Munroe, out of kindness, gives a bundle of clothes to the boy; Junius and Robbie had never before realized their poverty. The Lopez sisters can no longer give their favors to the men because Bert Munroe makes a suggestive joke to the wife of an innocent man whom Maria Lopez allows to ride in her wagon. Molly Morgan leaves town because the drunken tramp in Bert Munroe's car may be her father. Raymond Banks's pleasant visits to his friend, the warden at San Quentin, cease because Bert Munroe poisons his innocent mind. At first, Pat Humbert's desire to please Mae Munroe results in his opening the dreaded parlor where his parents died and from which their spirits still command him. However, when he goes to invite Mae to visit his expensive, remade "colonial room," he learns she is engaged to marry someone else. Whereas previously he had confined himself to the kitchen of the house, he now abandons the house altogether and goes to live in the barn. Finally, John Whiteside's ancestral home is destroyed by fire because Bert Munroe kindly suggests they burn the brush from around the house.

Each story revolves around this kind of irony, very reminiscent of some of Hardy's poems. They are "satires of circumstance," in each case the circumstance originating with a member of the Munroe family. Some of the stories, for example the one concerning the Whitesides, are completely saturated with this technique. Old Richard Whiteside comes to the valley intending to found a dynasty and build a lasting home for that dynasty. His wife can bear only one heir, his son John. John, in turn, has only one son, Bill, on whom to place his hopes. Bill marries Mae Munroe, who does not like to live on a farm and who takes him to live in Monterey. The house itself is then inadvertently destroyed by the father of the young girl who is taking Bill away to the city. This irony, which is especially apparent in the stories dealing with social themes, helps to give the book a unity of tone and mood, though the theme which embodies this irony may vary from one story to another.

The Raymond Banks story is interesting for the light it throws on Steinbeck's much-touted addiction to the use of "violence" and "animality." Raymond Banks is a big, hearty, simple man who raises thousands of chickens on the best kept and most admired farm in the valley. Two or three times a year he receives an invitation from the warden at San Quentin, his old high school chum, to be a witness at an execution. These trips are the only vacations Raymond takes, and they provide him with some excitement and the opportunity to talk over old times. Hearing of Raymond's trips to

San Quentin, Bert Munroe talks him into getting an extra invitation for him. When the time arrives, Bert not only refuses to go, but so firmly impresses Raymond with the gruesome possibilities of bungled hangings that he too gives up the trips. It would be wrong to see Bert Munroe as the normal man who pricks the bubble of Raymond Banks's naïve attitude, not only because Steinbeck consistently describes the Munroes as an "evil cloud," but because all Steinbeck's work, especially *The Red Pony,* denies this "unhealthy" view that violence and pain are necessary.

The complexity of the story and its real "meaning" lie in Steinbeck's portrayal of the two men. Bert Munroe's sensitivity and his dislike for fried chicken have their source in an incident of his youth, when he watched a man attempt to butcher a rooster and saw the badly mangled fowl running about in dying agonies. On the other hand, while Raymond likes hangings, he is not a cruel man nor a pervert. "The hanging itself was not the important part, it was the sharp, keen air of the whole proceeding that impressed him. . . . The whole thing made him feel a fullness of experience. . . . Raymond didn't think of the condemned any more than he thought of the chicken when he pressed the blade into its brain. No strain of cruelty nor any gloating over suffering took him to the gallows." Raymond butchers his chickens in the most painless, scientific way possible. Although he allows boys to watch him, he refuses to let them try it. " 'You might get excited and miss the brain,' he said. 'That would hurt the chicken, if you didn't stick him just right.' "

With Bert Munroe, however, it is clear that the attitude toward violence is morbid. He enjoys shivering at the horrible images of suffering which his mind readily conjures up. And it is obvious that he enjoys describing to Raymond in detail the incident from his youth and the possibility of a person's being strangled instead of having his neck broken, or of the head being pulled right off the body from the impact. He likes to horrify himself by imagining that it is he who is being hanged. Raymond listens painfully to his friend's elaborations and at the end cries, "I tell you, you don't think things like that. . . . If you think things like that you haven't got any right to go up with me." It is obvious that Steinbeck intends to show that Raymond has the healthy attitude and that it is Bert Munroe who has the sick one. Raymond's mind, however, has now been poisoned. He cannot go up to visit his friend, and some of his joy in the chicken ranch is also destroyed.

Like Hemingway, Steinbeck finds an important place for violence in his works; but whereas for Hemingway violence is part of a code, often to be sought as the final proof of manhood, Steinbeck merely accepts it as one of the facts of life which must be considered for a full understanding of man's nature and his place in the biological world of which he is a part. He once said about Ed Ricketts, whom he admired very much, "He hated pain inflicted without good reason. . . . When the infliction of pain was necessary, he had little feeling about it." (LSC, xviii-xix)

Except for the three stories about Raymond Banks, Pat Humbert, and John Whiteside, each of which serves its own purpose, the other stories in *The Pastures of Heaven* divide equally into two groups, each of which has a common theme. The stories concerning Shark Wicks, Helen Van Deventer, and Molly Morgan make up one of these groups. In each of the stories in this group the main theme is provided by a character who attempts to live happily by keeping up some illusion which is eventually destroyed.

Because his ambitions exceed his abilities and resources,

Shark Wicks gradually builds for himself a dream world in which he figures as a financial tycoon. He keeps a ledger in which he periodically records imaginary purchases of stocks and real estate, always discovering that he has sold out just in time and turned tremendous profits. As the secret life of Shark Wicks takes up more and more of his attention, the valley people become more and more convinced that he actually has this wealth, and he becomes respected as a financial wizard.

Helen Van Deventer insists on caring for her mad daughter, refusing to place her in an institution although there is a possibility of curing her. Also, she refuses to forget about her husband Hubert, a sporting, superficial man to whom she was married for three months. For twelve years she enjoys bearing the cross of her daughter and tries to make more real and painful the memory of her husband, whom she hardly knew.

All her life Molly Morgan has nursed childhood memories of a gay, fun-loving father who used to return home at long intervals from "business trips," loaded down with fascinating presents and full of wonderful stories which delighted all the children of the neighborhood. One day he went off on a longer trip than usual and did not return; but she believes that someday he surely will, with new, fantastic stories and delightful presents.

None of these illusions has a basis in fact. Shark Wicks has neither wealth nor talent; Helen Van Deventer feels no real love for either her daughter or her dead husband; Molly Morgan's father is actually an alcoholic who used to go off on long periodic drunks. Yet at the end of each story, despite revelations through catastrophe, the characters persist in their illusions. Shark Wicks is convinced that he is a man of ability who has just never had a chance before but will henceforth really make good; Helen Van Deventer abandons the painful memory of her husband and takes up the guilt of having killed her daughter; Molly Morgan prefers to leave her happy valley rather than chance losing her romantic memory of her father. The three stories are variations on a theme.

The stories about Tularecito, Junius Maltby, and the Lopez sisters can be taken as forming another group. Whereas the stories in the first group present characters with an orientation to life which can be held only by ignoring facts, the characters in this second group fail, not because their orientation is untenable in an absolute sense, but because of society's intrusion into the individual's adjustment.

Tularecito, though of subnormal intelligence, is a gentle and useful person as long as he is not tampered with. Gomez, with whom Tularecito lives, says of him, "He can work; he can do marvelous things with his hands, but he cannot learn to do the simple little things of the school. He is not crazy; he is one of those whom God has not quite finished." Society insists that he go to school. Although he cannot understand the lessons, Tularecito has a great talent for drawing animals and is encouraged to cover the blackboards with his art. When they are erased to make room for something else, he literally wrecks the school. The teacher, Miss Martin, tells Gomez that Tularecito is dangerous, but he replies, "He is not dangerous. No one can make a garden as he can. No one can milk so swiftly nor so gently. He is a good boy. He can break a mad horse without riding it; he can train a dog without whipping it, but the law says he must sit in the first grade repeating 'C–A–T, cat' for seven years." Tularecito does become dangerous, however. The new schoolteacher, Molly Morgan, thinking that it would enrich the poor boy's life, encourages him to believe in gnomes and fairies. It is while digging for gnomes in the Munroes' orchard that he is interrupted and strikes Bert Munroe with a shovel. Tularecito is then confined in an institution for the criminally insane.

Junius Maltby, his young son, Robbie, and Jakob live together very happily on a run-down farm. Junius left his city job and came to the Pastures of Heaven for his health and has not done a bit of work since. He and Jakob, his "hired man," who also does nothing, throw a few seeds on the ground every spring, let nature take its course, and eat what they can get with least effort. "Often they went hungry because they failed to find a hen's nest in the grass when it came suppertime." They wear their ragged clothes, go barefoot, and spend their days reading and talking while they sit on a tree branch and cool their feet in the river. They discuss the battle of Trafalgar, the frieze on the Parthenon, Carthaginian warfare, the Spartan virtues, why large things seem good and small things evil, and many other erudite topics. "They didn't make conversation; rather they let a seedling of thought sprout by itself, and then watched with wonder while it sent out branching limbs. They were surprised at the strange fruit their conversations bore, for they didn't direct their thinking, nor trellis nor trim it the way so many people do."

This pleasant existence is first threatened when Robbie is forced to attend school. Society has waited patiently for this legal opportunity to interfere. As it turns out, however, Robbie's ability to tell interesting stories from Thucydides, Herodotus, and Homer, to discuss the practices of certain cannibal tribes and the conquests of Hengist and Horsa, make him a fascinating person both to the teacher and the other children. Robbie soon emerges as a natural leader.

The trouble comes when the school board decides that Robbie must have feelings of inferiority, since his clothes are not as good as those of the other children. Although Molly Mcrgan pleads against it, Robbie is called before the board and Mrs. Munroe presents him with a bundle of shirts and overalls, "trying not to look too pointedly at his ragged clothes." But Robbie notices the stare. "For a moment he looked about nervously like a trapped animal and then he bolted through the door, leaving the little heap of clothing behind him." The next time we see Robbie, he and his father are boarding a bus. Junius explains to Molly Morgan that he is going to try to get a job because his son has "lived like an animal too long, you see. Besides, Miss Morgan, he doesn't know how nice it will be in San Francisco." The irony of Junius' words indicates Steinbeck's own attitude.

This attitude was made even clearer when the story appeared as a monograph in 1936. Its title, *Nothing So Monstrous,* was taken from Robert Louis Stevenson, whom Robbie says his father knows by heart: "There is nothing so monstrous but we can believe it of ourselves." (*Virginibus Puerisque,* II) The context in which this sentence occurs is significant, for it lays stress on the "unfading boyishness of hope and its vigorous irrationality," which is one of Steinbeck's main points in the story. One of Stevenson's analogies applies directly to Junius Maltby:

> We advance in years somewhat in the manner of an invading army in a barren land; the age we have reached, as the phrase goes, we but hold with an outpost, and still keep open our communications with the extreme rear and first beginnings of the march. There is our true base; that is not only the beginning, but the perennial spring of our faculties; and grandfather William can retire upon occasion into the green enchanted forest of his boyhood.

The separate publication of this story included an epilogue which makes Steinbeck's sympathies even more obvious: "I've often wondered whether Junius got a job and whether he kept it. . . . I for one should find it difficult to believe he could go under. I think rather he might have broken away again. For all I know he may have come back to the Pastures of Heaven." [5] There follows an imaginative reconstruction of Junius' return to the valley, and of the farmers coming in the evening to hear him tell his tales about Herodotus, Delphi, and Solomon. The last words in the book are, "I don't know that this is true. I only hope to God it is."

The third story in this group dealing with "social" themes is that of the Lopez sisters. This is Steinbeck's first extended treatment of the *paisanos,* who appeared briefly in *To a God Unknown* and were to provide material for all of his next book—*Tortilla Flat.* The story carries further the tolerant attitude toward prostitution held by Coeur de Gris and "The Other Burgundian" in *Cup of Gold;* but while in the first novel this attitude seems, in part, to be exploited for its shock value, in *The Pastures of Heaven* it becomes the basis for serious social criticism.

Left no means of support by their dead parents, Rosa and Maria establish a restaurant in which they sell "TORTILLAS, ENCHILADAS, TAMALES AND SOME OTHER SPANISH COOKINGS." Although their cuisine is of the best, business is not sufficient to provide a living and they stimulate their trade by giving their favors to the male customers. As Rosa puts it, "Do not make a mistake, I did not take money. The man had eaten three *enchiladas*—three!" Three *enchiladas* becomes the standard rate of exchange and their business prospers. They are happy; the men are happy; no one suffers. The sisters' knees polish the floor where they confess before the Virgin each evening, and they never take "the money of shame." So guileless are they that when Maria returns from Monterey one evening and hears from Rosa that the sheriff has been there she says, "The sheriff, he came? Now we are on the road. Now we will be rich. How many *enchiladas,* Rosa? Tell me how many for the sheriff." The sheriff, however, has come to close the restaurant because Bert Munroe told a joke about Allen Huenker's riding to town in Maria's wagon and Allen's jealous wife insisted that the sheriff take action. Knowing that they cannot live without selling *enchiladas,* Maria and Rosa are forced to go to San Francisco and become whores. Whereas the sisters had taken their activities as amateurs lightly, their decision to go to San Francisco and accept "the money of shame" is a tragic blow to them.

When, after a dozen such episodes of frustration and ironic reversals of fortune, the author leaves the inhabitants of the Pastures of Heaven to take his perspective from a group of tourists on the valley's ridge, the reader is confronted with the book's final ironies. Each of the four tourists in turn looks down upon the beautiful valley: a successful businessman, a young bridegroom, a priest, and an old man. Each sees in the valley only a peaceful place, an ideal spot to which to retire someday, far from the violence and strife of the world. Steinbeck does not leave the irony there, for the motives of the tourists are ironies in themselves. The businessman would like to start a real estate development there; the bridegroom is reminded by the bride that he has too much to accomplish to hide away in such a retreat; the priest mentally scourges himself for thus wishing to escape from the travails of his calling; the old man wants to settle in the valley to escape the troubles which have prevented him from thinking his way through to some meaningful philosophy of life.

After the bus is again in motion, the bus driver adds his

bit: "I guess it sounds kind of funny to you folks, but I always like to look down there and think how quiet and easy a man could live on a little place."

The Pastures of Heaven marks an important point in Steinbeck's career. It reveals his disengagement from the romantic materials of *Cup of Gold* and the unwieldy mythical paraphernalia of *To a God Unknown;* and it announces his preoccupation with fresh materials much closer at hand—the ordinary people of his "long valley." At the same time, through its carefully patterned structure and pervasive irony, *The Pastures of Heaven* promises a writer who will be capable of subjecting his realistic materials to the demands of significant form.

5 ⟩ *Tortilla Flat*

In January of 1933 Steinbeck was finishing his final draft of *To a God Unknown* and reading with detached amusement the book reviews of *The Pastures of Heaven*, especially those which commented on his choice of characters: "I notice that a number of reviewers (what lice they are) complain that I deal particularly in the subnormal and the psychopathic. If said critics would inspect their neighbors within one block, they would find that I deal with the normal and ordinary." (JS-RB, 1/?/33) With still a month's writing to do on *To a God Unknown,* he was already thinking of his next book:

I think that when this is sent off (this new novel) I shall do some short stories. I always think I will and they invariably grow into novels but I'll try anyway. There are some fine little things that happened in a big sugar mill where I was assistant chief chemist and Majordomo of about sixty Mexicans and Yuakis taken from the jails of northern Mexico. . . .

There was the ex-corporal of Mexican cavalry, whose wife had been stolen by a captain and who was training his baby to be a general so he could get even better women. . . . There is the saga of the C– – – – family. The son hanged himself for the love of a chippy and was cut down and married to the girl. His father aged sixty-five fell in love with a fourteen year old girl and tried the same thing, but a door with a spring lock fell shut and he didn't get cut down. . . . These are a few as they really happened. I could make some little stories of them I think. (JS-MO, 1/?/33)

In addition to giving the source for two of the stories in *Tortilla Flat*, this letter contains several important clues for an understanding of Steinbeck's method of writing. For one thing, almost without exception, he plans the next book while still working on the current one. This letter also illustrates the fact· that, from *The Pastures of Heaven* to his most recent work (with few exceptions), his books have drawn heavily on actual incidents he either knows about or has experienced at first hand. Concerning *Tortilla Flat*, for example, it is probable that, in addition to those incidents he observed while working in the sugar mill, a number of the others were told to Steinbeck by Susan Gregory, a long-time resident of Monterey to whom the book is dedicated.[1] In the Foreword which Steinbeck wrote for the Modern Library edition of the book he tells us that he wrote these stories "because they were true."

Another important aspect of Steinbeck's method, revealed also in the earlier letter about *The Pastures of Heaven*, is his tendency to think of his material in episodes. Although these episodes "invariably grow into novels," as Steinbeck put it, the books which originate in this manner are easily recognized by their retention of an episodic structure, their use of "inter-chapters," or both: *The Pastures of Heaven, Tortilla Flat, The Grapes of Wrath, Cannery Row, The Red Pony, Sweet Thursday.*

When Robert O. Ballou, who was Steinbeck's publisher in this early period, read the manuscript for *Tortilla Flat,* he was seriously worried about the book's structure. He wrote to the young author reminding him that *The Pastures of Heaven* did not sell because it was a collection of short stories and that *Tortilla Flat* seemed more of the same. Quite ironically, since this would be the first of Steinbeck's books to make any money, he urged Steinbeck to think more seriously of his reputation: "If *Tortilla Flat* were to my mind an important book and one which is representative of what you have to say, I would be the first to say, 'the hell with the critics and the public'; but it isn't an important book and it doesn't add to your stature as a novelist. My feeling of disappointment at the end of it lay in the fact that all the way through I had been looking for and waiting for some important story or argument and found it nowhere." (RB-JS, 1/10/34)

McIntosh & Otis, Steinbeck's agents, were also worried about the book's needing "something to hold it together," and were having a difficult time finding a publisher for it. (MO-JS, 12/28/33) Louis Kronenberger, then with Knopf, wrote the agents that he could not have the confidence in the book necessary in those hard times. He did, however, want to see the next book, saying, "I think the man has a future." (LK-MO, 9/18/34) There is a tradition that *Tortilla Flat* was turned down by eleven publishers, but the agents' files have a record of only two. That the book was published at all was the result of a happy accident. Pascal Covici happened to visit Ben Abramson's bookshop in Chicago and was pressed to read *The Pastures of Heaven* and *To a God Unknown,* which Abramson felt were the works of a very promising young writer. When Covici got back to his New York office he telephoned McIntosh & Otis, who passed on to him the manuscript for *Tortilla Flat*.[2] The book was finally published by Covici-Friede in May of 1935, a year and a half after Steinbeck had sent the manuscript to his agents. (MO-JS, 12/28/33) Quite contrary to expectation, the book became very popular. It was banned in Ireland and denounced by the Monterey Chamber of Commerce, who, fearing for its tourist trade, announced the book was a lie. (JS-MO, 6/12/35; MO-JS, late August, 1935) It appeared on best-seller lists for several months, received the California Commonwealth Club's annual gold medal for the best novel by a California writer, was produced as a stage play, obtained for Steinbeck a Hollywood contract, and was sold to Paramount Studios.

Steinbeck was much amused to receive, while in Mexico, a telegram offering $4,000 for "Tortilla," which the Mexicans must have thought was a code word or a race horse. (JS-MO, *ca.* Oct., 1935) He was also much amused by the fortunes of *Tortilla Flat* in Hollywood: "A moving-picture company bought *Tortilla Flat.* . . . And when, a few years later, the same company fired its editor, one of the reasons was that he had bought *Tortilla Flat.* So he bought it from the company for the original four thousand dollars and several years later sold it to M-G-M for ninety thousand dollars."[3]

The publishers were surprised at the book's financial success, but their doubts about the novel's loose structure were substantiated by book reviewers and subsequent critics.[4] It is interesting in this regard to examine an extensive quotation from a letter which Steinbeck had written to his agents in reply to various publishers' remarks about the book's form:

I want to write something about *Tortilla Flat* and about
some ideas I have about it. Perhaps you would care to show
this to Mr. Kronenberger. The book has a very definite theme.
I thought it was clear enough. I had expected that the plan of
the Arthurian cycle would be recognized, that my Gawaine
and Launcelot that my Arthur and Galahad would be recognized. Even the incident of the Sangreal in the search of the
forest is not clear enough I guess. The form is that of the
Malory version, the coming of Arthur and the mystic quality
of owning a house, the forming of the round table, the adventures of the knights and finally, the mystic adventures of
Danny. However, I seem not to have made any of this clear.
The main issue was to present a little known and, to me delightful people. Is not this cycle story or theme enough? Perhaps it is not enough because I have not made it clear enough.
Now, if it is not enough, then I must make it clearer. What
do you think of putting in an interlocutor, who between each
incident interprets the incident, morally, aesthetically, histori-
cally, but in the manner of the paisanos themselves. This would
give the book much the appeal of the *Gesta Romanorum,* those
outrageous tales with monkish morals appended, or of the *Song
of Solomon* in the King James version, with the delightful
chapter headings which go to prove that the Shulamite is in
reality Christ's Church. It would not be as sharp as this of
course. But the little dialogue, if it came between the incidents
would at least make clear the form of the book, its tragicomic
theme. . . . I don't intend to make the parallel of the Round
Table more clear, but simply to show that a cycle is there. You
will remember that the association forms, flowers and dies.
(JS-MO, winter, 1934)

Revealing as this letter may seem, it actually presents very
little that is not made obvious in the novel itself. The underlying scheme of the book is broadly stated in the Preface:
"For Danny's house was not unlike the Round Table, and

Danny's friends were not unlike the knights of it. And this is the story of how that group came into being, of how it flourished and grew to be an organization beautiful and wise. This story deals with the adventures of Danny's friends, with the good they did, with their thoughts and their endeavors. In the end, this story tells how the talisman was lost and how the group disintegrated." Another clue is provided by the chapter titles, which are modeled after those of the *Morte Darthur:* "How Danny, home from the wars, found himself an heir, and how he swore to protect the helpless"; "How the poison of possessions wrought with Pilon and how evil temporarily triumphed in him"; "How three sinful men, through contrition, attained peace. How Danny's friends swore comradeship."

The difficulty lies not in recognizing these general characteristics, but in squaring the details given in Steinbeck's letter with the incidents and characters of *Tortilla Flat.* It is not possible to identify with certainty and consistency his "Gawaine and Launcelot," his "Arthur and Galahad." If Danny is the Arthur of the saga, since he owns the property which corresponds to the Round Table, his identity is confused when, like Launcelot, he goes mad. Pilon, Jesus Maria, Danny, Big Joe Portagee: all are seduced by fleshly pleasures. While there are numerous examples in Malory of knights being seduced or tempted, none of the episodes seems to bear any resemblance to incidents in *Tortilla Flat.* Percival is not mentioned in the letter, but The Pirate bears him some resemblance in coming to the group from a boorish existence in the country. This similarity is strengthened by the fact that the Pirate's dogs see a vision of St. Francis. However, it is in Chrétien's *Perceval* that Percival sees the Grail; in Malory it is Galahad, the son of Launcelot.

Also, whereas in Malory the quest for the Grail results

in the disbanding of the Round Table knights, the *paisanos'* efforts to help The Pirate buy a golden candlestick for Saint Francis provide a strong bond among the group. The association breaks up from ennui shortly after The Pirate fulfills his vow. As for "the incident of the sangreal in the search of the forest," it is *not* "clear enough," though probably the reference is to chapter 8: "How Danny's Friends sought Mystic Treasure on St. Andrews Eve. How Pilon found it and later how a pair of serge pants changed ownership twice."

In this connection it is interesting that neither the Preface nor the chapter headings for *Tortilla Flat* are found in the handwritten manuscript for that book, but on a leaf of the handwritten manuscript for his next novel—*In Dubious Battle*.[5] After *Tortilla Flat* was published and Paramount had bought the motion-picture rights, Steinbeck wrote to his agents, "I do not see what even Hollywood can make of *Tortilla Flat* with its episodic treatment." (JS-MO, 11/3/35) Another time he wrote, "Curious that this second-rate book, written for relaxation, should cause this fuss. People are actually taking it seriously." [6] These remarks suggest that Steinbeck may have exaggerated the book's parallel to Malory in order to impress some publisher.

Nevertheless, as late as 1957 Steinbeck maintained that *Tortilla Flat* was "openly based" on the *Morte Darthur,* with which he had been intimately familiar since his school days and which had led him "to read extensively in every direction about the sources and versions of the Arthurian Cycle."

> You can imagine then that I was pretty excited in 1936 when the Winchester mss came to light and I could hardly wait until Dr. Vinaver brought out his great Oxford three volume edition. . . . I think this cycle has had enormous effect not only on our literature but on our mores and our ways of thinking about things. But over the years I have found that although everyone

knows the essence of the stories, very few people have read them. . . . They are the stuff psychiatry is made of. They are actually the lore on which our attitudes are based and still they have not been read except in saccharine rewritten and cut versions for children. (JS-CVW, 1/16/57)

At the time of writing this letter Steinbeck had been studying the manuscripts in the Morgan Library with a reading glass, and was planning a trip to England in June of that year "to associate with the Winchester manuscript and confer with Dr. Vinaver." Out of this study he expected to bring out his own edition of Malory in "not modern but at least recognizable English—trying to keep the tone, rhythms and meanings—adding nothing and subtracting nothing. And that I have been doing. And it is lovely work and I am enjoying it hugely." Steinbeck hoped that his version would be "a bridge between the scholarly few and the great mass of readers." (JS-CVW, 1/16/57)

Although a search for detailed parallels between *Tortilla Flat* and Malory will prove unfruitful, *Tortilla Flat* is not just a "sketch book." More important than any unity of action given the book by a superficial resemblance to the *Morte Darthur* is the unity of tone and style which makes more clear and effective what Steinbeck called "the strong but different philosophic-moral system of these people" and the book's "tragicomic theme."

The book's mock-epic tone is first indicated in Steinbeck's prefatory remarks, which in addition to comparing Danny's house to the Round Table contain a caution to readers: "It is well that this cycle be put down on paper so that in a future time scholars, hearing the legends, may not say as they say of Arthur and of Roland and of Robin Hood—'There was no Danny nor any house. Danny is a nature god and his friends primitive symbols of the wind, the sky, the sun.' This history is designed now and ever to keep the sneers from the lips of sour scholars." This mock-epic tone is also obvious in the chapter headings: "How Danny was ensnared by a vacuum-cleaner and how Danny's friends rescued him"; "How Danny brooded and became mad. How the devil in the shape of Torrelli assaulted Danny's House." Within the narrative itself, this spirit is sustained by the author's occasional interruptions:

> Some time a historian may write a cold, dry, fungus-like history of the Party. He may refer to the moment when Danny defied and attacked the whole party, men, women and children, with a table-leg. He may conclude, "A dying organism is often observed to be capable of extraordinary endurance and strength." Referring to Danny's super-human amorous activity that night, this same historian may write with unshaking hand: "When any living organism is attacked, its whole function seems to aim toward reproduction." But I say, and the people of Tortilla Flat would say, "To hell with it. That Danny was a man for you!"

While these author comments and chapter headings help to set the tone and style, the major part of this task falls upon the *paisanos* themselves. As in the speech of Hemingway's Italians and Spaniards, part of the effect results from translating the foreign idiom directly into English. Steinbeck, however, relies less than Hemingway on direct translation alone, often re-creating in English the very accents of the characters' speech. When Pilon learns of Danny's property, he sadly says to him: "Now the great times are done. Thy friends will mourn, but nothing will come of their mourning. . . . When one is poor, one thinks, 'If I had money I would share it with my good friends.' But let that money come and Charity flies away. So it is with thee my once-friend. Thou art lifted above thy friends who shared everything with thee, even their brandy." Another part of this effect, which can also be noted in the above quotation, is a conscious elevation of tone by the speakers themselves. When the friends welcome Danny back after his "madness," the accents of Pilon's speech are reminiscent of the Twenty-Third Psalm: "Where is there a friend like our friend? . . . He takes us into his house out of the cold. He shares his good food with us, and his wine. Ohee, the good man, the dear friend." This style of speech, while prominent in the book, is not used to the exclusion of more natural dialogue. Rather, it is reserved for high points of conversation.

In Mark Schorer's excellent essay, "Technique as Discovery," there is a particularly interesting passage on prose style as an aspect of form: "As for the resources of language, these, somehow, we almost never think of as part of the technique of fiction—language as used to create a certain texture and tone which in themselves state and define themes and meanings." This function of language is very crucial in *Tortilla Flat*, and it is the failure to perceive the fact that has resulted in that book's being hailed by critics as expressing Steinbeck's ideal of a primitivistic humanity and society,[7] and by the reading public as presenting a quaint and curious picture of the dispossessed. That neither of these was intended by Steinbeck is clear not only from the carefully sustained language of the book and the special Foreword he wrote for the Modern Library edition, but from the tenor of his next four books—*In Dubious Battle, Of Mice and Men, The Grapes of Wrath* and, especially, *The Forgotten Village*. In none of these is the "natural" state of man seen as ideal; nor are poor diet and filth considered quaint or superior to more civilized standards of living. Steinbeck did not write *Tortilla Flat* either to apotheosize "natural" man or to entertain what he called "literary slummers." Rather, as he wrote to his agents, he wished to explore "the strong but different philosophic-moral system" of these *paisanos*. And *Tortilla Flat* can be most profitably discussed by analyzing this "system" as it is revealed in plot and evaluated in prose style.

Before undertaking an analysis of the system itself, it is necessary to examine the manner in which the *paisanos* reckon with the larger society when such reckoning is unavoidable. Although on such occasions they temporarily accept its conventions, they can nevertheless see these conventions as arbitrary forms rather than absolute truths. When Danny "escapes" from the jail, with the jailer for company, he realizes that there is a ritualized behavior for escaped prisoners and enacts this ritual despite the lack of any pursuit. "When the brilliant sun awakened Danny about noon, he determined to hide all day to escape pursuit. He ran and dodged behind bushes. He peered out of the undergrowth like a hunted fox. And, at evening, the rules having been satisfied, he came out and went about his business." Similarly, when Danny learns that Pilon, Pablo, and Jesus Maria have burned down his other house he is in a dilemma. He realizes that as a man of property he has a certain pose and character to keep up. "He had thought over the ruin of his status as a man with a house to rent; and, all of this clutter of necessary and decent emotion having been swept away, he had finally slipped into his true emotion, one of relief that at least one of his burdens was removed." When the friends show up with their sad news, Danny faithfully goes through the forms of anger and sorrow. He calls them "dogs of dogs," "thieves of decent folk's other house," "spawn of cuttlefish";

and, "all of this clutter of necessary and decent emotion having been satisfied," he again welcomes his friends.

This same condescending observance of social convention is apparent throughout the book. When The Pirate gets his golden candlestick for St. Francis, his friends insist that he buy some decent clothes for the church service and that he leave his dogs at home. Even Danny's funeral is respected by his friends as a social form, and they who before gave as much thought to their raiment as do the lilies of the field do not attend the ceremonies because they cannot steal, beg, or even borrow the proper clothes for such an affair. Of course, the humor in these incidents cuts both ways, being also light satire on social customs.

In respect to their private social manners these *paisanos* are no less rigorous. If Danny sees Pilon going along with a jug under his coat, he does not ask him for a drink. Instead he throws his arm about his dear friend and offers to share some little thing he himself has, for friendship's sake. How then can Pilon refuse to share his jug? When Jesus Maria brings home the corporal and the baby, his *paisano* friends are consumed with curiosity about who these two are, how they came to Monterey, and what their trouble is, but their social customs prevent their asking a direct question concerning such personal matters, and only after the meal, when the jug is passing around, do they show, even indirectly, their curiosity.

This group code is also illustrated by the episode of The Pirate's money. Danny and his friends spend much time luring The Pirate to live with them so they can more easily discover where his treasure is hidden. They spend a sleepless week trying to track him through the forest to his sack of money, trying everything short of violence. But when The Pirate comes home one morning with his treasure and gives it to them for safekeeping, they ask if he will not take some out before putting it in their hands. When The Pirate shrewdly refuses, they know "it was all over, all hope of diverting the money. . . . There was nothing in the world they could do about it. Their chance had come, and it had gone." They could not break the sacred trust of friendship. Later, when the outcast Big Joe Portagee steals some of The Pirate's money, the friends pursue and torture him with a vengeance.

While the *paisanos* are so careful to observe the niceties of social intercourse, possessions hold no fascination for them, and even the necessary ones are burdensome. As Pilon watches Danny inspecting his inherited house, he "noticed that the worry of property was settling on Danny's face. No more in life would that face be free of care. No more would Danny break windows now that he had windows of his own to break." To buy wine for their housewarming, Pilon sells the washbowl and pitcher, two red glass vases, and a bouquet of ostrich plumes, explaining, "It is not good to have so many breakable things around. When they are broken you become sad. It is much better never to have had them."

As Danny eases his own burden by "renting" to Pilon, Pilon "rents" to Pablo, and both pass on the responsibility to Jesus Maria Corcoran. Later, when Jesus Maria comes to inform Danny that one of his houses is on fire and calls for him persistently, the bedroom window of Mrs. Morales opens and Danny asks, "Is the fire department there?" "Yes," cries Jesus Maria. "Well," says Danny, "If the fire department can't do anything about it, what does Pilon expect me to do?" From this fire Pilon draws a profound moral: "By this we learn never to leave wine in a house overnight."

Having no respect for their own property, the group of friends of course have no respect for the property of those outside their social circle. They subsist by a series of very petty larcenies and divine interventions in the form of "miracles." The miracle of the dollar not only expresses the *paisanos'* attitude towards property, but demonstrates their perfect defense against exploitation: "One night he [Pilon] had a dollar, acquired in a manner so astounding that he tried to forget it immediately for fear the memory might drive him mad. A man in front of the San Carlos hotel had put the dollar in his hand, saying, 'Run down and get four bottles of ginger-ale. The hotel is out.' Such things were almost miracles, Pilon thought. One should take them on faith, not worry and question them."

Another time a "nice little rowboat," complete with oars, is washed up at the feet of Jesus Maria, who sells it for seven dollars. Once Danny finds a keg of copper shingling nails, obviously "lost," since no member of the supply company is nearby. When a coast guard cutter goes on the rocks, the *paisanos* gather up the flotsam: "a five pound can of butter, several cases of canned goods, a water-soaked Bowditch, two pea jackets, a water barrel from a life boat and a machine gun." This manna they sell on the spot. Even deadly botulism comes to the aid of these innocents. When Mrs. Morales feeds her chickens some spoiled jars of beans they all die. "Someone" tells her those chickens are inedible, but Danny helps her scrape the insides well and sell them to the butcher.

In Steinbeck's presentation of the *paisanos'* theory of property the account of Dolores "Sweets" Ramirez and the vacuum cleaner occupies a key place; it is a satire on the conventional prestige value of possessions—on "conspicuous consumption." After Danny, in return for certain favors, presents Dolores with a vacuum sweeper, she "climbed to the peak of the social scale of Tortilla Flat."

People who did not remember her name referred to her as "that one with the sweeping-machine." Often when her enemies passed the house, Sweets could be seen through the window, pushing the cleaner back and forth. . . . She excited envy in many houses. Her manner became dignified and gracious, and she held her chin high as befitted one who had a sweeping-machine. In her conversation she included it. "Ramon passed this morning, while I was pushing the sweeping-machine." "Louise Meater cut her hand this morning not three hours after I had been pushing the sweeping-machine."

This prestige value is pointed up by the fact that there is no electricity in Dolores' house. Indeed, it eventually turns out that the sweeper itself has no motor.

The *paisanos'* adjustment toward property, their delicate code of manners: both are a part of "the strong but different philosophic-moral system of these people." There is one more characteristic of this "system," however—the most pervasive of all and the most incisive in its social comment. A psychologist might call it "rationalization"; George Orwell's term for it in *1984,* "doublethink," is perhaps better. In *Tortilla Flat* this becomes a highly developed technique whereby socially unacceptable modes of behavior are metamorphosed into socially acceptable, even praiseworthy ones, and predatory instincts transformed into dictates of the moral conscience—all without compromising the original goal. Almost every incident in *Tortilla Flat* has this logical substructure, the essence of which can be shown in two episodes.

When Pilon, out for a casual stroll, comes upon an unattended chicken, he thinks: "Poor little fowl. How cold it must be for you in the early morning, when the dew falls and the air grows cold with the dawn. The good God is not always so good to little beasts. . . . Here you play in the street little chicken. Some day an automobile will run over you; and if it kills you, that will be the best that can happen. It may only break your leg or your wing. Then all of your life you will drag along in misery. Life is too hard for you, little bird." Aware that other, more hardened people may not appreciate his humanitarian views, Pilon carefully plucks and dismembers the chicken before bringing it home, for without feathers, head, or feet a chicken cannot be identified. The train of thought is similar to the one by which Pilon at another time talks himself into stealing Big Joe's only pair of pants, which the victim happens to be wearing: "Then he remembered how badly the pants fit Big Joe, how tight the waist was even with two flybuttons undone, how the cuffs missed the shoe tops by inches. 'Some one of decent size would be happy in those pants.'" These two incidents illustrate the technique in its simplest form.

An example *par excellence* is the reasoning whereby Danny's request for two dollars rent from Pilon and Pablo results in these two getting the money from Jesus Maria and then getting drunk on it:

"Danny wants to buy a box of candy for Mrs. Morales." [begins Jesus Maria]

"Candy is not good for people," Pablo observed. "It makes their teeth ache."

"That is up to Danny," said Jesus Maria. "If he wants to ache Mrs. Morales' teeth, that is his business. What do we care for Mrs. Morales' teeth?"

A cloud of anxiety settled on Pilon's face. "But," he interposed sternly, "if our friend Danny takes big candy to Mrs. Morales, he will eat some too. So it is the teeth of our friend will ache."

Pablo shook his head anxiously, "It would be a bad thing if

Danny's friends, on whom he depends, should bring about the aching of his teeth."

"What should we do, then?" asked Jesus Maria, although he and everyone else knew exactly what they would do. They waited politely, each one for another to make the inevitable suggestion. . . .

"A gallon of wine makes a nice present for a lady," he [Jesus Maria] suggested in a musing tone. . . .

"But maybe Danny will pay no heed to our warning. If you give money to that Danny, you can't tell what he will do with it. He might buy candy anyway and then all our time and worry are wasted."

. . . "Maybe if we buy the wine ourselves and then give it to Danny there is no danger," he [Jesus Maria] suggested. "That is the thing," cried Pilon. "Now you have it."

Of course the logical sequence does not end here. After sending Jesus Maria on an errand, Pilon and Pablo devote their full attention to the wine and Pilon remarks: "It is just as well that we do not take two gallons of wine to Danny. He is a man who knows little restraint in drinking." And Pablo adds: "Danny looks healthy, but it is just such people you hear of dying every day."

While these characteristics do make clear the "strong" philosophic-moral system of these people, one is not quite certain that it is "different." In this lies the book's social comment, not in its praise of primitivistic man. If the state of civilization can be distinguished from the primitivistic or naturalistic state by its having an intricate pattern for satisfying wants through socially acceptable channels, then the *paisanos* of Tortilla Flat are extremely civilized. The *paisanos'* method of satisfying desires becomes more than acceptable; it becomes altruistic. That is why they can derive so much pleasure from such small things with so little effort. Take the simple matter of raising a pig, as one of them expresses it: "There is nothing nicer to have than a pig. He will eat anything. He is a nice pet. You get to love that little pig. But then that pig grows up and his character changes. That pig becomes mean and evil-tempered, so that you do not love him anymore. Then one day that pig bites you, and you are angry. And so you kill that pig and eat him." Pilon aptly expresses the moral: "See how many satisfactions he has made with his pig—affection, love, revenge and food." Similarly, if through the theft of Big Joe's pants Pilon could "avenge Danny, discipline Big Joe, teach an ethical lesson and get a little wine, who in the world could criticize him?"

Considering the intricacy and subtlety of this "philosophic-moral system," it is not really possible to say, as does Edmund Wilson, that these *paisanos* are "human beings so rudimentary that they are almost on the animal level," or that they are "cunning little living dolls that amuse us like pet guinea pigs or rabbits." [8] Neither is it possible to agree with Freeman Champney that *Tortilla Flat* shows "man as animal . . . without any other pretensions." [9]

As is frequent in Steinbeck's novels, there is in *Tortilla Flat* one episode which serves as a parable for its theme. This is the story of the corporal and his son, and it comes immediately after its companion piece—the story of "Sweets" Ramirez and her vacuum sweeper. When Jesus Maria rescues the young corporal and his baby son from the policeman and brings them to the *paisanos'* house, the corporal satisfies their curiosity by telling his story. It seems that while he was serving in the Mexican army his wife was taken from him by a captain. Now, he is raising his son to become a general. A certain "wise man" (obviously a psychologist of the environmentalist school) has told him that to accomplish this, he need only repeat constantly to the child, "You will become

a general. You will wear epaulets and carry a golden sword."
(The Pirate wonders "whether the same method would work
on a dog.")

The baby dies soon after arriving at the *paisanos*' house
and they all feel sad, for this seems the end of what they
thought to be the corporal's noble plan: " 'This baby would
grow up, and he would be a general; and in time he would
find that captain, and he would kill him slowly. It was a good
plan. The long waiting, and then the stroke.' " The young
corporal is shocked at this idea. " 'What is this?' he demanded. 'I have nothing to do with this captain. He is the
captain.' " He explains his plan: " 'Well,' said the corporal,
'my wife was so pretty, and she was not any *puta*, either. She
was a good woman, and that captain took her. He had little
epaulets, and a little sash, and his sword was only of a silver
color. Consider,' said the corporal; and he spread out his
hands, 'if that captain, with the little epaulets and little
sash could take my wife, imagine what a general with a big
sash and a gold sword could take!' " This is not merely an
amusing anecdote, but an allegory of the basic tenets of a
predatory social system which the *paisanos* have successfully
avoided, which will never give them ulcers, and which
Tortilla Flat criticizes in the comic spirit.

Ten years after *Tortilla Flat*, Steinbeck wrote the script
for a motion picture called "A Medal for Benny," which
further defines the virtues of his *paisanos*' "philosophic-moral
system." Benny, a Danny-like character, dies a hero's death
in World War II, and his indigent, illiterate father is to receive his son's posthumous decoration. The small town's
chamber of commerce builds this up to a big thing for tourist
purposes, surrounding the ceremony with all the boosterism
and chicanery they can. When the father realizes that his
private sorrow and pride and his son's honor are being ex-

ploited for commercial purposes, he refuses to go through with the public ceremony and says to the publicity manager, "Mister Lovekin—Benny was a wild boy, but even *Benny* would not do a thing like this. . . . Never would he use the bravery and a beautiful medal to sell a lot of hot dogs and real estate. . . . No—even Benny would not do that." [10]

Although *Tortilla Flat* points out certain advantages of the *paisanos*' "philosophic-moral system," Steinbeck has his reservations. As he wrote to his agents, ". . . rarely does any theme in the lives of these people survive the night." Helping The Pirate to buy his golden candlestick provides a focal point for the *paisanos*' energies, but with this accomplished they fall into a depressed lassitude from which only the riotous and fatal party awakens them. Steinbeck uses the comic spirit of *Tortilla Flat* to criticize certain aspects of society, but there is no indication that the life depicted in its pages, though it has its virtues, is the ideal for which man should strive.

Steinbeck's achievement lies in the fact that his reservations never intrude in the novel. Rather, they are implicit in his major strategy—the burlesque of epic language and action. More important than the fact that it imposes a form on his assorted incidents, this strategy enables the author to keep his characters at an aesthetic distance through its inherent humor—a humor which, while making us fully conscious of the *paisanos*' shortcomings as moral human beings, at the same time allows us to respect what is good and even noble in them.

6 $\rbrace$ *The Long Valley*

As the episodic structures of *Tortilla Flat* and *The Pastures of Heaven* attest, Steinbeck's talents at this stage in his career seemed inclined toward the short story form. And in fact he had been writing steadily in this genre even before *Cup of Gold*, but except for two stories printed in *The Stanford Spectator* and the *Stanford Lit*, none of his short stories was published until *North American* printed the first two parts of *The Red Pony* in November and December of 1933. This same periodical published "The Murder" and "The Raid" in April and October of 1934 and "The White Quail" in March of the following year.

Even this flurry of publication did not gain his stories entrance to other magazines. In July of 1935 Steinbeck wrote his agents that he had given "The Snake," which could find no other publisher, to a magazine "run in conjunction with a stable" [*The Monterey Beacon*] in return for six months' use of a big bay hunter.[1] He humorously suggested that the agents could get their 10 per cent of the riding, but would have to come out to California for it. (JS-MO, 7/20/35) Later, this story was rejected by both *Atlantic* and *Harper's*. (*Atlantic*-MO, 7/14/37; *Harper's*-MO, 9/9/37) "Saint Katy the Virgin" is mentioned in the letters as early as May of 1932, when Steinbeck wrote, "As for St. Katy—I shall send you a copy, and this time keep her if you want her. She was a pleasant afternoon to me, when I was tired of trying to convince taxpayer and Old Subscriber that I could write the English language." (JS-MO, 5/17/32) Three years later it had still not found a publisher, and Steinbeck wrote that he "would like to make someone print St. Katy." (JS-MO, 6/13/35) Finally his publishers, Covici-Friede, issued it as a monograph in 1936. "Flight," rejected in 1937 by both *Scribner's* and *Saturday Evening Post,* was not published until it appeared in *The Long Valley*. (*Scribner's*-MO, 6/29/37; *Sat. Eve. Post*-Mo, 8/18/37)

By this time *In Dubious Battle* and especially *Of Mice and Men* were making Steinbeck's reputation, and magazines which had turned him down earlier now vied for his short stories. "The Chrysanthemums" and a third part of *The Red Pony* ("The Promise") were published by *Harper's* in August and October of 1937. *Esquire* accepted "The Ears of Johnny Bear" in September of the same year, and in June of 1938 *Atlantic* printed "The Harness." "The Leader of the People" first appeared in *The Long Valley* and, while included in the 1945 edition of *The Red Pony*, was not a part of the 1937 edition, although it had probably been written by then. It is found in the same manuscript book with *Tortilla Flat*, "The Murder," and "The Chrysanthemums."

As may be suspected from the five books Steinbeck had

published up to that time, these stories show a wide range of technique and subject matter. Two of the stories are studies of valley people such as might well have appeared in *The Pastures of Heaven*. In fact, "The Murder" has much in common with the stories in that earlier book. It will be recalled that while in a letter to his agents Steinbeck mentions two murders in the valley of Nuestra Señora, the book includes only one. Also, the story's basically ironic structure fits well in *The Pastures of Heaven*. One need only substitute a Munroe for the "George" who unexpectedly turns Jim back home to find his wife with her lover. There is one good reason why the story was not included in the earlier volume, however. Its happy ending would have jarred with the book's predominant tone. "The Harness" is similar in setting to the stories in *The Pastures of Heaven* and is similar in theme to the Pat Humbert section, but lacks both the ironic tone and "black cloud" which characterize all the stories in that book.

Another story, "St. Katy the Virgin," illustrates Steinbeck's early versatility by being a goliardic farce in the best fabliau tradition. St. Katy is a pig who becomes converted from her sinful life, works miraculous cures, and, after her bones have become holy relics, is added to the "Calendar of the Elect." The story is rife with hilarious parodies of medieval arguments concerning the power of exorcism, the nobility of the lion ("a beast built for parables"), the power of the crucifix ("two great tears squeezed out of the eyes of Katy"), the true definition of virginity ("to differentiate between the Grace of God knocking it [the hymen] out from the inside or the wickedness of man from the outside"), and even the "usual scandal" about monks: "For a while it was thought that, because of her sex, she [Katy] should leave the monastery and enter a nunnery." "St. Katy the Virgin" is an altogether delightful tale that even Chaucer's Reeve or

Miller would have been proud to present as his claim to the free dinner.

The dominant interest in many of these stories collected in *The Long Valley* is psychological, and in them, as in *To a God Unknown,* there is a certain resemblance to the preoccupations of D. H. Lawrence, for whom Steinbeck has expressed some admiration.[2] Elisa Allen in "The Chrysanthemums," Mary Teller in "The White Quail," Amy Hawkins in "Johnny Bear," and the anonymous woman in "The Snake" are psychological portraits of frustrated females.

Elisa's silent rebellion against the passive role required of her as a woman (symbolized by her masculine manner of gardening) is triggered by the old pot-mender, who throws away the chrysanthemums she has given him. However, in rejecting her first impulse to violence (which is to witness a bloody boxing match), she lapses into frustration, and the story ends with her "crying weakly—like an old woman." This story was much admired by André Gide, who said it was "remarkable for its adroitness" and seemed "like a short story by Chekhov; one of the best by Chekhov."[3]

In "The White Quail" Mary Teller's lack of sexual vigor is aptly symbolized by her prim garden and her self-identification with the single albino quail which comes to drink at its pool. The tangled thickets at the garden's edge and a prowling cat symbolize the rough, natural world which constantly endangers her ordered, artificial one of trimmed bushes and white quail. Although her cowed husband finds symbolic assertion in killing the white quail rather than the prowling cat she asked him to kill, this reaction, like Elisa Allen's desire to see violence, is a temporary one.

In "The Snake" a strange woman objectifies her frustration by watching a male rattlesnake eat a white rat; she first insists that she buy both. According to Steinbeck, the story is an accurate account of an incident which happened to Ricketts, his biologist friend. (LSC, xxiii-xxiv)

"Johnny Bear" is a story about a cretin with a remarkable memory and mimetic talent. On one level, it is an exploration of the artist's role in society; for, like the artist, Johnny Bear holds the mirror up to mankind and reveals through his mimetic talent the hidden festers of society. He is described as "a kind of recording and reproducing device, only you use a glass of whiskey instead of a nickel." The central interest, however, is neither Johnny Bear nor the aristocratic spinster whose secret love affair with a Chinese laborer he so innocently divulges. Rather, it is the social group within which these characters exist, and the conflict between its innate curiosity and its desire to perpetuate the symbols of its decorum despite the further revelation by Johnny Bear that the spinster, aided by her sister, committed suicide —to hide her pregnancy. It is curious that such a story should, in narrative style and setting, be so reminiscent of O. Henry and Bret Harte: the atmosphere of the outpost saloon and boardinghouse; the stranger in town; the unexpected twist in the last sentence.

The psychological interest of these explorations of character is carried on into the two stories dealing with the current social scene, "Vigilante" and "The Raid." Dick and Root in "The Raid" are early studies for Mac and Jim of *In Dubious Battle;* they are party organizers coming into a small town. Whereas in the novel the action is physical and dramatic, in the short story the action takes place in the mind of the frightened neophyte. The story builds up its intensity through Root's struggles to conquer his growing fear of the beating they are in for at the hands of the raiding party. The narrative skilfully keeps the reader's sympathy with the two organizers without requiring approval of their cause. In fact, their Communism provides a fine ironical turn to the story. Dick, the more experienced one, is a veritable apostle of the class struggle. To strengthen his weak companion he points to a portrait they have hung on the wall and says, "He wasn't scared. Just remember what he did." Later he tells Root, "If someone busts you, it isn't him that's doing it, it's the System. And it isn't you he's busting. He's taking a crack at the Principle." In the hospital, when the neophyte tells Dick how he had felt during the beating, the latter says, "It wasn't them. It was the System. You don't want to hate them. They don't know no better." And Root replies, "You remember in the Bible, Dick, how it says something like 'Forgive them because they don't know what they're doing?'" Dick's reply is stern: "'You lay off that religion stuff, kid.' He quoted, 'Religion is the opium of the people.'"

Like "The Raid," the story "Vigilante" avoids dramatic presentation of violence and focuses instead on the psychological action. Whereas "The Raid" depicts the victim of a mob before and after he is beaten up, "Vigilante" concerns itself with the psychological state of a man after he has helped lynch a Negro. The story explores the character's motivations, which become clear through his thoughts, and his conversations with a bartender and his own wife. As might be expected, the story has some development of Steinbeck's group-man theories. The vigilante, like the grandfather in "The Leader of the People," fully lives only for that time when he is part of a group, and when that group disperses the single man is left a hull. "Half an hour before, when he had been hauling with the mob and fighting for a chance to help pull the rope, then his chest had been so full that he had found he was crying. But now everything was dead, everything unreal." A study of the several other passages describing the character's feelings makes clear that there is perhaps an even stronger drive than gregariousness. "He could feel the let down in himself. He was as heavily weary as though he had gone without sleep for several nights, but it was a dream-like weariness, a grey comfortable weariness." This and similar descriptions come sharply into focus when the vigilante is greeted by his wife as follows: "You been with a woman. . . . You think I can't tell by the look on your face that you been with a woman?" The story ends with the vigilante looking into a mirror and saying, "By God, she was right. . . . That's just exactly how I do feel."

One of the best stories in *The Long Valley* is "Flight," whose firm prose style once again attests Steinbeck's debt to Hemingway. Everything which has been admired in such passages of Hemingway prose as the bus ride to Pamplona in *The Sun Also Rises* and the bullfighting scenes in "The Undefeated" can be found in this short story. Its style is a crisp rendering of factual details which, while staying always close to the actual object and action, avoids the myopic distortions of "realistic" writing. Take, for example, the scene in which Pepé, behind a rock on a high slope, is wounded in a duel with his pursuer far below:

> The rifle swung over. The frontsight nestled in the V of the rear sight. Pepé studied for a moment and then raised the rear sight a notch. The little movement in the brush came again. The sight settled on it. Pepé squeezed the trigger. The explosion crashed down the mountain and up the other side, and came rattling back. The whole side of the slope grew still. No more movement. And then a white streak cut into the granite of the slit and a bullet whined away and a crash sounded up from below. Pepé felt a sharp pain in his right hand. A sliver

of granite was sticking out from between his first and second knuckles and the point protruded from his palm. Carefully he pulled out the sliver of stone. The wound bled evenly and gently. No vein nor artery was cut.

The surface story is a simple one. A young boy kills a man, takes flight, is pursued and shot. Through this uncomplicated plot, however, Steinbeck weaves a thread of moral allegory—the growth of a boy to manhood and the meaning of that manhood. When the boy Pepé throws his dead father's knife into a man as unerringly as he has been playfully throwing it into a wooden post, the cards are dealt. Sticking the post was a boy's game, but when he takes the stranger's insults as a man would and throws his knife, he has bid into a man's game and must play it to the end. Most of the story concerns itself with the time between Pepé's return home to prepare himself for flight into the desolate granite mountains and the time when, realizing there is no escape from the gangrene of his wound, he stands fully exposed on a high rock and recieves the fatal bullet from his mysterious pursuer.

The flight itself has meaning on two planes. On the physical level, Pepé's penetration into the desert mountains is directly proportional to his increasing separation from civilized man and his reduction to the state of a wild animal. The extent to which this process has gone is measured by his encounters with a wildcat and later a mountain lion, both of whom regard Pepé with a calm curiosity, not yet having learned to fear man. The symbolic meaning of Pepé's flight moves in the opposite direction. On this level, the whole action of the story goes to show how man, even when stripped of all his civilized accouterments (like Ahab of his pipe, sextant, and hat), is still something more than an animal. This is the purpose of Pepé's losing consecutively his horse (escape), his hat (protection from nature), and his gun (physical defense), to face his inevitable death not with the headlong retreat or futile death struggle of an animal, but with the calm and stoicism required by the highest conception of manhood, forcing fate to give him a voice in the "how" if not the "what" of his destiny.

It is worth remarking that perhaps Steinbeck achieves this significant symbolic meaning of the story's ending at some expense of verisimilitude. The boy standing exposed on the high rock and taking his death is "theatrical" in the same way that the ending of almost every one of Steinbeck's novels is "theatrical"—not incredible or contrived so much as disjunctive, incongruous in realistic terms because of its too perfect symbolic congruity. This type of ending is one of Steinbeck's most consistent stylistic devices, and his persistent use of it in the face of almost unanimous adverse criticism must indicate that for him, at least, the important action to be terminated in his novels exists not on the physical plane, but on the symbolic. When these endings are examined in the light of the whole work, it becomes evident that their incongruity with the surface "realism" is overshadowed by their bringing into sharper focus the substrata of symbolism and allegory.

Although the four stories about Jody do not have plot continuity, they do have a continuity of theme—the education of a young boy. The three stories collected in the 1937 edition of *The Red Pony* show Jody's education through Nature, and "The Leader of the People" continues this education through Grandfather, who represents history, a sense of the past. Like "Flight," these stories are remarkable for the lyric realism of their prose style, a style which while coming to grips with the essentials of violence and death still retains a rhythm and tone more akin to the idyllic and pastoral than to the naturalistic. The result of this rhythm and tone is the creation of what Mr. T. K. Whipple has called "the middle distance." In this perspective the characters "cannot touch us, and yet we can see their performances with the greatest clarity and fullness. . . . We feel the appropriate emotions—pity, sympathy, terror and horror even—but with the delightful sense that we are apart, in the audience, and that anyhow nothing can be done or needs be done." [4] This effect is very important in Steinbeck's work, and its presence is often a touchstone for his more successful works. It is through this technique of distance that the stories about Jody escape both the infantilism and the excessive psychological distortions which are the usual literary pitfalls of these stories' subject matter.

The central experience in each of the first three stories ("The Gift," "The Great Mountains," and "The Promise") is physical death: the red pony, Gitano, and the mare. Each shows death in a different perspective. The red pony comes from a broken-down "show," and its superficial prettiness is emphasized by the tinsel-hung, red morocco saddle that comes with it. " 'It's just a show saddle,' Billy Buck said disparagingly. 'It isn't practical for the brush. . . .' " The red pony's death is in part the result of Jody's carelessness. Twice he falls asleep and allows the pony to escape into the storm, which aggravates the cold it caught from getting wet. Billy Buck has remarked, "—why a little rain don't hurt a horse." But it is fatal to the red pony. When Jody comes upon his red pony, already being devoured by the buzzards, anger seems a normal reaction. Carl Tiflin says, "Jody, the buzzards didn't kill the pony. Don't you know that?" The function of this incident in Jody's education becomes clear from Billy Buck's reprimand. " 'Course he knows

it, Jesus Christ! man, can't you see how he'd feel about it?"
It is important to note that he does not contradict the father's words, but merely relates Jody's action to its context
of incomplete education. The reader may "feel" with Jody
and "understand" with Carl, but he identifies himself with
Billy Buck, the complete man whose perspective includes
both the buzzards' place in the chain of being and their
repulsiveness. And Billy Buck is the model on whom Jody is
fashioning himself.

While the death of the red pony is associated with violence, pain, and disgust, the death of Gitano in "The Great
Mountains" is as calm and peaceful as the title. Before the
old Mexican comes "home" to the Tiflin ranch to die, Jody
has already identified the western mountains, the "Great
Ones," with death and the eastern ones, the Gabilans, with
life. Symbolically, the Tiflin ranch lies in a valley cup formed
by the two ranges. When Gitano disappears with the old
horse, Easter, who is also waiting to die, Carl remarks, "They
never get too old to steal. I guess he just stole old Easter."
Jody, who has seen Gitano's old basket-hilted rapier (handed
down from father to son since the conquistadores), who feels
the significance of Gitano's journey into the symbolic "Great
Ones," knows the truth. "Jody thought of the rapier and of
Gitano. And he thought of the great mountains. A longing
caressed him, and it was so sharp that he wanted to cry to
get it out of his breast. He lay down in the green grass
near the round tub [which Jody associates with life] at the
brush line. He covered his eyes with his crossed arms and lay
there a long time, and he was full of nameless sorrow." This
sorrow comes not from grief for Gitano or the old horse,
but rather from an emotional perception of that whole of
which Gitano, Old Easter, the rapier, and the Great Mountains are parts, a recognition of the symbolic significance

of their conjunction—"nameless" because intuitive and sub-conscious. Jody's sorrow is very much like that of the girl Margaret in Hopkins' poem "Spring and Fall: To a Young Child."

Like "The Gift," "The Promise" is a story about a pony. Whereas the first concerns itself with the pony's increasing sickness, ending in death, the second begins with a pony's conception and ends with its birth. And as Jody was spared no detail of the first pony's suffering and death, so he is spared no fact of life in the mare's pregnancy and the colt's birth. He is present at the violent copulation, cares for the mare during the progress of her pregnancy, sees the agonies of her labor pains, watches Billy Buck attempt to turn the colt in her uterus and, this failing, kill her with a hammer and cut the living colt from its dead mother. Jody's vital relation to this colt is as different from his relation to the red pony as the red pony's carnival background and useless red morocco saddle are different from the violence and suffering which bring the colt into the world. And the colt's birth provides Jody with a new insight into death. The red pony's suffering and terror had been the process of death, which meant life to the buzzards. Gitano had gone to his death calmly, of his own free will and accepting the inevitable. The mare's suffering and death are the price of life and give to Jody a new sense of his responsibility to that life.

In *Sea of Cortez* Steinbeck tells an anecdote, probably autobiographical, which further clarifies his attitude toward the natural processes of life in these Jody stories:

A man we know once long ago worked for a wealthy family in a country place. One morning one of the cows had a calf. The children of the house went down with him to watch her. It was a good normal birth, a perfect presentation, and the cow needed no help. The children asked questions and he answered them. And when the emerged head cleared through the sac, the little black muzzle appeared, and the first breath was drawn, the children were fascinated and awed. And this was the time for their mother to come screaming down on the vulgarity of letting the children see the birth. This "vulgarity" had given them a sense of wonder at the structure of life, while the mother's propriety supplanted that feeling with dirtiness. (SC, 68)

Because the style of the Jody stories is so perfectly suited to their theme and subject matter (as well suited, for example, as is the style of *The Pearl* to its own materials), the myriad specific details imbedded in these stories remain unobtrusive. Jody, however, is engaged in learning not only about such larger things as death, birth, and suffering, but also about the many particulars of ranch life and nature. The source for much of this information is Billy Buck, who, along with other men of skill, occupies the place in the Steinbeck world that bullfighters do in that of Hemingway. Throughout his fiction Steinbeck pays tribute to the man who is skilled with his hands: the man who can, like Billy Buck and Slim, work with horses; the man who can, like Raymond Banks, kill chickens painlessly and with efficiency; the man who can, like Alec and Juan Chicoy, repair motors and gear assemblies. In *Cannery Row* Steinbeck refers to Gay, a self-made mechanic, as "the Saint Francis of all things that turn and twist and explode." This type of character is often depicted by Steinbeck, who thus expresses his admiration for the man who is close to life, whether that life be spent on a ranch, in a garage, or behind a lunch counter. In Doc of *Cannery Row* Steinbeck creates his ideal character by combining the man of skill with the man of contemplation.

While the boy Jody appears in "The Leader of the People," it is not *about* him in the sense that the stories in *The Red Pony* are about him. This is why Steinbeck did not include this story in the first edition of *The Red Pony*, although he had probably written it by then since it is found in the same manuscript book as the earlier *Tortilla Flat*, "The Murder," and "The Chrysanthemums," where it is called "Grandfather." Although this story was later included in the 1945 edition of *The Red Pony*, in *The Long Valley* (1938) it appears under a separate title. The central character is Jody's grandfather, who was once "the leader of the people." It is Steinbeck's first explicit statement of his group-man theory, which was hinted at in the earlier stories and novels and which was to be developed at such great length in his next four books.

Through the garrulous grandfather Steinbeck poses the question of the meaning and place which the frontier spirit should have in our time. Through each character's attitude toward the grandfather, in whom the tradition is embodied, the author explores a distinct reaction to the American pioneer past. For Carl, it is something done with. The West Coast has been reached and the job now is one of consolidation. It is boring and pointless to dwell on the heroic deeds of our past: "Now it's finished. Nobody wants to hear about it over and over." In this dismissal there is perhaps an unconscious resentment of his own unheroic life. To Carl's wife, the daughter of Grandfather, the stories of the past are just as boring, but her attitude is more respectful. She listens out of loyalty, knowing what this past meant to her forebears. Billy Buck's attitude is a little more complicated. His own father was a mule packer under Grandfather's leadership, and he himself retains much of the self-reliant, able-handed spirit of the heroic past. He listens with respect born of understanding. For Jody, as for any other American youngster, this past was a time of excitement: Indians, wagon trains, scouts, crossing the plains.

Yet it is to Jody that the grandfather is finally able to communicate the double aspect of the meaning behind his tales of Indians and wagon trains: "It wasn't Indians that were important, nor adventures, nor even getting out here. It was a whole bunch of people made into one big crawling beast. And I was the head. It was westering and westering. Every man wanted something for himself, but the big beast that was all of them wanted only westering. I was the leader, but if I hadn't been there, someone else would have been the head. The thing had to have a head." This is an important statement for an understanding of Steinbeck's group-man concept. The analogy of men to a "big crawling beast" was not intended to put, and in the context of Steinbeck's work does not put, men on the same moral basis as animals. Rather, it points out the energy that is released when the many desires of men can find expression in one unifying activity or aspiration. As the old man continues, it becomes evident that although "westering" may bear a superficial resemblance to animal migration, the impetus which drove his people had its roots not in the flesh but in the human spirit. "No place to go, Jody. Every place is taken. But that's not the worst—no, not the worst. Westering has died out of people. Westering isn't a hunger any more. It's all done."

Grandfather's statement is supported not only by Carl Tiflin and his wife, but by a continuum of symbols firmly imbedded in the story. The physical setting is alive not with Indians and buffaloes but with small and petty game— gophers, snakes, pigeons, crows, rabbits, squirrels, and mice. And these mice which Jody sets out to kill early in the story are, significantly, still alive at its end, fat and comfortable in a rotting haystack. Yet, the story is not a sentimental glorification of a heroic past set against a mean and complacent present. The frontier *is* gone; Jody's excitement about killing the mice is not, as Grandfather sees it, a symbol of a degenerating race; Carl Tiflin and his wife are not cruel and stupid, but competent for the tasks at hand; and their boredom with the old man's garrulousness is made understandable. Furthermore, in a very important sense it is Grandfather who has failed, in two ways. He has failed to adjust himself to the unavoidable fact that he could not go on being "the leader of the people" after the Pacific Ocean was reached. More important, despite his garrulousness he has failed to communicate to the new generation that "westering" was not just killing Indians and eating buffalo meat.

Perhaps the ultimate wisdom in the story belongs only to Billy Buck. When Jody remarks to him that the fat mice he intends to kill "don't know what's going to happen to them today," Billy Buck replies philosophically, "No, nor you either, nor me, nor anyone." Jody is "staggered" by this thought; he "knew it was true." This is Jody's lesson in history, the meaning of the past. Grandfather's frontier, like Frederick Jackson Turner's, was not so much a physical manifestation as an attitude of mind and a spirit which needs reviving in our time. Life is always a risk. The call for heroism is heard today as it was yesterday. The need for a leader of the people is still real, for we are all pioneers, forever crossing the dangerous and the unknown.

This attitude and spirit Steinbeck was to explore more fully in his account of a new migration—the trek from the dust bowl in *The Grapes of Wrath.*

7 } *In Dubious Battle*

Only one year after Steinbeck's new publishers, Covici-Friede, brought out *Tortilla Flat,* typed as "charming sentimentality," they published his *In Dubious Battle*—"left-wing melodrama." Actually, Steinbeck had been working on a second draft of his strike novel as early as September, 1934, and it was completed in February of 1935, three months before the publication of *Tortilla Flat,* which had been seeking a publisher for a year and a half. (JS-MO, 9/?/34; 2/4/35) This change of pace was no less startling to his publishers than it was to the reading public. As Robert O. Ballou had earlier been worried about publishing *Tortilla Flat* after *The Pastures of Heaven,* so Covici-Friede, in almost the same language, expressed concern that Steinbeck should wish to risk his reputation and reading audience by following the popular *Tortilla Flat* with a strike novel. They reminded

Steinbeck that, in spite of recent agitation, none of the strike novels of the last two or three years had succeeded. And, like the earlier publishers, Covici-Friede suggested revisions. (CF-JS, 4/2/35) To these considerations Steinbeck himself had a ready answer: "We've gone through too damn much trying to keep the work honest and in a state of improvement to let it slip now in consideration of a little miserable popularity. It has ruined everyone I know. That's one of the reasons I would like Dubious Battle printed next. Myths form quickly and I want no tag of humorist on me, nor any other kind." (JS-MO, 6/13/35)

Cup of Gold, The Pastures of Heaven, To a God Unknown, Tortilla Flat: these earlier volumes did not prepare Steinbeck readers for a red-hot strike novel. Among his published works only "The Raid" (*North American*, October, 1934) suggested this aspect of his interests. Even in this story, the emphasis is not on the social issues involved, but on the psychological state of the protagonists. What clues there are for the sources of this social interest can be found in certain aspects of Steinbeck's biography. Salinas, the seat of Steinbeck's home county of Monterey, was often the scene of labor migrations and strikes. Mr. Freeman Champney describes one of these strikes, which took place while *In Dubious Battle* was coming off the presses:

> In 1936 a strike by lettuce packing shed workers was crushed at a cost of around a quarter of a million dollars. Civil liberties, local government, and normal judicial processes were all suspended during the strike and Salinas was governed by a general staff directed by the Associated Farmers and the big lettuce growers and shippers. The local police were bossed by a reserve army officer imported for the job and at the height of the strike all male residents of Salinas between 18 and 45 were mobilized under penalty of arrest, were deputized and

armed. Beatings, tear gas attacks, wholesale arrests, threats to lynch San Francisco newpapermen if they didn't leave town, and machine guns and barbed wire all figured in the month-long struggle which finally broke the strike and destroyed the union.[1]

This is the same strike which Steinbeck referred to in his *San Francisco News* series, "The Harvest Gypsies" (October 5–12, 1936), and described again nineteen years later in "Always Something to do in Salinas" (*Holiday*, June, 1955). But Steinbeck's familiarity with the labor problems of the Salinas Valley was not merely that of an observer, for he had himself worked with migrant laborers on ranches, farms, and road gangs since his boyhood.

While this type of background does not inevitably lead to what may for the present be described as "proletarian" writing, it can, and for Steinbeck did, provide an intimate knowledge of the working man—his attitudes, habits, language. It is this intimate knowledge which gives to *In Dubious Battle, Of Mice and Men,* and *The Grapes of Wrath* that solidity of observation conspicuously absent from the majority of ideological, parlor-proletarian novels of the thirties. That Steinbeck was consciously aware of the working man's language, as opposed to the view that he either spoke it naturally or merely invented a haphazard grammar for his purposes, is evident from a letter to his agents about *In Dubious Battle:*

The speech of working men may seem a little bit racy to ladies' clubs, but, since ladies' clubs won't believe that such things go on anyway, it doesn't matter. I know this speech and I'm sick of working men being gelded of their natural expression until they talk with a fine Oxonian flavor.

There are curious things about the language of working men. I do not mean the local idioms, but the speech which is universal in this country among traveling workers. Nearly every man uses it individually, but it has universal rules. It is not grammatical error but a highly developed speech form. The use of the final "g" in "ing" is tricky, too. The "g" is put on for emphasis and often to finish a short hard sentence. It is sometimes used for purpose of elision but not always. Certain words like "something" rarely lose the final "g" or if they do, the word becomes "somepin" or "sompm." A man who says "thinkin' " will say "morning" if it comes on the end of a sentence. I tell you these things so you will understand why, in one sentence having two present participles, one "g" will be there and the other left off. This is a pretty carefully done mss. If you will read such a sentence over, aloud, you will see that it naturally falls that way. (JS-MO, 2/4/35)

It should be noted that Mac, the organizer in *In Dubious Battle*, has this same sensitivity to the spoken word:

"Mac," Burton said wearily. "You're a mystery to me. You imitate any speech you're taking part in. When you're with London and Dakin you talk the way they do. You're an actor."

"No," said Mac. "I'm not an actor at all. Speech has a kind of feel about it. I get the feel, and it comes out, perfectly naturally. I don't try to do it. I don't think I could help doing it. You know, Doc, men are suspicious of a man who doesn't talk their way. You can insult a man pretty badly by using a word he doesn't understand."

Among some of the changes in manuscript proposed by the publishers must have been some cleaning-up of the book's language, for at another time Steinbeck wrote his agents, "I should like the speech of the men to remain intact if that is possible. A working man bereft of his profanity is a silent man. I've used only those expressions that are commonly used. I hope it won't be necessary to remove them. To try to reproduce the speech of these people and to clean it up, is to make it sound stiff, unnatural and emasculated. I think it is vulgar only in the latin sense." (JS-MO, *ca.* February, 1935)

Although Steinbeck's experiences as a working man provided him with the necessary knowledge of language and daily life, *In Dubious Battle* is not a mere transcript of personal experience. "I have usually avoided using actual places to avoid hurting feelings," writes Steinbeck, "for, although I rarely use a person or a story as it is—neighbors love only too well to attribute them to someone. . . . as for the valley in *In Dubious Battle*—it is a composite valley as it is a composite strike. If it has the characteristics of Pajaro nevertheless there was no strike there. If it's like the cotton strike, that wasn't apples." [2] The main incidents of the conflict were taken from an actual strike near Fresno a few years earlier.[3]

Another of Steinbeck's sources of information was a person called Tom Collins, who knew about labor strikes from personal experience and was willing to show Steinbeck some things the writer had not yet seen.[4] This is the same "Tom, who lived it," to whom *The Grapes of Wrath* is dedicated. Mr. Collins' experiences included being a director of a mobile-camp unit under the Farm Security Administration and he may be the source for Steinbeck's characterization of such a director in *The Grapes of Wrath*.[5] These facts support the observation, made earlier in another connection, that Steinbeck has almost invariably written directly about things which he has either experienced himself or of which he has had a firsthand account.

So much for Steinbeck's intimate knowledge of working men and working conditions. There is also the problem of his knowledge of Communist organizers, tactics, and theory as these are reflected in *In Dubious Battle*. Of this aspect of the book, André Gide has written, "It is the best (psychological) portrayal that I know of communism. . . ." [6] There are several clues to Steinbeck's sources of information. About the time that he was working on *Tortilla Flat,* he had also begun a realistic biographical sketch in the first person based on information given him by a Communist district organizer. This work was not completed and some of the material went into *In Dubious Battle.* [7] Another source for Steinbeck's knowledge is acknowledged in a letter to his agents: "My information for this book came mostly from Irish and Italian communists whose training was in the field not in the drawing room. They don't believe in ideologies and ideal tactics. They do what they can under the circumstances." (JS-MO, 5/13/35)

Steinbeck's use of information from organizers "in the field" aroused unforeseen reactions. After he had sent the manuscript for *In Dubious Battle* to Covici-Friede, he received a three-page, closely typed letter from one of the publisher's readers criticizing the ideology and practice of the book's party organizers and suggesting various ways in which these deviations could be corrected. Steinbeck refused to consider such changes and asked that the manuscript be returned. [8] The agents then submitted the manuscript to Bobbs-Merrill, who were willing to publish it. Macmillan was also interested. But Covici-Friede asked Steinbeck to disregard the reader's letter; they would bring the book out after all, if he really wanted it published. There ensued a wrangle over publishing rights which was settled only upon Miss Otis' return from abroad. [9] The book was finally issued by Covici-Friede, though they were still worried about its protagonists being Communists. (CF-JS, 4/2/35)

Steinbeck's letters of this period are valuable documents of his artistic integrity. He insisted that he would change "neither thesis nor point of view" (JS-MO, 5/9/35) and made clear his stand: "Does no one in the world want to see and judge this thing coldly? Answering the complaint that the ideology is incorrect, this is the silliest of criticism. There are as many communist systems as there are communists. They postulate either an ideal communist or a thoroughly damnable communist and neither side is willing to suspect that the communist is a human subject to the weaknesses of humans and to the greatnesses of humans." (JS-MO, spring, 1935) This statement is of particular interest because it not only defines Steinbeck's intention in the novel, but also poses his aesthetic problem. He was not concerned with the protagonists as communists or capitalists but rather as humans.

It was because of this aspect that he wrote to Ben Abramson, "What a critical panning the book will take. And it's a good book I think. But both sides will jump on it. . . ." (JS-BA, early spring, 1936) On the first sheet of the second handwritten draft of the manuscript is a note in Steinbeck's hand addressed to "George," [10] which says of the book, in part, "Communists will hate it and the other side will too." After its publication, Steinbeck said he was trying to write this story without looking through "the narrow glass of political or economic preconception." [11] That *In Dubious Battle* was not to be a piece of propaganda for one of its conflicting ideologies is emphasized by the words "cold" and "brutal," which come up repeatedly in the letters of that period. The manuscript note referred to above, for example, stresses the fact that "this is a brutal cold book." In one of his first letters about the work in progress, he wrote, "I guess it is a brutal book, more brutal because there is no author's moral point of view." (JS-MO, 2/4/35) Another time he referred to *In Dubious Battle* as "a conscientious piece of work." (JS-MO, 1/21/36)

Contrary to Steinbeck's expectations, the book was not jumped on by both sides; nevertheless, the reviews did not please him: "So far Burton Rascoe and Ben Abramson are the only two reviewers who have discovered that *In Dubious Battle* is a novel and not a tract. Perhaps more will later." [12] (JS-MO, 2/14/36) And in the same vein he wrote Lewis Gannett that the book was "a novel rather than a treatise on social reform." (JS-LG, 2/3/36) Since Steinbeck himself considered *In Dubious Battle* to be "a novel and not a tract," any analysis of the book must address itself to two problems: First, does Steinbeck succeed in aesthetically fusing what he calls a "cold," "conscientious" observation having "no author's moral point of view" with what he refers to as the "human" elements?

The problem posed by this kind of ambivalence has been one of Steinbeck's major concerns not only as a writer of fiction (especially in *In Dubious Battle, The Grapes of Wrath,* and *The Moon Is Down*), but even more essentially as a thinker and observer. Six years after writing the strike novel he ended his Introduction to *Sea of Cortez* as follows:

> We determined to go doubly open so that in the end we could, if we wished, describe the sierra thus: "D. XVII-15-IX; A. II-15-IX," but also we could see the fish alive and swimming, feel it plunge against the lines, drag it threshing over the rail, and even finally eat it. And there is no reason why either approach should be inaccurate. Spinecount description need not suffer because another approach is also used. Perhaps out of the two approaches, we thought, there might emerge a picture more complete and even more accurate than either alone could produce. And so we went. (SC, 4)

Sea of Cortez is not a piece of fiction and in that book these two approaches lie side by side. *In Dubious Battle,* however, as a piece of fiction, raises a second problem: What are the techniques by which a fusion of these two approaches is attempted or effected?

Steinbeck attempts to bring together the ambivalent aspects of his material by resorting to that strategy of "middle distance," which he used so effectively in some of the stories in *The Long Valley*. Whereas in the Jody stories, for example, this effect of distance is created by a rich lyric prose which surrounds violence with an idyllic or pastoral mood, the prose of *In Dubious Battle* is harsh, factual, catalogue-like in its complete objectivity. It does not soften the violence, but neither does it exploit it. Near the end of the novel, for example, one of the town's high school boys, armed with a .22 rifle, is caught on the strikers' camping ground. The strikers tie his hands behind him and bring him to Mac, who decides to make an example of him. " 'I want a billboard,' said Mac, 'not a corpse. All right, kid. I guess you're for it.' The boy tried to retreat. He bent down trying to cower. Mac took him firmly by the shoulder. His right fist worked in quick, short hammer blows one after another. The nose cracked flat, the other eye closed, and the dark bruises formed on the cheeks. The boy jerked wildly to escape the short, precise strokes. Suddenly the torture stopped." This cold, itemizing prose is no different from that used to describe more ordinary actions: "Jim stepped to the washstand in the corner and washed his hands and combed water through his hair with his fingers. Looking into the mirror fastened across the corner of the room above the washstand, he peered into his own small grey eyes for a moment. From an inside pocket he took a comb fitted with a pocket clip and combed his straight brown hair, and parted it neatly on the side. He wore a dark suit and a grey flannel shirt, open at the throat."

Steinbeck's descriptions of nature usually display a poetic

prose; but in *In Dubious Battle* these descriptions are totally absent and the necessary setting of scene is done in this same itemizing, cataloguing fashion. Whether the action described is one of violence or tenderness, whether the scene is a sordid boardinghouse room or a beautiful apple orchard, the prose style is the same. It is a monotone which does not attempt either to soothe or jar the reader's sensibilities.

The objectivity of this prose style is reinforced by the novel's dramatic presentation of its materials. A note in Steinbeck's hand scribbled on the cover sheet of the novel's second draft makes it evident that this dramatic technique is part of the calculated strategy. "It [*In Dubious Battle*] is mostly done in dialogue thus permitting many varying opinions but keeping out any author's opinion. . . ." André Gide has written that in this dialogue, "the variegated aspects of the problem are set forth without the discussion's ever cluttering and interrupting the action." [13] This dramatic technique is carried so far that the reader is never let into any of the characters' minds directly. The characters are perceived only as they speak or execute physical movements. At any point in the novel the reader may change the verbs from past to present tense and go on reading as if the book were a play with completely objective stage directions. Indeed, at one point Steinbeck abandons the quotation tags altogether and merely places a colon after the speakers' names.

Although the novel is divided into fifteen sections or chapters, these sections, unlike those of his next book, *Of Mice and Men,* cannot be taken as separate stage scenes. They are not interlocked by tag-lines and within these sections the action often shifts its locale. But Steinbeck did write to his agents that *In Dubious Battle* might make a good play (JS-MO, 2/4/36), and the producer Herman Shumlin at one time had plans for dramatizing it.[14]

Steinbeck's "cold" prose and his dramatic presentation are important techniques for driving a wedge of objectivity not only between the author and his artifact, but also between the artifact and its audience. There is, however, an even more important technique for achieving these results, a technique based on what Steinbeck has called his "phalanx theory." [15] In *In Dubious Battle* this concept of group-man is used primarily to explain mob psychology: " 'I know,' London agreed. 'Take one guy that you know eve' thing about him, an' take ten more the same, an' you can't tell what in hell they'll do.' " In "The Leader of the People" Steinbeck uses the image of a great, crawling beast to explain the organized westering movement of pioneers. This image is repeated in the strike novel. Jim describes the mob of strikers as "just one big—animal, going down the road. Just all one animal." Mac elaborates this idea: "That's right what you said. It *is* a big animal. It's different from the men in it. And it's stronger than all the men put together. It doesn't want the same things men want—it's like Doc said—and we don't know what it'll do."

It is this mob, this group-man, and the strike through which it exists which are the real protagonist and subject matter of *In Dubious Battle*. Mac, Jim, and London are its head, but one feels, as does Grandfather in "The Leader of the People," that if they hadn't been there, "someone else would have been the head. The thing had to have a head." As Doc Burton points out, "You might be an effect as well as a cause, Mac. You might be an expression of group-man, a cell endowed with a special function, like an eye cell, drawing your force from group-man, and at the same time directing him, like an eye." This idea of leadership, similar to Tolstoy's conclusions on heroes in *War and Peace*, is repeated in *Sea of Cortez:* "Non-teleological notion: that the people we call leaders are simply those who, at the given moment, are moving in the direction behind which will be found the greatest weight, and which represents a future mass movement." (SC, 138) This theory is further elaborated in *The Moon Is Down,* where people who have leadership imposed on them are seen, in the long run, as less efficient than "leaderless" people, people whose leaders are, like Grandfather, but expressions of the body politic.

In *Sea of Cortez,* this idea of the relationship between leaders and the group is developed by an analogy to the amoeba and its pseudopodia. Steinbeck also applies this method of explication by biological analogy to his group-man concept, this time using a school of fish:

> In their millions they followed a pattern minute as to direction and depth and speed. There must be some fallacy in our thinking of these fish as individuals. Their functions in the school are in some as yet unknown way as controlled as though the school were one unit. We cannot conceive of this intricacy until we are able to think of the school as an animal itself, reacting with all its cells to stimuli which perhaps might not influence one fish at all. And this larger animal, the school, seems to have a nature and drive and ends of its own. It is more than and different from the sum of its units.[16] (SC, 240)

To perceive how deeply this idea has affected Steinbeck it is only necessary to compare in detail this statement from *Sea of Cortez* with those made about the mob of strikers in *In Dubious Battle* six years earlier.

In this development of a group-man concept, Doc Burton of *In Dubious Battle* plays an important part. While Mac, Jim, and London know, through experience, that a mob is a different thing from the sum of its parts, it remains for Doc to speculate about the possible explanation of this phenomenon. After comparing a mob of men to a human body and the strike to a local infection, he continues his explanation, with frequent interruptions from Mac:

> "A man in a group isn't himself at all; he's a cell in an organization that isn't like him any more than the cells in your body are like you. . . . It might be like this Mac: When group-man wants to move, he makes a standard. 'God wills that we recapture the Holy-Land'; or he says, 'We fight to make the world safe for democracy'; or he says, 'We will wipe out social injustice with communism.' But the group doesn't care about the Holy-Land, or Democracy, or Communism. Maybe the group simply wants to move, to fight, and uses these words simply to reassure the brains of individual men. . . . Yes it might be worthwhile to know more about group-man, to know his nature, his ends, his desires. They're not the same as ours. The pleasure we get in scratching an itch causes death to a great number of cells. Maybe group-man gets pleasure when individual men are wiped out in a war."

Although Steinbeck has denied any autobiographical connection with Doc Burton, it is evident that many passages in *Sea of Cortez,* such as the following, are but further developments of Burton's ideas:

> We have looked into the tide pools and seen the little animals feeding and reproducing and killing for food. We name them and describe them and, out of long watching, arrive at some conclusion about their habits so that we say, "This species typically does thus and so," but we do not objectively observe our own species as a species, although we know the individuals fairly well. When it seems that men may be kinder to men, that wars may not come again, we completely ignore the record of our species. If we used the same smug observation on ourselves that we do on hermit crabs we would be forced to say, with the information at hand, "It is one diagnostic

trait of *Homo Sapiens* that groups of individuals are periodically infected with a feverish nervousness which causes the
individual to turn on and destroy, not only his own kind, but
the works of his own kind. It is not known whether this be
caused by. . . ." (SC, 16–17)

What has happened between *In Dubious Battle* and *Sea of
Cortez* is that the hypothesis has shifted from psychological
to biological grounds. But the attempt to see man as a group
animal persists.

In *In Dubious Battle*, this technique of treating the strikers
as group-man is paralleled by Steinbeck's treatment of the
Communist leaders, Mac and Jim, who voluntarily renounce
their individuality in order to find their true definition in the
proletarian adventure.[17] The quality of this renunciation
differs markedly in the two men. Mac, the long-time party
organizer, has rejected individuality before the book begins.
Even his cigarette smoking is an asset to the cause. As he
explains to Jim, "You ought to take up smoking. It's a nice
social habit. You'll have to talk to a lot of strangers in your
time. I don't know any quicker way to soften a stranger
down than to offer him a smoke, or even to ask him for one.
And lots of guys feel insulted if they offer you a cigarette
and you don't take it. You better start." Mac once stops to
pet a dog when this may influence its master to help the
party, but, because he knows that his sorrow would not
benefit the party, he shows no sympathy when the same dog
is later burned alive. When his friend Joy, the "slug-nutty"
organizer, is killed, Mac uses his body to stir up spirit among
the strikers, saying, "He's done the first real, useful thing in
his life." But underneath this tough exterior, we sense a
humane individuality which insists on asserting itself more
and more as the strike progresses. For example, although he
does make a "billboard" of the high school boy, he is so

revolted by his act that he collapses when it is over. On a few occasions this individuality is so strong that he acts on impulse and in passion, losing all efficiency as a party leader.

This renunciation of humanity takes an opposite course in Jim, the neophyte. Early in the novel, he is a normal, frustrated individual, having moral objections to his mentor's use of humans as party tools. By the end, he has progressed so far in his renunciation that it is he who is master. He can coldly watch Mac administer the beating and say to him, "It wasn't a scared kid, it was a danger to the cause. . . . Sympathy is as bad as fear. That was like a doctor's work. It was an operation, that's all." Sensing this growing quality in his protégé, Mac says, "I'm getting scared of you. I've seen men like you before. . . . it's not human." Jim's words leave no doubt about his transformation. " 'I'm stronger than you, Mac . . . because I'm going in a straight line. You and all the rest have to think of women and tobacco and liquor and keeping warm and fed.' His eyes were as cold as wet river stones." This difference between Mac and Jim is precisely the difference which exists between the old and the new leaders in Koestler's *Darkness at Noon*. The old ones have a method superimposed on their humanity; the new ones are all method. For the rest of the novel it is Jim who is master, even at the very end—his headless body propped up on a platform before the mob of strikers. Even then he is important not as an individual, but as giving cause and credence to Mac's words, the last in the novel, "He didn't want nothing for himself—."

Steinbeck's use of a "cold" prose and dramatic structure, his application of "phalanx theory" and his de-personalization of the protagonists do succeed in creating in the novel an objective distance. He uses one more device, however, which, while contributing to this sense of objectivity, also imparts credibility and life to the novel. If one examines closely the structure of such fictional characters as Milton's Satan and Shakespeare's Falstaff, it becomes evident that to a great extent their "reality," their ability to make themselves "felt" by the reader, rather than merely perceived, is based on their ability to effect in the reader a dichotomy between his emotion and his intellect. This dichotomy or reception on two planes is what is often referred to as "depth" of character. The reader experiences emotional empathy for Falstaff and even Satan; but, within the framework of the artifact, his intellect must reject them. It is largely this tension within the mind of the reader which makes the characters "live," become "real." They dramatize for the reader in archetypal form the constant conflict within himself of id and ego.

The group of strikers in *In Dubious Battle* has this same dual structure. Very early in the novel, it is established that they have been tricked into coming to the orchards by wage promises which are immediately broken. The new wages are too low to live on. When they attempt to get better wages by striking, the owners import hoodlums as paid strike-breakers and do all they can to drive the strikers from their camp by both spuriously legal and outright illegal use of violence and by using lies to turn the townspeople's sympathies against the strikers. On the two occasions that the owners' representative appears, he incites hatred not only in the strikers, but in the reader as well. It is the owners who draw first blood and they who have all the advantages of guns, deputies, food, tear gas, and the law. The reader's sympathies go out to the strikers as to wronged underdogs.

The situation so far sounds very like that of any dozen strike novels of the thirties. But there are three essential differences. First, the strikers are far from being a noble folk, an idealized proletariat. Jim's father was killed by company guns, true, but he was killed while trying to blow up a slaughterhouse. In the orchard, before any violence has broken out, we see workers carelessly bruising fruit, making it worthless, and breaking off the tree branches because too lazy to reach out. When cautioned about these things, they react with profanity and further carelessness. That working men are not by nature altruistic, kind or honest, even with one another, is demonstrated again and again. They suspect London, their leader, of living in luxury from a store of canned goods while they are starving. They will not cooperate with sanitation measures to the extent of kicking a little dirt into their outside toilet when the lime is all gone. London brags about the number of cats he has managed to run over with his car. Unless aroused by violence or stuffed with food, at which time they are equally dangerous to friend and foe, the men are cowardly and apathetic. That they are not imbued with the spirit of brotherly love and cooperation is dramatically brought out in the first contact the two organizers have with the proletariat, the boxcar scene in chapter 4. A thoroughly proletarian novel would have the three men kindly and altruistically sharing the available paper for bedding. Instead, their fellow traveler tries to take all of it, and only a show of force by Mac compels sharing. Even such little bits of detail as workers blowing their noses into their fingers are more than gratuitous realism.

A second factor in the reader's ambivalent attitude toward the strikers' cause is the revelation of the Communist organizers' methods and real aims in fomenting the strike. Mac's purpose in acting as midwife is not to alleviate suffering, but to get into the confidence of the strikers. And, not having any real knowledge, he risks two lives to do it: " 'Course it was nice to help the girl, but hell, even if it killed her—we've got to use everything." When the old worker, Dan, falls out of a tree and breaks his hip, Mac comments, "The old buzzard was worth something after all," and uses the incident to start the strike. Mac ruthlessly uses the Andersons, neutrals in the strike, and they are eventually destroyed. When Jim says of the older Anderson, on whose farm they have been allowed to camp, "I like him," Mac replies, "Don't go liking people, Jim. We can't waste time liking people." Although he instructs London that the strikers must vote on everything, he also instructs him on how to get them to vote as he wants them to. Near the end of the novel, when it is clear that the strike is lost and that the men will be literally butchered if they attempt further violence, Mac nevertheless rallies them to bloodshed by means of Jim's mangled body. Yet he has carefully laid plans for the escape of himself and London. Mac's actions make it increasingly evident that he is exploiting the workers for party agitation rather than helping them.

It must be pointed out that the workers themselves are suspicious of and even antagonistic toward communists. Mac and Jim do not dare reveal their identity until it is unavoidable and the strike is at its height. Nevertheless, the fact that these workers are being led into an action whose consequences and direction are determined by Mac and Jim do much to limit the reader's sympathy for their cause.

The third means by which Steinbeck qualifies the reader's sympathy for the strikers is his use of Doc Burton as an objective chorus. It is he who frequently remarks on Mac's inhumanity, and who points out that the strikers are compromising their cause by resorting to violence: "But in my little experience the end is never very different in its nature from the means. Damn it, Jim, you can only build a violent thing with violence." And it is Doc Burton who elaborates the group-man theory which puts the strike into a context of vast forces transcending individual will and particular incident. That Doc's view is very close to Steinbeck's is evident not only from a comparison of their ideas on group-man, but also from a comparison of their attitudes toward the technique of observation:

> "Listen to me, Mac. My senses aren't above reproach, but they're all I have. I want to see the whole picture—as nearly as I can. I don't want to put on blinders of 'good' and 'bad,' and limit my vision. If I used the term 'good' on a thing I'd lose my license to inspect it, because there might be bad in it. Don't you see? I want to be able to look at the whole thing." (IDB, 149)

> The best reception of all is that which is easy and relaxed, which says in effect, "Let me absorb this thing. Let me try to understand it without private barriers. When I have understood what you are saying, only then will I subject it to my own scrutiny and my own criticism." This is the finest of all critical approaches and the rarest. (SC, 258)

As Steinbeck's letters demonstrate, both these quotations are but restatements of principles he had in mind when writing *In Dubious Battle*. While *Sea of Cortez* was in progress, Steinbeck wrote to Pascal Covici, "When this work is done I will have finished a cycle of work which has been biting me for many years. . . ." (JS-PC, 6/19/41) Certainly it had been "biting" him when he created Doc Burton. And while Doc Burton does not control the action of *In Dubious Battle*, it is his attitude which the author uses as the basis of his technique throughout the book.

Concerning the novel's "disorder," its lack of controlled meaning and climactic ending, Steinbeck wrote to his agents,

"I hardly expect you to like the book. I don't like it. It is terrible. But I hope when you finish it, in the disorder you will feel a terrible kind of order. . . . A story of the life of a man ends with his death, but where can you end a story of man-movement that has no end. No matter where you stop there is always more to come. I have tried to indicate this by stopping on a high point but it is by no means an ending." (JS-MO, 2/4/35) It is this very objectivity, actually the result of a self-neutralizing ambivalence, which determines the book's technique and structure. It is this very quality of "a terrible kind of order" which caused **André Gide** to refer to the novel as "this beautiful and painful book" (*ce beau livre atroce*).[18]

While Steinbeck's intensive application of distance techniques does make possible the overall pattern which informs *In Dubious Battle*, it has certain important consequences for character depiction. These consequences are interesting because, while a great deal of Steinbeck criticism revolves about his inability to create "living" characters, very little of objective value has been said. It has not been generally recognized that because an author's characters are as much a part of the total fiction as is the plot, a truly critical approach must address itself to the relationship of these parts. Certainly it is true that *In Dubious Battle*, for example, contains no character who "lives" or is "real" in the sense that Hamlet "lives" or in the sense that Dickens' characters are "real." But it is equally true that Hamlet "lives" at the expense of *Hamlet*, and that Dickens' characters have a reality quite independent of the hackneyed plots and circumstances in which they move. Furthermore, a character's "lifelikeness" is no test whatsoever of his effectiveness. Volpone and Subtle the Alchemist are flat objectifications of humors, yet will bear no criticism of being "un-lifelike." The reason for this is that these characters of humors are but integral parts of a comedy, an action, of humors. Mac and Jim of *In Dubious Battle* have precisely this organic relationship to the substance of the novel. They effect no rift between themselves and the other parts of the fictive substance, because they have been consciously de-personalized to fit their part in that struggle of vast forces which is the novel. They draw no undue attention to themselves.

Returning now to the problem of whether Steinbeck succeeded in creating "real" characters in *In Dubious Battle*, it seems most fair to say that while they are not as vivid as Hamlet, neither are they mere robots. Rather, they have been made as individual and "real" as their roles permit. In a very definite sense, it can be high praise to say of Steinbeck's characters that they have no reality apart from the fiction in which they exist. Whether one approves or disapproves of this conception of character, there is no doubt that this was Steinbeck's intention. On one of the sheets of the ledger which contains the strike novel is a notation in Steinbeck's hand saying that he has "always had a feeling of the texture of a story rather than an idea of characters or theme or plot."

Concerning this problem of the role of the individual in Steinbeck's work there is a paradox. For while many of his novels concern themselves with men primarily as mystical, social, psychological, or biological unit-protagonists, rather than individuals *per se,* his thought as a whole rejects the values of the group and asserts the primacy of the individual. For only the individual is capable of initiating the new directions and departures which prevent the species from losing its "survival quotient." "In a thoroughly collectivized state," says Steinbeck, "mediocre efficiency might be very great, but only through the complete elimination of the swift, the clever, and the intelligent, as well as the incompetent. Truly collective man might in fact abandon his versatility." (SC, 214) Yet Steinbeck is always conscious that man's necessary individuality is meaningless apart from its social context. In one of his little essays for *The Saturday Review* in 1955, he said, "But also I believe that man is a double thing—a group animal and at the same time an individual. And it occurs to me that he cannot successfully be the second until he has fulfilled the first." [19]

The protagonists of *In Dubious Battle* have taken the first step—submitting themselves to the group animal; but, as Doc Burton constantly points out, they fail to use this experience to fashion their own individuality. In his great strike novel, Steinbeck does not champion group-man; rather, he uses this concept as a strategy for selecting, exploring, and eventually evaluating his materials.

8 *Of Mice and Men*

Although *Of Mice and Men* appeared almost exactly one year after *In Dubious Battle,* two years had elapsed since the strike novel had been completed. The delay this time, however, was not in publication. Covici-Friede received the completed manuscript in September of 1936, and *Of Mice and Men* was published in February of the following year. Steinbeck had hardly finished the final draft of *In Dubious Battle* when he wrote to his agents, "I'm doing a play now. I don't know what will come of it. If I can do it well enough it will be a good play. I mean the theme is swell." (JS-MO, *ca.* February, 1935)

While this reference to "a play" probably indicates that *Of Mice and Men* was in progress two years before its publication, Steinbeck was doing so many other things during this time that attention to the new work must have been sporadic. For one thing, he was deeply involved in the wrangle over the publication of *In Dubious Battle,* which was not settled until the summer of 1935. For another, his father was very ill that spring and died in June. Also, Steinbeck was once again trying to get to Mexico for a year to do a novel, but the trip was put off because of the rainy season. (JS-MO, 6/13/35) At the end of August, royalties from *Tortilla Flat* began coming in, and Steinbeck was once again busy with plans for a Mexican trip to gather material for a new novel. (JS-MO, 8/29/35; JS-BA, 7/14/35) Finally, in September, Steinbeck and his wife drove down to Mexico. He stayed there until the end of the year, but was anxious to get back because by then the "new book" was working him up. On his return he sent his agents two copies of a "new little manuscript," saying he liked the new title better. (JS-MO, *ca.* January, 1936) The "new little manuscript" is probably a reference to "The Leader of the People," since about the same time, Steinbeck wrote Ben Abramson that he was "writing a book for children" (*The Red Pony*).

Despite these interruptions, however, *Of Mice and Men* was pretty well along by April, when Steinbeck wrote he was working very hard on the new novel, and again that he had "struck a snag" in the new work. (JS-MO, 4/15/36; 4/20/36) In May he was planning to collect octopi in the low spring tides of Baja California. (JS-MO, 5/15/36) That same month he underwent a baptism which many authors have undergone at some time or other. "Minor tragedy stalked," he wrote. "My setter pup, left alone one night, made confetti of about half of my manuscript book. Two months work to do over again. It sets me back. There was no other draft. I was pretty mad, but the poor little fellow may have been acting critically. I didn't want to ruin a good dog for a manuscript I'm not so sure is good at all. He only got an ordinary spanking." (JS-MO, 5/27/36) It was not until late in August that Steinbeck finished the job of rewriting.[1]

Steinbeck's growing reputation and the publishers' promotion created an eager market for *Of Mice and Men* even before the book appeared. But although Steinbeck was so poor that he could write excitedly about the acquisition of a kerosene heater for his workroom (". . . warm hands are fine."), he looked on the hullabaloo with suspicion. "About the Mice book—already, before publication, there has been a lot of nonsense written about it. I'm not sure that I like adulation. I could defend myself against attack. I wish I were as sure I could defend myself against flattery." (JS-MO, 1/27/37) On the eve of publication he wrote again: "I wish I could be personally elated about all this fuss but I can't. The book isn't that good. It's just one of these crazy streams starting. I'm still not sure Toby didn't know what he was doing when he ate the first draft. I have promoted Toby to be Lieutenant Colonel in charge of literature. But as for the unpredictable literary enthusiasms of this country—I have little faith in them." (JS-MO, 2/12/37) This opinion that "The book isn't that good" is repeated in an article which Steinbeck wrote for *Stage* just before *Of Mice and Men*'s Broadway première, but after it had been performed directly from the book by the San Francisco labor-theater group: "The book *Of Mice and Men* was an experiment and, in what it set out to do, it was a failure." [2]

Since, in this article and elsewhere, Steinbeck is explicit about what the book "set out to do," it may be well to examine these intentions before undertaking a critical analysis of the work itself. Steinbeck's remarks on technique are particularly pertinent because *Of Mice and Men* was the first of four attempts (to date) in the play-novelette form, the beginnings of which can be seen in some chapters of *In Dubious Battle*.

As set forth in the *Stage* article, Steinbeck's intention was to write a play "in the physical technique of the novel." This technique was to offer certain advantages. First, "it would go a great way towards making the play easy to read [avoiding awkward and interrupting stage directions]." Second, "the novel's ability to describe scene and people in detail would not only make for a better visual picture to the reader, but would be of value to the director, stage designer, and actor. . . ." Third, "it would be possible for the playwright by this method to set his tone much more powerfully. . . . And this tone is vastly important." Steinbeck observes that George Bernard Shaw uses his prefaces for this purpose, but that "the novel form would integrate tone and play in one entity. . . ."

While these advantages would accrue to the play, "the novel itself would be interfered with by such a method in only one way, and that is that it would be short." But several advantages for the novel would result. For one thing, "the necessity of sticking to the theme (in fact of knowing what the theme is), the brevity and necessity of holding an audience could influence the novel only for the better." In a play, "wandering, discussion, and essay are impossible." There is another advantage for the novel which can be "played," one related to Steinbeck's group-man theories: "For whatever reasons . . . the recent tendency of writers has been to deal in those themes and those scenes which are best understood and appreciated by groups of people." Some things (such as war, prize fights on the radio) "cannot be understood in solitude. . . . the thing that is missing is the close, almost physical contact with other people. . . ." He gives *Waiting for Lefty* as an example of a work which requires a mass audience for its full effect. Steinbeck explicitly states that he is not advocating this method for the whole field of the novel. The novel of "contemplation, of characterization through analysis, of philosophic discussion is not affected at all by this form."

So much for the technique. Concerning the book's theme, Steinbeck wrote his agents, "I'm sorry that you do not find the new book as large in subject as it should be. I probably did not make my subjects and my symbols clear. The microcosm is rather difficult to handle and apparently I did not get it over—the earth longings of a Lennie who was not to represent insanity at all but the inarticulate and powerful yearning of all men. Well, if it isn't there it isn't there." (JS-MO, 9/1/36) To Ben Abramson he wrote a similar comment on the book's theme: ". . . it's a study of the dreams and pleasures of everyone in the world." (JS-BA, *ca.* September, 1936)

Such words as "microcosm," "of all men," and "everyone in the world" indicate that the problem he set himself in *Of Mice and Men* was similar to that he had solved in his previous novel, *In Dubious Battle.* But whereas in the earlier work the de-personalized protagonists were easily absorbed into a greater pattern because that pattern was physically present in the novel, in *Of Mice and Men* the protagonists are projected against a very thin background and must suggest or create this larger pattern through their own particularity. To achieve this, Steinbeck makes use of language, action, and symbol as recurring motifs. All three of these motifs are presented in the opening scene, are contrapuntally developed through the story, and come together again at the end.

The first symbol in the novel, and the primary one, is the little spot by the river where the story begins and ends.

The book opens with a description of this place by the river, and we first see George and Lennie as they enter this place from the highway to an outside world. It is significant that they prefer spending the night here rather than going on to the bunkhouse at the ranch.

Steinbeck's novels and stories often contain groves, willow thickets by a river, and caves which figure prominently in the action. There are, for example, the grove in *To a God Unknown*, the place by the river in the Junius Maltby story, the two caves and a willow thicket in *The Grapes of Wrath*, the cave under the bridge in *In Dubious Battle*, the caves in *The Wayward Bus*, and the thicket and cave in *The Pearl*. For George and Lennie, as for other Steinbeck heroes, coming to a cave or thicket by the river symbolizes a retreat from the world to a primeval innocence. Sometimes, as in *The Grapes of Wrath*, this retreat has explicit overtones of a return to the womb and rebirth. In the opening scene of *Of Mice and Men* Lennie twice mentions the possibility of hiding out in a cave, and George impresses on him that he **must** return to this thicket by the river when there is trouble.

While the cave or the river thicket is a "safe place," it is physically impossible to remain there, and this symbol of primeval innocence becomes translated into terms possible in the real world. For George and Lennie it becomes "a little house an' a couple of acres." Out of this translation grows a second symbol, the rabbits, and this symbol serves several purposes. Through synecdoche it comes to stand for the "safe place" itself, making a much more easily manipulated symbol than the "house an' a couple of acres." Also, through Lennie's love for the rabbits Steinbeck is able not only to dramatize Lennie's desire for the "safe place," but to define the basis of that desire on a very low level of consciousness—the attraction to soft, warm fur, which is for Lennie the most important aspect of their plans.

This transference of symbolic value from the farm to the rabbits is important also because it makes possible the motif of action. This is introduced in the first scene by the dead mouse which Lennie is carrying in his pocket (much as Tom carries the turtle in *The Grapes of Wrath*). As George talks about Lennie's attraction to mice, it becomes evident that the symbolic rabbits will come to the same end—crushed by Lennie's simple, blundering strength. Thus Lennie's killing of mice and later his killing of the puppy set up a pattern which the reader expects to be carried out again. George's story about Lennie and the little girl with the red dress, which he tells twice, contributes to this expectancy of pattern, as do the shooting of Candy's dog, the crushing of Curley's hand, and the frequent appearances of Curley's wife. All these incidents are patterns of the action motif and predict the fate of the rabbits and thus the fate of the dream of a "safe place."

The third motif, that of language, is also present in the opening scene. Lennie asks George, "Tell me—like you done before," and George's words are obviously in the nature of a ritual. "George's voice became deeper. He repeated his words rhythmically, as though he had said them many times before." The element of ritual is stressed by the fact that even Lennie has heard it often enough to remember its precise language: *"An' live off the fatta the lan'. . . . An' have rabbits. Go on George! Tell about what we're gonna have in the garden and about the rabbits in the cages and about. . . ."* This ritual is performed often in the story, whenever Lennie feels insecure. And of course it is while Lennie is caught up in this dream vision that George shoots him, so that on one level the vision is accomplished—the dream never interrupted, the rabbits never crushed.

The highly patterned effect achieved by these incremental motifs of symbol, action, and language is the knife edge on which criticism of *Of Mice and Men* divides. For although Steinbeck's success in creating a pattern has been acknowledged, criticism has been divided as to the effect of this achievement. On one side, it is claimed that this strong patterning creates a sense of contrivance and mechanical action,[3] and on the other, that the patterning actually gives a meaningful design to the story, a tone of classic fate.[4] What is obviously needed here is some objective critical tool for determining under what conditions a sense of inevitability (to use a neutral word) should be experienced as mechanical contrivance, and when it should be experienced as catharsis effected by a sense of fate. Such a tool cannot be forged within the limits of this study; but it is possible to examine the particular circumstances of *Of Mice and Men* more closely before passing judgment.

Although the three motifs of symbol, action, and language build up a strong pattern of inevitability, the movement is not unbroken. About midway in the novel (chapters 3 and 4) there is set up a countermovement which seems to threaten the pattern. Up to this point the dream of "a house an' a couple of acres" seemed impossible of realization. Now it develops that George has an actual farm in mind (ten acres), knows the owners and why they want to sell it: "The ol' people that owns it is flat bust an' the ol' lady needs an operation." He even knows the price—"six hundred dollars." Also, the old workman, Candy, is willing to buy a share in the dream with the three hundred dollars he has saved up. It appears that at the end of the month George and Lennie will have another hundred dollars and that quite possibly they "could swing her for that." In the following chapter this dream and its possibilities are further explored through Lennie's visit with Crooks, the power of the dream manifesting itself in Crooks's conversion from cynicism to optimism. But at the very height of his conversion the mice symbol reappears in the form of Curley's wife, who threatens the dream by bringing with her the harsh realities of the outside world and by arousing Lennie's interest.

The function of Candy's and Crooks's interest and the sudden bringing of the dream within reasonable possibility is to interrupt, momentarily, the pattern of inevitability. But, and this is very important, Steinbeck handles this interruption so that it does not actually reverse the situation. Rather, it insinuates a possibility. Thus, though working against the pattern, this countermovement makes that pattern more credible by creating the necessary ingredient of free will. The story achieves power through a delicate balance of the protagonists' free will and the force of circumstance.

In addition to imposing a sense of inevitability, this strong patterning of events performs the important function of extending the story's range of meanings. This can best be understood by reference to Hemingway's "fourth dimension," which has been defined by Joseph Warren Beach as an "aesthetic factor" achieved by the protagonists' repeated participation in some traditional "ritual or strategy," [5] and by Malcolm Cowley as "the almost continual performance of rites and ceremonies" suggesting recurrent patterns of human experience.[6] The incremental motifs of symbol, action, and language which inform *Of Mice and Men* have precisely these effects. The simple story of two migrant workers' dream of a safe retreat, a "clean well-lighted place," becomes itself a pattern or archetype which exists on three levels.

There is the obvious story level on a realistic plane, with

its shocking climax. There is also the level of social protest, Steinbeck the reformer crying out against the exploitation of migrant workers. The third level is an allegorical one, its interpretation limited only by the ingenuity of the audience. It could be, as Carlos Baker suggests, "an allegory of Mind and Body." [7] Using the same kind of dichotomy, the story could also be about the dumb, clumsy, but strong mass of humanity and its shrewd manipulators. This would make the book a more abstract treatment of the two forces of *In Dubious Battle*—the mob and its leaders. The dichotomy could also be that of the unconscious and the conscious, the id and the ego, or any other forces or qualities which have the same structural relationship to each other that do Lennie and George. It is interesting in this connection that the name Leonard means "strong or brave as a lion," and that the name George means "husbandman."

The title itself, however, relates the whole story to still another level which is implicit in the context of Burns's poem.

But, Mousie, thou art no thy lane,
In proving foresight may be vain:
The best laid schemes o' mice an' men
            Gang aft a-gley
An' lea'e us nought but grief an' pain
            For promis'd joy.

In the poem, Burns extends the mouse's experience to include that of mankind; in *Of Mice and Men*, Steinbeck extends the experience of two migrant workers to the human condition. "This is the way things are," both writers are saying. On this level, perhaps the most important, Steinbeck is dramatizing the non-teleological philosophy which had such a great part in shaping *In Dubious Battle* and which would be fully discussed in *Sea of Cortez*. This level of meaning is indicated by the title originally intended for the book—"Something That Happened." [8] In this light, the ending of the story is, like the ploughman's disrupting of the mouse's nest, neither tragic nor brutal, but simply a part of the pattern of events. It is amusing in this regard that a Hollywood director suggested to Steinbeck that someone else kill the girl, so that sympathy could be kept with Lennie. (JS-MO, 3/?/38)

In addition to these meanings which grow out of the book's "pattern," there is what might be termed a subplot which defines George's concern with Lennie. It is easily perceived that George, the "husbandman," is necessary to Lennie; but it has not been pointed out that Lennie is just as necessary to George. Without an explanation of this latter relationship, any allegory posited on the pattern created in *Of Mice and Men* must remain incomplete. Repeatedly, George tells Lennie, "God, you're a lot of trouble. I could get along so easy and so nice if I didn't have you on my tail." But this getting along so easy never means getting a farm of his own. With one important exception, George never mentions the dream except for Lennie's benefit. That his own "dream" is quite different from Lennie's is established early in the novel and often repeated: "God a'mighty, if I was alone I could live so easy. I could go get a job an' work, an' no trouble. No mess at all, and when the end of the month come I could take my fifty bucks and go into town and get whatever I want. Why, I could stay in a cat house all night. I could eat any place I want, hotel or anyplace, and order any damn thing I could think of. An' I could do all that every damn month. Get a gallon whiskey, or set in a pool room and play cards or shoot pool." Lennie has heard this from George so often that in the last scene, when he realizes that he has "done another bad thing," he asks, "Ain't you gonna give me hell? . . . Like, 'If I didn't have you I'd take my fifty bucks—'."

Almost every character in the story asks George why he goes around with Lennie—the foreman, Curley, Slim, and Candy. Crooks, the lonely Negro, doesn't ask George, but he does speculate about it, and shrewdly—"a guy talkin' to another guy and it don't make no difference if he don't hear or understand. The thing is, they're talkin'. . . ." George's explanations vary from outright lies to a simple statement of "We travel together." It is only to Slim, the superior workman with "God-like eyes," that he tells a great part of the truth. Among several reasons, such as his feeling of responsibility for Lennie in return for the latter's unfailing loyalty, and their having grown up together, there is revealed another: "He's dumb as hell, but he ain't crazy. An' I ain't so bright neither, or I wouldn't be buckin' barley for my fifty and found. If I was even a little bit smart, I'd have my own little place, an' I'd be bringin' in my own crops, 'stead of doin' all the work and not getting what comes up outa the ground."

This statement, together with George's repeatedly expressed desire to take his fifty bucks to a cat house and his continual playing of solitaire, reveals that to some extent George needs Lennie as a rationalization for his failure. This is one of the reasons why, after the body of Curley's wife is discovered, George refuses Candy's offer of a partnership which would make the dream a reality and says to him, "I'll work my month an' I'll take my fifty bucks an' I'll stay all night in some lousy cat house. Or I'll set in some poolroom till ever'body goes home. An' then I'll come back an' work another month an' I'll have fifty bucks more." The dream of the farm originates with Lennie and it is only through Lennie, who also makes the dream impossible, that the dream has any meaning for George. An understanding of this dual relationship will do much to mitigate the frequent charge that Steinbeck's depiction of George's attachment is concocted of pure sentimentality. At the end of the novel, George's going off with Slim to "do the town" is more than an escape from grief. It is an ironic and symbolic twist to his dream.

The "real" meaning of the book is neither in the realistic action nor in the levels of allegory. Nor is it in some middle course. Rather, it is in the pattern which informs the story both on the realistic and the allegorical levels, a pattern which Steinbeck took pains to prevent from becoming either trite or mechanical.

But whether because of its realism, its allegory, or its pattern, *Of Mice and Men* was an immediate popular success. It appeared on best-seller lists, was a Book-of-the-Month Club selection, and was sold to Hollywood. This financial success made it possible for Steinbeck to do some traveling, and in the spring of 1937 he left San Francisco for New York, traveling his favorite way, by freighter via the Panama Canal. Steinbeck stayed briefly in New York to see his agents and publishers, reluctantly attended a dinner for Thomas Mann (in a borrowed suit), and in the middle of May sailed for England aboard a Swedish freighter. He traveled to his mother's homeplace in Ireland, over to Sweden, and then to Russia, which country he found as bewildering in its own way as Mexico had been.

Before leaving on this trip, Steinbeck had been working on a dramatization of *Of Mice and Men,* and on his return to New York early in August (aboard another freighter) he stayed at George Kaufman's farm in Bucks County, Pennsylvania, and with some advice from Kaufman, who was to direct it, finished the final version of the play. *Of Mice and Men* opened on November 23, 1937, on the stage of the Music Box theater in New York and won great critical and popular acclaim. It brought Steinbeck the Drama Critics' Circle Award in a season which had also seen *Our Town, The Cradle Will Rock, Golden Boy,* and *Prologue to Glory.* On the very first ballot, *Of Mice and Men* got nine votes to a total of seven for all the others. The citation ran as follows:

> The New York Drama Critics' Circle awards its prize to John Steinbeck's "Of Mice and Men" for its direct force and perception in handling a theme genuinely rooted in American life; for its bite into the strict quality of its material; for his refusal to make this study of tragical loneliness and frustration either cheap or sensational; and finally for its simple, intense and steadily rising effect on the stage.[9]

Steinbeck had not stayed for the laurels. Upon completing the stage version, and not even waiting for the play to be produced, he went to Detroit, bought a car, and, after visiting Ben Abramson in Chicago, drove to Oklahoma. There he joined a group of migrant workers heading west, lived with them in their Hoovervilles, and worked with them when they got to California. He was already writing *The Grapes of Wrath.*

9 *The Grapes of Wrath*

Steinbeck's trek from Oklahoma to the cotton fields of California in the fall of 1937 was not the first of such forays made to observe his materials at first hand. He had made several trips into the agricultural areas of California in preparation for his strike novel, and immediately after completing *Of Mice and Men* in September of 1936 he had gone to observe the squatters' camps near Salinas and Bakersfield. There he gathered materials for "Dubious Battle in California" (*Nation*, Sept. 12, 1936) and a series of seven other articles called "The Harvest Gypsies," which appeared in the *San Francisco News*, October 5–12, 1936.[1] On his return from this trip he wrote to Ben Abramson, "California is not very far from civil war. I hope it can be averted." (JS-BA, 10/?/36) He expressed the same concern to his agents: "I just returned yesterday from the strike area of Salinas and from my migrants in Bakersfield. This thing is dangerous.

Maybe it will be patched up for a while, but I look for the lid to blow off in a few weeks. Issues are very sharp here now. . . . My material drawer is chock full." (JS-MO, 10/?/36)

During one period that autumn Steinbeck lived in one of the federal migrant camps in central California and wrote to Lawrence Clark Powell, "I have to write this sitting in a ditch. I'm out working—may go south to pick a little cotton. Migrants are going south now and I'll probably go along." [2] After the publication of *The Grapes of Wrath* these migrants sent Steinbeck a patchwork dog sewn from pieces of shirt-tails and dresses and bearing around its neck a tag with the inscription "Migrant John."

The *San Francisco News* articles are straight-forward reports of living conditions among migrant workers, along with suggestions and appeals for a more enlightened treatment of these people. Although they contain several details which were later incorporated in *The Grapes of Wrath,* these articles are significant primarily as a record of Steinbeck's attitude toward the people and conditions which he was to use as the materials of his great novel. Actually, the extremes of poverty, injustice, and suffering depicted in these articles are nowhere equaled in *The Grapes of Wrath.*

Steinbeck was still trying to understand the total situation. He did not go into the field to substantiate a ready-made theory. When the editors of *Occident* asked him for an article of a political nature, he refused, saying, "Generalities seem to solidify so quickly into stupidities. A writer can only honestly say—'This is the way it seems to me at this moment.'" He didn't think he knew enough about the situation and didn't wish to retire into some "terminology." Steinbeck did, however, allow the editors to print his letter of refusal, part of which follows:

The changes go on so rapidly and it is so hard to see! Sad that it will be so easy in fifty years. Of course there is a larger picture one can feel. I suppose the appellations communist and fascist are adequate. I don't really think they are. I'm probably making a mistake in simply listening to men talk and watching them act, hoping that the projection of the microcosm will define the outlines of the macrocosm. There will come a time and that soon, I suppose, when such a position will be untenable, when we'll all put on blinders and put our heads down, and yelling some meaningless rallying cry, we'll do what men of every other time have done—tear the guts out of our own race.[3]

Unlike Doc in *In Dubious Battle*, however, Steinbeck's attempt to understand did not make him a dispassionate observer. In the autumn of that same year he was planning to accept a Hollywood contract of a thousand dollars a week for six weeks' work on *Of Mice and Men* so that he could give two dollars apiece to three thousand migrants. Pascal Covici flew out to the coast to talk him out of it. Early in 1938, in the midst of work on the new novel, he wrote his agents, "I must go over into the interior valleys. There are five thousand families starving to death over there, not just hungry, but actually starving. . . . In one tent there are twenty people quarantined for smallpox and two of the women are to have babies in that tent this week. . . . Talk about Spanish children. The death of children by starvation in our valleys is simply staggering. . . . I'll do what I can. . . . Funny how mean and how little books become in the face of such tragedies." [4] When *Life* offered to send him into the field with a photographer to write about the migrants, he informed his agents that he would accept no money other than expenses—"I'm sorry but I simply can't make money on these people. . . . The suffering is too great for me to cash in on it." (JS-MO, 3/?/38) It is this great compassion which accounts for the difference in tone between *In Dubious Battle* and *The Grapes of Wrath*.

But this compassion, this honest indignation, did not carry Steinbeck into propagandism or blind him to his responsibilities as a novelist. "The subject is so large that it scares me," he wrote. "And I am not going to rush it. It must be worked out with care." (JS-MO, 1/?/37) By June of 1938 he finished a sixty-thousand-word novel called *L'Affaire Lettuceberg*. To his agents and publishers, who were expecting the book and had announced it variously as *Oklahoma* and *Lettuceberg*, he sent the following joint letter:

This is going to be a hard letter to write. I feel badly about it. You see this book is finished and it is a bad book and I must get rid of it. It can't be printed. It is bad because it isn't honest. Oh! the incidents all happened but—I'm not telling as much of the truth about them as I know. In satire you have to restrict the picture and I just can't do satire. . . . I know that a great many people would think they liked this book. I, myself, have built up a hole-proof argument on how and why I liked it. I can't beat the argument, but I don't like the book. And I would be doing Pat a greater injury in letting him print it than I would by destroying it. Not once in the writing of it have I felt the curious warm pleasure that comes when work is going well. My whole work drive has been aimed at making people understand each other and then I deliberately write this book, the aim of which is to cause hatred through partial understanding. My father would have called it a smart-alec book. It was full of tricks to make people ridiculous. If I can't do better I have slipped badly. And that I won't admit—yet. . . . (JS-MO, 6/?/38)

Such a letter makes ridiculous any insinuation that Steinbeck's "social protest" was literary opportunism. It is Steinbeck's corollary to Hemingway's ideal of writing "truly," without "tricks," and without "cheating."

Steinbeck continued to work on his big novel all that summer, and by autumn it was in its final stages. "I am desperately tired," he wrote, "but I want to finish. And mean. I feel as though shrapnel were bursting about my head. I only hope the book is some good. Can't tell yet at all. And I can't tell whether it is balanced. It is a slow plodding book but I don't think that it is dull." [5] On September 16, 1938, he sent Pascal Covici the book's title—*The Grapes of Wrath* —saying, "I like the soft with the hard and the marching content and the American revolutionary content." Three months later he suggested to Covici that the "Battle Hymn of the Republic" be printed somewhere in the book, possibly as end pages. (JS-PC, 12/22/38)

The completion of *The Grapes of Wrath* late in 1938 left Steinbeck exhausted. He was confined to bed for some weeks and forbidden on doctor's orders to read or write. But he conscientiously saw the book through the press. As in the publication of *In Dubious Battle*, there arose the problem of printable language. Steinbeck's stand was again firm. He warned the publishers that no words must be changed; even "shit-heels" must remain. (JS-PC, 1/15/39) Also, he refused to have included in the book a page reproduced in his own handwriting. He insisted on keeping his personality out of it. The book was to stand on its own merits, even if it meant a loss in sales. He didn't want "that kind" of reader anyway. (JS-PC, 2/23/39) In April, 1939, the Viking Press brought out *The Grapes of Wrath*.

The Grapes of Wrath did not have a chance of being accepted and evaluated as a piece of fiction. From the very beginning it was taken as substantial fact and its merits debated as a document rather than as a novel. This was to be expected in a decade which had produced such motion pictures as Pare Lorentz' *The River* and *The Plow that Broke the Plains;* such books as Dorothea Lange's and Paul S. Taylor's *An American Exodus: A Record of Human Erosion,* Archibald MacLeish's *Land of the Free,* Erskine Caldwell's and Margaret Bourke-White's *You Have Seen Their Faces,* and the WPA collection of case histories called *These Are Our Lives,* to cite only a few. The line between social documentation and fiction has never been so hazy, and this lack of a definite line resulted in works like *Land of the Free,* which is neither an illustrated text nor a book of pictures with captions, but a form in itself. Often what was intended as social documentation and reportage had a literary value achieved only rarely in proletarian fiction—Ruth McKenney's *Industrial Valley* being an example.

Even aside from the fact that *The Grapes of Wrath* came in such a period, Steinbeck's novel had the vulnerability of all social fiction—it was subject to attack on its facts. It is not within the scope of this study to present an exhaustive analysis either of the attack made on his facts and their defense or of the sociological and political consequences of the book, but a small sampling of the relevant literature may indicate the nature of that social-political-economic controversy which eclipsed *The Grapes of Wrath* as a novel.

Within two months after the publication of *The Grapes of Wrath,* there appeared a slim volume called *Grapes of Gladness: California's Refreshing and Inspiring Answer to John Steinbeck's "Grapes of Wrath."* This title, a remnant from the age of pamphleteering, was affixed to the story of a family of migrants who came to California poverty-stricken and found that everyone, including the banks and growers, welcomed them with open arms. They were given free land, loaned money, and lionized. In an "Addenda" to this soap opera, the author tries to break down some of Steinbeck's "facts." [6]

Another book, *The Truth About John Steinbeck and the Migrants,* tells of its author's own experiences on a trip which he made, disguised as a migrant, just to see what conditions really were. This "migrant" found that he was able to average four dollars a day on wages and that almost all the growers begged him to stay with them and live in the ranch house all year round. In an essay which prefaces this sojourn in the land of Canaan, the author calls *The Grapes of Wrath* "a novel wherein naturalism has gone berserk, where truth has run amuck drunken upon prejudice and exaggeration, where matters economic have been hurled beyond the pale of rational and realistic thinking." [7]

Defenses of the book's accuracy were no less vehement. Professors of sociology, ministers, and government officials put themselves on record that Steinbeck's information was accurate.[8] The subject was debated on radio programs such as "Town Meeting," and the book was publicly reviewed before mass audiences. Before making the motion picture, Zanuck sent private detectives to ascertain the accuracy of the novel and found conditions even worse than described by Steinbeck.[9] The author himself, accompanied by a photographer, visited hundreds of migrant camps, took notes and made a pictorial record which was later printed in *Life* as evidence that the motion picture had not exaggerated. The book itself was both banned and burned on both political and pornographic grounds from Buffalo, New York, to California, and Archbishop Spellman's denunciation of it appeared in all the Hearst papers. Not the least antagonism was fomented in Oklahoma, whose native sons found them-

selves degraded and abused and whose bookstores found
that the novel's circulation exceeded even that of *Gone With
the Wind*. Oklahoma Congressman Lyle Boren denounced
the book in Congress, maintaining that "the heart and brain
and character of the average tenant farmer of Oklahoma
cannot be surpassed and probably not equaled by any other
group. . . ." He called the book itself "a black, infernal
creation of a twisted, distorted mind." The Oklahoma
Chamber of Commerce tried to stop the filming of the picture.[10] No American novel since *Uncle Tom's Cabin* has
created such an immediate reaction on so many levels.

While the exploration of these frenzied reactions to the
factual details of *The Grapes of Wrath* is more pertinent to
sociology and perhaps even psychology than it is to either
the history or criticism of literature, critical reactions to the
novel's social philosophy do come within the scope of this
study.

One extreme position is best stated by the author of *The
Truth About John Steinbeck and the Migrants*, who "can
think of no other novel which advances the idea of class
war and promotes hatred of class against class . . . more
than does *The Grapes of Wrath*." [11] It is directly opposed by
Stanley Edgar Hyman: "Actually, as a careful reading makes
clear, the central message of *The Grapes of Wrath* is an
appeal to the owning class to behave, to become enlightened,
rather than to the working class to change its own conditions." [12]

That it could not have been Steinbeck's intention to urge
organized revolt is indicated not only in his letter retracting
L'Affaire Lettuceberg, but also in the series of articles which
he wrote for the *San Francisco News* in October of 1936.
The first of these articles ends with the warning that "California . . . is gradually building up a human structure

which will certainly change the State, and may, if handled with the inhumanity and stupidity that have characterized the past, destroy the present system of agricultural economics." [13] Steinbeck makes a similar point at the end of his article in *The Nation:* "It is fervently to be hoped that the great group of migrant workers so necessary to the harvesting of California's crops may be given the right to live decently, that they may not be so badgered, tormented, and hurt that in the end they become avengers of the hundreds of thousands who have been tormented and starved before them." [14] In his third article of the *News* series appears another warning that "a continuation of this approach [intimidation and repression] constitutes a criminal endangering of the peace of the State." [15] In the final article of this series, Steinbeck offers three suggestions: first, that migrant laborers be allotted small "subsistence" farms on which they can live and work when there is no call for migrant labor; second, that a Migratory Labor Board be created to help allot labor where needed and to determine fair wages; third, that vigilante-ism and terrorism be punished. Steinbeck's proposed alternative to this solution has a keen logic: "If, on the other hand, as has been stated by a large grower, our agriculture requires the creation and maintenance of a peon class, then it is submitted that California agriculture is economically unsound under a democracy." [16] There is certainly no Marxian class war or Bolshevik revolutionary ardor here. Steinbeck's statement about an American "peon" class is milder even than that of Walt Whitman in "Notes Left Over." "If the United States," said Whitman, "like the countries of the Old World, are also to grow vast crops of poor, desperate, dissatisfied, nomadic, miserably-waged populations . . . then our republican experiment, not withstanding all its surface-success, is at heart an unhealthy failure."

Actually, as Frederick I. Carpenter has observed, Steinbeck's social philosophy had three roots: "For the first time in history, *The Grapes of Wrath* brings together and makes real three skeins of American thought. It begins with the transcendental oversoul, Emerson's faith in the common man, and his Protestant self-reliance. To this it joins Whitman's religion of the love of all man and his mass democracy. And it combines these mystical and poetic ideas with the realistic philosophy of pragmatism and its emphasis on effective action." Jim Casy "translates American philosophy into words of one syllable, and the Joads translate it into action." [17]

Another critic, Chester E. Eisinger, taking note of Carpenter's observations, suggests that there must be added a fourth skein of American thought—the agrarianism of Jefferson: "Because he had faith in the common man and thus gave his thinking a broad popular basis, Steinbeck was closer to Jeffersonianism than were the Southern Agrarians, who sought to resurrect not only an agricultural way of life but also the traditional cultural values of Europe. Steinbeck was concerned with democracy, and looked upon agrarianism as a way of life that would enable us to realize the full potentialities of the creed. Jefferson, of course, held the same." [18]

Steinbeck had dealt with this theme of man's relationship to the land earlier—in *To a God Unknown* and *Of Mice and Men*. In these works the relationship is mystical, symbolic, and mythical. While these values persist in *The Grapes of Wrath*, man's identification with the growth cycle is also seen as pragmatic, socially practical in Jeffersonian terms. The human erosion pictured in the book is as much the result of a separation from the land as it is of poverty. And because for the absentee growers their land has become a column of figures in a book, they too are suffering an erosion —a moral one. Jefferson would have had no difficulty understanding what Steinbeck was getting at in one of his *San Francisco News* articles—that the loss of land led to a loss of dignity, which he defined not as a sense of self-importance, but as "a register of man's responsibility to the community": "We regard this destruction of dignity, then, as one of the most regrettable results of the migrant's life since it does reduce his responsibility and does make him a sullen outcast who will strike at our government in any way that occurs to him." [19]

Although *The Grapes of Wrath* brings together these four important skeins of American thought, it can be considered one of our great American novels only to the extent that it succeeds in realizing these ideas in the concrete forms of art. As Alex Comfort has put it, "The critical importance of a writer's ideas is this: if their scope is insufficient to cover the material he deals with, and to cover it in a coherent manner, irrespective of their immediate truth, they may render him unable to write at that level which, by common agreement, we call major literature." [20]

The ideas and materials of *The Grapes of Wrath* presented Steinbeck with the most difficult problem of structure he had faced so far. Neither the variations on a single line of action and development that he had used in *Cup of Gold, To a God Unknown, In Dubious Battle,* and *Of Mice and Men* nor the episodic structure of *The Pastures of Heaven* and *Tortilla Flat* could handle the scope and diversity of *The Grapes of Wrath.* His position was not unlike that of Tolstoy in writing *War and Peace.* Tolstoy's materials were, roughly, the adventures of the Bezukhov, Rostov, and Bolkonski families on the one hand, and the Napoleonic wars on the other. And while these two blocks of material were brought together in the plot development, there was enough material about the Napoleonic wars left over so that the author had to incorporate it in separate, philosophic interchapters. Steinbeck's materials were similar. There were the adventures of the Joad family and there was also the Great Depression. And, like Tolstoy, he had enough material left over to write separate, philosophic interchapters.

In the light of this basic analogy, Percy Lubbock's comments on the structural role of these two elements in *War and Peace* become significant for an analysis of structure in *The Grapes of Wrath:* "I can discover no angle at which the two stories will appear to unite and merge in a single impression. Neither is subordinated to the other, and there is nothing above them . . . to which they are both related. Nor are they placed together to illustrate a contrast; nothing *results* from their juxtaposition. Only from time to time, upon no apparent principle and without a word of warning, one of them is dropped and the other resumed." [21]

In these few phrases Lubbock has defined the aesthetic conditions not only for *War and Peace*, but for any other piece of fiction whose strategies include an intercalary construction—*The Grapes of Wrath*, for example. The test is whether anything *"results"* from this kind of structure.

Counting the opening description of the drought and the penultimate chapter on the rains, pieces of straightforward description allowable even to strictly "scenic" novels (Lubbock's term for materials presented entirely from the objective point of view), there are in *The Grapes of Wrath* sixteen interchapters, making up a total of just under a hundred pages—almost one sixth of the book. In none of these chapters do the Joads, Wilsons, or Wainwrights appear.

These interchapters have two main functions. First, by presenting the social background they serve to amplify the pattern of action created by the Joad family. To this purpose, thirteen of the sixteen chapters are largely devoted. Chapter 1, for example, describes in panoramic terms the drought which forces the Joads off their land. Chapter 5 is mostly a dialogue between two generalized forces, the banks and the farmers, presenting in archetype the conflict in which the Joads are caught up. Chapters 7 and 9 depict, respectively, the buying of jalopies and the selling of household goods. Chapter 11 describes at length a decaying and deserted house which is the prototype of all the houses abandoned in the dust bowl. Other chapters explore, through the collage technique of chapters 7 and 9, the nature of that new, nomadic society which the Joads are helping to form (14, 17, 23). Almost every aspect of the Joads' adventures is enlarged in the interchapters and seen as part of the social climate.

The remaining three intercalary chapters (19, 21, and 25) have the function of providing such historical information as the development of land ownership in California, the consequent development of migrant labor, and certain economic aspects of the social lag. These three "informative" chapters make up only nineteen of the novel's six hundred odd pages. Scattered through the sixteen interchapters are occasional paragraphs whose purpose is to present, with choric effect, the philosophy or social message to which the current situation gives rise. For the most part, these paragraphs occur in four chapters—9, 11, 14, and 19.

While all these various materials are obviously ideologically related to the longer, narrative section of the novel (five hundred pages), there remains the problem of their aesthetic integration with the book as a whole. Even a cursory reading will show that there is a general correspondence between the material of each intercalary chapter and that of the current narrative portion. The magnificent opening description of the drought sets forth the condition which gives rise to the novel's action. Chapter 5 deals with the banks' foreclosing of mortgages, which forces the sharecroppers to emigrate. Highway 66 is given a chapter as the Joads begin their trek on that historic route. The chapters dealing with migrant life on the highway appear interspersed with the narrative of the Joads' actual journey. The last intercalary chapter, 29, describes the rain and flood in which the action of the novel ends.

A more careful reading will make it evident that this integration of the interchapters into a total structure goes far beyond a merely complementary juxtaposition. There is in addition an intricate interweaving of specific details. The chapter about the banks, for example, comes immediately after Tom and Casy see the deserted Joad farmhouse and is itself followed by a narrative chapter particularizing many of that chapter's generalities: As with the anonymous house in the intercalary chapter (5), one corner of the Joad house has been knocked off its foundation by a tractor. The man who in the interchapter threatens the tractor driver with his rifle becomes Grampa Joad, except that where the anonymous tenant does not fire, Grampa shoots out both headlights. The tractor driver in the intercalary chapter, Joe Davis, is a family acquaintance of the anonymous tenant, as Willy is an acquaintance of the Joads in the narrative chapter. The general dialogue between banks and tenants in the intercalary chapter is particularized by Muley in the narrative chapter: "Well, the guy that come aroun' talked nice as pie. 'You got to get off. It ain't my fault.' 'Well,' I says, 'Whose fault is it? I'll go an' nut the fella.' 'It's the Shawnee Lan' an' Cattle Company. I jus' got orders.' 'Who's the Shawnee Lan' an' Cattle Company?' 'It ain't nobody. It's a company.' Got a fella crazy. There wasn't nobody you could lay for." The jalopy sitting in the Joads' front yard is the kind of jalopy described in chapter 7. Chapter 8 ends with Al Joad driving off to sell a truckload of household goods. Chapter 9 is an intercalary chapter describing destitute farmers selling such goods, including many items which the Joads themselves are selling—pumps, farming tools, furniture, a team and wagon for ten dollars. In the following chapter the Joads' truck returns empty, the men having sold everything for eighteen dollars—including ten dollars they got for a team and wagon. Every chapter is locked into the book's narrative portion by this kind of specific cross-reference, which amplifies the Joads' typical actions to the dimensions of a communal experience.

Often, this interlocking of details becomes thematic or symbolic. The dust which is mentioned twenty-seven times in three pages of chapter 1 comes to stand not only for the land itself, but also for the basic situation out of which the novel's action develops. Everything which moves on the ground, from insects to trucks, raises a proportionate amount of dust; "a walking man lifted a thin layer as high as his waist." When Tom returns home after four years in prison and gets out of the truck which has given him a lift, he steps off the highway, and performs the symbolic ritual of taking off his new, prison-issue shoes and carefully working his bare feet into the dust. He then moves off across the land, "making a cloud that hung low to the ground behind him."

One of the novel's most important symbols, the turtle, is presented in what is actually the first intercalary chapter (3). And while this chapter is a masterpiece of realistic description (often included as such in Freshman English texts), it is also obvious that the turtle is symbolic and its adventures prophetic allegory. "Nobody can't keep a turtle though," says Jim Casy. "They work at it and work at it, and at last one day they get out and away they go. . . ." (p. 28) The indomitable life force which drives the turtle drives the Joads, and in the same direction—southwest. As the turtle picks up seeds in its shell and drops them on the other side of the road, so the Joads pick up life and take it across the country to California. (As Grandfather in "The Leader of the People" puts it, "We carried life out here and set it down the way those ants carry eggs.") As the turtle survives the truck's attempt to smash it on the highway and as it crushes the red ant which runs into its shell, so the Joads endure the perils of their journey.

This symbolic value is retained and further defined when the turtle specifically enters the narrative. The incident with the red ant is echoed two hundred and seventy pages later when another red ant runs over "the folds of loose skin" on Granma's neck and she reaches up with her "little wrinkled claws"; Ma Joad picks it off and crushes it. In chapter 3 the turtle is seen "dragging his high-domed shell across the grass." In the next chapter, Tom sees "the high-domed back of a land turtle" and, picking up the turtle, carries it with him. It is only when he is convinced that his family has left the land that he releases the turtle, which travels "southwest, as it had been from the first," a direction which is repeated in the next two sentences. The first thing which Tom does after releasing the turtle is to put on his shoes, which he took off when he left the highway. Thus, not only the turtle but also Tom's connection with it is symbolic, as symbolic as Lennie's appearance in *Of Mice and Men,* with a dead mouse in his pocket.

In addition to this constant knitting together of the two kinds of chapters, often the interchapters themselves are further assimilated into the narrative portion by incorporating in themselves the techniques of fiction. There are no more than a half-dozen paragraphs in the book which are aimed directly at the reader or delivered by the author. The general conflict between small farmers and the banks, for example, is presented as an imaginary dialogue, each speaker personifying the sentiments of his group. And although neither speaker is a "real" person, they are dramatically differentiated and their arguments embody details particular to the specific social condition. Each speaker is like the chorus in a Greek tragedy.[22] This kind of dramatization is also evident in those chapters concerned with the buying of used cars, the selling of household goods, the police intimidation of migrants, and others.

These structural techniques for integrating the two parts of *The Grapes of Wrath* are greatly implemented by a masterful command of prose style. In his novels after *To a God Unknown*, Steinbeck had demonstrated the variety of prose styles that he could weld into the very meaning of a novel—prose styles as different as those of *Tortilla Flat* and *In Dubious Battle*. In *The Grapes of Wrath* there is such a number of strategically employed prose styles that the novel almost amounts to a *tour de force*. No Steinbeck novel begins so auspiciously.

To the red country and part of the gray country of Oklahoma, the last rains came gently, and they did not cut the scarred earth. The plows crossed and recrossed the rivulet marks. The last rains lifted the corn quickly and scattered weed colonies and grass along the sides of the roads so that the gray country and the dark red country began to disappear under a green cover. In the last part of May the sky grew pale and the clouds that had hung in high puffs for so long in the spring were dissipated. The sun flared down on the growing corn day after day until a line of brown spread along the edge of each green bayonet. The clouds appeared, and went away, and in a while they did not try any more. The weeds grew darker green to protect themselves, and they did not spread any more. The surface of the earth crusted, a thin hard crust, and as the sky became pale, so the earth became pale, pink in the red country and white in the gray country.

This opening paragraph is as carefully worked out as an overture to an opera. The themes of *red, gray, green,* and *earth* are announced and given parallel developments: *red* to pink, *gray* to white, *green* to brown, and ploughed *earth* to thin hard *crust*. The pervading structural rhythm of each sentence is echoed in the paragraph as a whole, a paragraph promising a story of epic sweep and dignity.

The extent to which this style is indebted to the Old Testament can be strikingly demonstrated by arranging a similar passage from the novel according to phrases, in the manner of the Bates Bible, leaving the punctuation intact.

The tractors had lights shining,
For there is no day and night for a tractor
And the disks turn the earth in the darkness
And they glitter in the daylight.

And when a horse stops work and goes into the barn
There is a life and a vitality left,
There is a breathing and a warmth,
And the feet shift on the straw,
And the jaws champ on the hay,
And the ears and the eyes are alive.
There is a warmth of life in the barn,
And the heat and smell of life.

But when the motor of a tractor stops,
It is as dead as the ore it came from.
The heat goes out of it
Like the living heat that leaves a corpse.

The parallel grammatical structure of parallel meanings, the simplicity of diction, the balance, the concrete details, the summary sentences, the reiterations—all are here. Note also the organization: four phrases for the tractor, eight for the horse, four again for the tractor. Except for the terms of machinery, the passage might be one the Psalms.

It is this echo—more, this pedal point—evident even in the most obviously "directed" passages of the interchapters, which supports their often simple philosophy, imbuing them with a dignity which their content alone could not sustain. The style gives them their authority:

> Burn coffee for fuel in the ships. Burn corn to keep warm, it makes a hot fire. Dump potatoes in the rivers and place guards along the banks to keep the hungry people from fishing them out. Slaughter the pigs and bury them, and let the putrescence drip down into the earth.
>
> There is a crime here that goes beyond denunciation. There is a sorrow here that weeping cannot symbolize. There is a failure here that topples all our success. The fertile earth, the straight tree rows, the sturdy trunks, and the ripe fruit. And children dying of pellagra must die because a profit cannot be taken from an orange.

These passages are not complex philosophy, but they may well be profound. The Biblical resonance which gives them power is used discreetly, is never employed on the trivial and particular, and its recurrence has a cumulative effect.

There are many other distinct prose styles in the interchapters of *The Grapes of Wrath,* and each is just as functional in its place. There is, for example, the harsh, staccato prose of chapter 7, which is devoted to the sale of used cars:

Cadillacs, La Salles, Buicks, Plymouths, Packards, Chevvies, Fords, Pontiacs. Row on row, headlights glinting in the afternoon sun. Good Used Cars.

Soften 'em up, Joe. Jesus, I wisht I had a thousand jalopies! Get 'em ready to deal, an' I'll close 'em.

Goin' to California? Here's jus' what you need. Looks shot, but they's thousan's of miles in her.

Lined up side by side. Good Used Cars. Bargains. Clean runs good.

A good contrast to this hectic prose is offered by chapter 9, which presents the loss and despair of people forced to abandon their household goods. Here the style itself takes on a dazed resignation:

The women sat among the doomed things, turning them over and looking past them and back. This book. My father had it. He liked a book. *Pilgrim's Progress*. Used to read it. Got his name on it. And his pipe—still smells rank. And this picture—an angel. I looked at that before the first three come—didn't seem to do much good. Think we could get this china dog in? Aunt Sadie brought it from the St. Louis Fair. See? Wrote right on it. No, I guess not. Here's a letter my brother wrote the day before he died. Here's an old-time hat. These feathers—never got to use them. No, there isn't room.

At times, as in the description of a folk dance in chapter 23, the prose style becomes a veritable chameleon:

Look at that Texas boy, long legs loose, taps four times for ever' damn step. Never see a boy swing aroun' like that. Look at him swing that Cherokee girl, red in her cheeks and her toe points out. Look at her pant, look at her heave. Think she's tired? Think she's winded? Well, she ain't. Texas boy got his hair in his eyes, mouth's wide open, can't get air, but he pats four times for ever' darn step, an' he'll keep a-goin' with the Cherokee girl.

No other American novel has succeeded in forging and making instrumental so many prose styles.

The number of such passages which could be cited is almost endless. Those cited thus far suggest a number of influences—the Bible, Dos Passos' "Newsreel" technique, folk idiom, Walt Whitman, Hemingway, and perhaps Carl Sandburg's *The People, Yes,* although the latter's diction is much more strident than that of *The Grapes of Wrath.* Another influence on this prose is certainly the narrative style of Pare Lorentz in his scripts for the motion pictures *The Plow That Broke the Plains* and *The River.* Steinbeck had met Lorentz and discussed this style with him, listening to recordings of Lorentz' radio drama *Ecce Homo!* [23] Lorentz too had made use of the Old Testament, but the influence on him of Whitman and Sandburg was perhaps stronger, as the following passage from *The River* makes clear:

Down the Missouri three thousand miles from the Rockies;
Down the Ohio a thousand miles from the Alleghenies;
Down the Arkansas fifteen hundred miles from the Great Divide;
Down the Red, a thousand miles from Texas;
Down the great Valley, twenty-five hundred miles from Minnesota,
Carrying every rivulet and brook, creek and rill,
Carrying all the rivers that run down two-thirds the continent—
The Mississippi runs to the Gulf.[24]

The debt of Steinbeck's intercalary chapter on Highway 66 to this kind of writing is obvious: "Clarksville and Ozark and Van Buren and Fort Smith on 64, and there's an end of

Arkansas. And all the roads into Oklahoma City, 66 down from Tulsa, 270 up from McAlester. 81 from Wichita Falls south, from Enid north. Edmond, McLoud, Purcell. 66 out of Oklahoma City; El Reno and Clinton, going west on 66. Hydro, Elk City. . . ." But Steinbeck demonstrates a much greater range than Lorentz, and was capable of much greater variety; only in this chapter did he resort to the easy device of cataloguing America. And in this chapter the catalogue is functional, representing the more detailed progress the Joads are making.

The great variety of prose style and subject matter found in these interchapters not only has value as Americana, but creates a "realism" far beyond that of literal reporting. In addition, this variety is important because it tends to destroy any impression that these interchapters, as a group, constitute a separate entity. They are a group only in that they are not a direct part of the narrative. They have enough individuality of subject matter, prose style, and technique to keep the novel from falling into two parts, and to keep the reader from feeling that he is now reading "the other part."

Because Steinbeck's subject in *The Grapes of Wrath* is not the adventures of the Joad family so much as the social conditions which occasion them, these interchapters serve a vital purpose. As Percy Lubbock has pointed out, the purely "scenic" or objective technique "is out of the question . . . whenever the story is too big, too comprehensive, too widely ranging to be treated scenically, with no opportunity for general and panoramic survey. . . . These stories . . . call for some narrator, somebody who *knows,* to contemplate the facts and create an impression of them." [25]

Steinbeck's story certainly is "big," "comprehensive," and "wide ranging." As we have seen, however, he took pains to keep the novel from falling into two independent parts. The cross-reference of detail, the interweaving symbols, the dramatization, and the choric effects are techniques designed to make the necessary "panoramic" sections tend toward the "scenic." An examination of the narrative portion of *The Grapes of Wrath* will reveal, conversely, that its techniques make the "scenic" or narrative sections tend toward the "panoramic." Steinbeck worked from both sides to make the two kinds of chapters approach each other and fuse into a single impression.

This tendency of the narrative or dramatic portion of *The Grapes of Wrath* toward the pictorial can be seen readily by comparing the book with another of Steinbeck's group-man novels, *In Dubious Battle*, which has a straightforward plot development and an involving action. Of course, things happen in *The Grapes of Wrath*, and what happens not only grows out of what has gone before but grows into what will happen in the future. But while critics have perceived that plot is not the organizational principle of the novel, they have not attempted to relate this fact to the novel's materials as they are revealed through other techniques, assuming instead that this lack of plot constitutes one of the novel's major flaws.[26]

Actually, this lack of an involving action is effective in at least two ways. It could reasonably be expected that the greatest threat to the novel's unity would come from the interchapters' constant breaking up of the narrative's line of action. However, the very fact that *The Grapes of Wrath* is *not* organized by a unifying plot works for absorbing these intercalary chapters smoothly into its texture. A second way in which this tendency of the "scenic" towards the "panoramic" is germane to the novel's materials becomes evident when it is considered that Steinbeck's subject is not an action so much as a situation. Description, therefore, must often substitute for narration.[27]

This substitution of the static for the dynamic also gives us an insight into the nature and function of the novel's characters, especially the Joads, who have been called "essentially symbolic marionettes" [28] and "puppets with differentiating traits," [29] but seldom real people. While there are scant objective grounds for determining whether a novel's characters are "real," one fruitful approach is to consider fictional characters not only in relation to life, but in relation to the *rest* of the fiction of which they are a part.

In his Preface to *The Forgotten Village*, which immediately followed *The Grapes of Wrath*, Steinbeck comments on just these relationships:

A great many documentary films have used the generalized method, that is, the showing of a condition or an event as it affects a group of people. The audience can then have a personalized reaction from imagining one member of that group. I have felt that this is the more difficult observation from the audience's viewpoint. It means very little to know that a million Chinese are starving unless you know one Chinese who is starving. In *The Forgotten Village* we reversed the usual process. Our story centered on one family in one small village. We wished our audience to know this family very well, and incidently to like it, as we did. Then, from association with this little personalized group, the larger conclusion concerning the racial group could be drawn with something like participation.[30]

This is precisely the strategy in *The Grapes of Wrath*. Whatever value the Joads have as individuals is "incidental" to their primary function as a "personalized group." Kenneth Burke has pointed out that ". . . most of the characters derive their role, which is to say their personality, purely from their relationship to the basic situation." [31] What he takes to be a serious weakness is actually one of the book's greatest accomplishments. The characters are so absorbed into the novel's materials that the reader's response goes beyond sympathy for the individuals to moral indignation at their social condition. This is, of course, precisely Steinbeck's intention. And certainly the Joads are adequate for this purpose. This conception of character is a parallel to the fusing of the "scenic" and "panoramic" techniques in the narrative and interchapters.

Although the diverse materials of *The Grapes of Wrath* made organization by a unifying plot difficult, nevertheless the novel does have structural form. The action progresses through three successive movements, and its significance is revealed by an intricate system of themes and symbols.

The Grapes of Wrath is divided into thirty consecutive chapters with no larger grouping, but even a cursory reading reveals that the novel is made up of three major parts: the drought, the journey, and California. The first section ends with chapter 10. It is separated from the second section, the journey, by *two* interchapters. The first of these chapters presents a picture of the deserted land—"The houses were left vacant on the land, and the land was vacant because of this." The second interchapter is devoted to Highway 66 and is followed by chapter 13, which begins the Joads' journey—"The ancient overloaded Hudson creaked and grunted to the highway at Sallisaw and turned west, and the sun was blinding." The journey section extends past the geographical California border, across the desert to Bakersfield. This section ends with chapter 18, "And the truck rolled down the mountain into the great valley," and the next chapter begins the California section by introducing the reader to labor conditions in that state. Steinbeck had this tripartite division in mind as early as September of 1937, when he told Joseph Henry Jackson that he was working on "the first of three related longer novels." [32]

Like the prose style of the philosophical passages in the interchapters, this structure has its roots in the Old Testament. The novel's three sections correspond to the oppression in Egypt, the exodus, and the sojourn in the land of Canaan, which in both accounts is first viewed from the mountains. This parallel is not worked out in detail, but the grand design is there: the plagues (erosion), the Egyptian (banks), the exodus (journey), and the hostile tribes of Canaan (Californians).

This Biblical structure is supported by a continuum of symbols and symbolic actions. The most pervasive symbolism is that of grapes. The novel's title, taken from "The Battle Hymn of the Republic," ("He is trampling out the vintage where the grapes of wrath are stored") is itself a reference to Revelation: "And the angel thrust in his sickle into the earth, and gathered the vine of the earth, and cast it into the great winepress of the wrath of God." (14:19) Similarly, in Deuteronomy: "Their grapes are grapes of gall, their clusters are bitter. Their wine is the poison of serpents. . . . (32:32); in Jeremiah: "The fathers have eaten sour grapes, and their children's teeth are set on edge." (31:29) Sometimes this meaning of the symbol is stated in the novel's interchapters: "In the souls of the people the grapes of wrath are filling and growing heavy, heavy for the vintage."

Steinbeck also uses grapes for symbols of plenty, as the one huge cluster of grapes which Joshua and Oshea bring back from their first excursion into the rich land of Canaan is a symbol of plenty, a cluster so huge that "they bare it between two on a staff." (Numbers, 12:23) It is this meaning of grapes that is frequently alluded to by Grampa Joad: "Gonna get me a whole big bunch a grapes off a bush, or whatever, an' I'm gonna squash 'em on my face an' let 'em run offen my chin." Although Grampa dies long before the Joads get to California, he is symbolically present through the anonymous old man in the barn (stable), who is saved from starvation by Rosasharn's breasts: "This thy stature is like to a palm tree, and thy breasts to clusters of grapes." [33] (Canticles, 7:7) Rosasharn's giving of new life to the old man is another reference to the orthodox interpretation of Canticles: "I [Christ] am the rose of Sharon, and the lily of the valleys" (2:1); and to the Gospels: "take, eat; this is my body." Still another important Biblical symbol is Jim Casy (Jesus Christ), who will be discussed in another connection.

Closely associated with this latter symbolic meaning of grapes and the land of Canaan is Ma Joad's frequent assertion that "We are the people." She has not been reading Carl Sandburg; she has been reading her Bible. As she tells Tom when he is looking for a suitable verse to bury with Grampa, "Turn to Psalms, over further. You kin always get somepin outa Psalms." And it is from Psalms that she gets her phrase: "For he is our God; and we are the people of his pasture, and the sheep of his hand." (95:7) They are the people who pick up life in Oklahoma (Egypt) and carry it to California (Canaan) as the turtle picks up seeds and as the ants pick up their eggs in "The Leader of the People." These parallels to the Israelites of Exodus are all brought into focus when, near the end of the novel, Uncle John sets Rose of Sharon's still-born child in an old apple crate (like Moses in the basket), sets the box in a stream "among the willow stems," and floats it toward the town saying, "Go down an' tell 'em."

As the Israelites received the new Law in their exodus, so the migrants develop new laws: "The families learned what rights must be observed—the right of privacy in the tent; the right to keep the past black hidden in the heart; the right to refuse help or accept it, to offer help or to decline it; the right of son to court and the daughter to be courted; the right of the hungry to be fed; the rights of the pregnant and the sick to transcend all other rights." Chapter 17 can be seen as the Deuteronomy of *The Grapes of Wrath*. It is this context which makes of the Joads' journey "out west" an archetype of mass migration.[34]

Through this supporting Biblical structure and context there are interwoven two opposing themes which make up the book's "plot." One of these, the "negative" one, concerns itself with the increasingly straitened circumstances of the Joads. At the beginning of their journey they have $154 their household goods, two barrels of pork, a serviceable truck, and their good health. As the novel progresses they become more and more impoverished, until at the end they are destitute, without food, sick, their truck and goods abandoned in the mud, without shelter, and without hope of work. This economic decline is paralleled by a similar decline in the family's morale. In his *San Francisco News* articles Steinbeck had described the gradual deterioration of family and of human dignity which accompanies impoverished circumstances. This is illustrated by the Joads, who start off as a cheerful group full of hope and will power and by the end of the novel are spiritually bankrupt. As Steinbeck had noted about the migrants around Bakersfield three years earlier, they "feel that paralyzed dullness with which the mind protects itself against too much sorrow and too much pain."[35] When the Joads enter their first Hooverville they catch a glimpse of the deterioration which lies ahead of them. They see filthy tin and rug shacks littered with trash, the children dirty and diseased, the heads of families "bull-simple" from being roughed up too often, all spirit gone and in its place a whining, passive resistance to authority. Although the novel ends before the Joads come to this point, in the last chapter they are well on their way.

And as the family declines morally and economically, so the family unit itself breaks up. Grampa dies before they are out of Oklahoma and lies in a nameless grave; Granma is buried a pauper; Noah deserts the family; Connie deserts Rosasharn; the baby is born dead; Tom becomes a fugitive; Al is planning to leave as soon as possible; Casy is killed; and they have had to abandon the Wilsons.

These two "negative" or downward movements are balanced by two "positive" or upward movements. Although the primitive family unit is breaking up, the fragments are going to make up a larger group. The sense of a communal unit grows steadily through the narrative—the Wilsons, the Wainwrights—and is pointed to again and again in the interchapters: "One man, one family driven from the land; this rusty car creaking along the highway to the west. I lost my land, a single tractor took my land. I am alone and I am bewildered. And in the night one family camps in a ditch and another family pulls in and the tents come out. The two men squat on their hams and the women and children listen. . . . For here 'I lost my land' is changed; a cell is split and from its splitting grows the thing you [owners] hate—'We lost *our* land!' " Oppression and intimidation only serve to strengthen the social group; the relief offered by a federal migrant camp only gives them a vision of the democratic life they can attain by cooperation, which is why the local citizens are opposed to these camps.

Another of the techniques by which Steinbeck develops this theme of unity can be illustrated by the Joads' relationship with the Wilson family of Kansas, which they meet just before crossing the Oklahoma border. This relationship is developed not so much by explicit statements, as in the interchapters, as by symbols. Grampa Joad, for example, dies in the Wilsons' tent and he is buried in one of the Wilsons' blankets. Furthermore, the epitaph which is buried with Grampa (in Oklahoma soil) is written on a page torn from the Wilsons' Bible—that page usually reserved for family records of births, marriages, and deaths. In burying this page with Grampa, the Wilsons symbolize not only their adoption of the Joads, but their renouncing of hope for continuing their own family line. Also, note that it is the more destitute Wilson family which embraces the Joads. Steinbeck makes of the two families' relationship a microcosm of the migration's total picture, its human significance.

This growing awareness on the part of the people *en masse* is paralleled by the "education" and "conversion" of Tom and Casy. At the beginning of the book, Tom's attitude is individualistic. He is looking out for himself. As he puts it, "I'm still laying my dogs down one at a time," and "I climb fences when I got fences to climb." His first real lesson comes when Casy strikes out against the trooper to save his friend and then gives himself up in his place. The section immediately following is that of the family's stay at a federal migrant camp, and here Tom's education is advanced still further. By the time Casy is killed, Tom is ready for his conversion, which he seals by revenging his mentor. While Tom is hiding out in the cave, after having struck down the vigilante, he has time to think of Casy and his message, so that in his last meeting with his mother, in which he asserts his spiritual unity with all men, it is evident that he has moved from material and personal resentment to ethical indignation, from particulars to principles.

This last meeting between mother and son takes place

under conditions reminiscent of the prenatal state. The entrance to the cave is covered with black vines, and the interior is damp and completely dark, so that the contact of mother and son is actually physical rather than visual; she gives him food. When Tom comes out of the cave after announcing his conversion, it is as though he were reborn. When Tom says, "An' when our folks eat the stuff they raise an' live in the houses they build—why I'll be there," he is paraphrasing Isaiah: "And they shall build houses and inhabit them, they shall not build and another inhabit; they shall not plant and another eat." (65:21-22)

The development of Jim Casy is similar to that of Tom. He moves from Bible-belt evangelism to social prophecy. At the beginning of the book he has already left preaching and has returned from his sojourn "in the hills, thinkin', almost you might say like Jesus went into the wilderness to think His way out of a mess of troubles." But although Casy is already approaching his revelation of the Oversoul, it is only through his experiences with the Joads that he is able to complete his vision. As Tom moves from material resentment to ethical indignation, from action to thought to action again, so Casy moves from the purely speculative to the pragmatic. Both move from stasis to action. Casy's Christ-like development is complete when, pointed out as "that shiny bastard" and struck on the head with a pick handle, he dies saying, "You don' know what you're a-doin'." [36]

Those critics are reading superficially who think that Steinbeck "expects us to admire Casy, an itinerant preacher, who, over-excited from his evangelistic revivals, is in the habit of taking one or another of the girls of his audience to lie in the grass." [37] Actually, Casy himself perceives the incongruity of this behavior, which is why he goes "into the wilderness" and renounces his Bible-belt evangelism for a species of social humanism, and his congregation for the human race. His development, like that of Tom, is symbolic of the changing social condition which is the novel's essential theme, paralleling the development of the Joad family as a whole, which is, again, but a "personalized group." Casy resembles Emerson more than he does Sinclair Lewis' Elmer Gantry or Erskine Caldwell's Semon Dye. For like Emerson, Casy discovers the Oversoul through intuition and rejects his congregation in order to preach to the world.

Because these themes of "education" and "conversion" are not the central, involving action of the novel, but grow slowly out of a rich and solid context, the development of Tom and Casy achieves an authority lacking in most proletarian fiction. The novel's thematic organization also makes it possible for Steinbeck successfully to incorporate the widest variety of materials, and, with the exception of romantic love, to present the full scale of human emotions. This accomplishment is a great one when it is considered that the point of view in the narrative sections is absolutely objective. At no point are we told what the characters feel or think, only what they do or say.

The ability of this thematic structure to absorb incidents is illustrated by the early morning "breakfast" scene. One version of this little scene, a first-person narrative, had appeared as a short sketch in *The Long Valley*. This earlier version is a well-written piece of description—the girl and her baby, the three men, the smell of early morning breakfast, the hospitality extended a stranger. But somehow the emotion apparently felt by the author is not conveyed to the reader. Steinbeck concludes the piece lamely: "That's all. I know, of course, some of the reasons why it was pleasant. But there was some element of great beauty there that makes the rush of warmth when I think of it." (LV, 92) Although this incident was completely rewritten for *The Grapes of Wrath,* what makes it effective there is its context. This bit of normal human activity, warmth, and tenderness is Tom's first experience in the refuge of the federal migrant camp, immediately following a night of vigilante horror and cringing flight. It constitutes for him a renewal of faith in his fellow man. In this connection, it is significant that whereas both Dos Passos' *U.S.A.* and *Manhattan Transfer* end with the protagonist hitchhiking *away from* home, the group, Steinbeck's novel begins with Tom coming home, joining the group.[38]

This ability of Steinbeck's thematic organization to absorb incidents organically into its context is also important for an understanding of the last scene, of which there has been much criticism. Typical of this criticism is Bernard De Voto's contention that the ending of the novel is "symbolism gone sentimental." [39] The novel's materials do make a climactic ending difficult. Steinbeck had faced the same problem in *In Dubious Battle,* where he had solved it by "stopping on a high point." (JS-MO, 2/4/35) By this same solution in *The Grapes of Wrath,* Steinbeck avoids three pitfalls: a *deus ex machina* ending; a summing-up, moral essay; and a new level of horror. The novel's thematic treatment makes it possible for him to avoid these choices by bringing his novel to a "symbolic" climax without doing violence to credulity, structure, or theme.[40]

This climax is prepared for by the last interchapter, which parallels in terms of rain the opening description of drought. The last paragraphs of these chapters are strikingly similar:

The women studied the men's faces secretly. . . . After a while the faces of the watching men lost the bemused perplexity and became hard and angry and resistant. Then the women knew that they were safe and that there was no break.

The women watched the men, watched to see whether the break had come at last. . . . And where a number of men gathered together, the fear went from their faces, and anger took its place. And the women sighed with relief, for they knew it was all right—the break had not come. . . .

With this latter paragraph the novel is brought full circle. The last chapter compactly re-enacts the whole drama of the Joads' journey in one uninterrupted continuity of suspense. The rain continues to fall; the truck and household goods must be abandoned; the little mud levee collapses; Rosasharn's baby is born dead; the boxcar must be abandoned; they take to the highway in search of food and find instead a starving man. Then the miracle happens. As Rose of Sharon offers her breast to the old man (this is my body and my blood), the novel's two counterthemes are brought together in a symbolic paradox. Out of her own need she gives life; out of the profoundest depth of despair comes the greatest assertion of faith.

Steinbeck's great achievement in *The Grapes of Wrath* is that while minimizing what seem to be the most essential elements of fiction—plot and character—he was able to create a "well-made" and emotionally compelling novel out of materials which in most other hands have resulted in sentimental propaganda.[41]

10 } *Sea of Cortez*
War Writings
The Moon Is Down

The immediate and overwhelming popular success of *The Grapes of Wrath* subjected Steinbeck to pressures he was not temperamentally suited to bear. Overnight he became a national figure whose time was considered public property by innumerable organized groups. "I'm so busy being a writer," he complained, "that I haven't time to write. Ten thousand people have apparently put aside all other affairs to devote themselves to getting me to speak. And I'm so increasingly afraid in crowds that I do not talk comfortably to a pair of dice any more." [1] Steinbeck was not a man to enjoy public attention. He had not stayed in New York to relish the fame of *Of Mice and Men,* and to Alexander Woollcott's request for publicity material he had replied, via his agents. "I think you know my hatred of personal matter. I hope you will get some of that impression over to

Mr. Woollcott. On the other hand I should like to have him talk about the work . . . but tell him please no personalities." (JS-MO, 3/19/37)

Steinbeck's dislike of publicity was not so much a sign of his natural shyness as of his fear of what public attention would do to his artistic integrity. "Everything the people admires, it destroys," he once said. "It imposes a personality on him [the artist] it thinks he should have." [2] Shortly before the publication of *Of Mice and Men* he had discussed the success of *Gone With the Wind* and *Anthony Adverse* with Lawrence Clark Powell and had remarked, "I hope that doesn't happen to me. A single best-seller can ruin a writer forever." [3] To his agents, he had written in the same vein: "I simply can't write books if a consciousness of self is thrust upon me." (JS-MO, 3/19/37) This suspicion is evident as early as *Tortilla Flat*, when he wrote of popularity, "It has ruined everyone I know." (JS-MO, 6/13/35) Steinbeck's letters contain literally dozens of references to this subject.

In addition to being plagued by public demands, Steinbeck was increasingly concerned with the war. His state of mind is evident in a letter he wrote to Pascal Covici on New Year's Eve, 1940: "So we go into this happy new year, knowing that our species has learned nothing, can as a race learn nothing—that the experience of ten thousand years has made no impression on the instincts of the million years that preceded." A few months later he wrote, in the introductory part of *Sea of Cortez*, that war seemed a "diagnostic trait of *Homo sapiens*," like the tendency of crayfish to fight when they meet each other:

And perhaps our species is not likely to forego war without some psychic mutation which at present, at least, does not seem imminent. And if one places the blame for killing and destroying on economic insecurity, on inequality, on injustice, he is simply stating the proposition in another way. We have what we are. Perhaps the crayfish feels the itch of jealousy, or perhaps he is sexually insecure. The effect is that he fights. . . . So far the murder trait of our species is as regular and observable as our various sexual habits.

It was in such a frame of mind that, early 1940, Steinbeck was preparing for a scientific expedition to the Gulf of California with his friend Ed Ricketts, the marine biologist. The object of this expedition, or "trip" as they preferred to call it, was "to collect and preserve the marine invertebrates of the littoral." Steinbeck's association with Ed Ricketts had done much to stimulate and expand his scientific interests. Late in 1939 he had accompanied Ricketts on a similar expedition to the littoral north of San Francisco (JS-PC, 12/22/39), and in that year Ricketts published his book on marine biology, *Between Pacific Tides*, which was reissued in 1948 with an introduction by Steinbeck. It is quite probable, however, that part of the interest on Steinbeck's part lay in a desire to escape the pressures of popularity and to ease his growing concern with the possibilities of global war. In March of 1940 the Mexican government granted the two men permits for their expedition along the Mexican coasts, and on the 11th of that month they lifted anchor for the Gulf of California, which they preferred to call by its older name—Sea of Cortez.

Steinbeck returned to Monterey the 20th of April and almost immediately set off again for Mexico to work on the motion picture *The Forgotten Village*, which also appeared in the form of a book of pictures accompanied by Steinbeck's script.[4] It is a simple and moving account of one Mexican village in its struggles to fight disease, a fight hindered by its own superstitions and ignorance. This he completed in January of 1941, and he immediately began work on the manuscript for *Sea of Cortez*, which occupied him until August of that year.

Although the material for the narrative and speculative portion of the book came in part from two journals, one kept by Ricketts and the other by Steinbeck, and is probably an accurate sampling of both men's metaphysical speculations,[5] it is clear from constant references in the letters to "my part" that this portion itself was actually composed by Steinbeck, while Ricketts was working on the highly technical biological sections. Steinbeck was very excited about the book; he wanted to do a "good job" and refused to be rushed. (JS-PC, 4/14/41) He was planning the book very carefully and found "a great poetry in scientific thinking." (JS-PC, 7/4/41) Another time he wrote, "It will only outrage the second rate scientists who are ready to yell mysticism the moment anything gets dangerously close to careful thinking and a little bit out of their range." (JS-PC, 6/19/41)

It is not to the purpose here to analyze *Sea of Cortez* as a book. It is neither a piece of fiction nor a system of philosophy, but rather a leisurely journal of informal speculation (and often genial "spoofing") which makes explicit several working concepts which had been implicit in all Steinbeck's work thus far: non-teleological thinking, ecology, the possible individuality of a group-animal, "survival of the fittest," group psyche-memory, and the mystic unity of all life. These are germinal concepts in Steinbeck, but it would be misleading to discuss them as part of his world view without taking into consideration their modification in the context of his literary works. (Numerous references to *Sea of Cortez* occur throughout the present study.)

It is true, for example, that in his "scientific" book Steinbeck notes the survival of the "strong and hungry," speaks approvingly of our "benevolently hostile planet," and finds a place even for "disease and sorrow and hunger and alcoholism." But this does not indicate, as has been asserted, that he is abandoning social responsibility for the Darwinian *laissez-faire* of literary naturalism.[6] (The first thing he wrote after returning from his trip to the Gulf of California was *The Forgotten Village*, published a few months before *Sea of Cortez*.) Actually, this Darwinian element was present in the very first novel Steinbeck published, *Cup of Gold*, in which he describes the "weak survival quotient" of a town long accustomed to ease and security. The same idea is repeated many times in *The Grapes of Wrath:* "The Mexicans were weak and fed. They could not resist, because they wanted nothing in the world as frantically as the Americans wanted land"; when the Californians are established and become complacent, secure, and self-satisfied, they in turn succumb to the migrants—"the new barbarians who wanted only two things—land and food." (GW, 315, 318) In *Sea of Cortez* Steinbeck sees a similar example in the struggle between Pizarro and the Incas. It is this vital energy, an energy which can be renewed only by constant struggle, that Grandfather in "The Leader of the People" calls the spirit of "westering."

Similarly, in *Sea of Cortez* Steinbeck may seem to be qualifying his previous social views when he rejects a "collectivized state" because "this process of integration must destroy all tendencies toward improvisation, must destroy the habit of creation, since this is sand in the bearings of the system." (SC, 214; LSC, xlvi) But *In Dubious Battle* had made the same point in dramatic terms; and in *A Russian Journal* (1948) this criticism is turned on actual conditions.

Even the famous Easter Sunday sermon on non-teleological thinking is but a further elucidation of Doc Burton's position in *In Dubious Battle* and Steinbeck's attitude toward his materials in *The Grapes of Wrath:* "Usually it seems to be true that when even the most definitely apparent cause-effect situations are examined in the light of wider knowledge, the cause-effect aspect comes to be seen as less rather than more significant, and the statistical or relational aspects acquire larger importance. It seems safe to assume that non-teleological is more 'ultimate' than teleological reasoning." This concept that all phenomena exist in a *Gestalt* or "field" enables Steinbeck, as it does Doc Burton, to become both participant and observer, to avoid both regimentation and *laissez-faire.* For the ecological view makes it clear that unsuccessful units of society "may be blamed as individuals, but as members of society they cannot be blamed." If one has "strength and energy of mind," Steinbeck asserts, "the tide pool stretches both ways, digs back to electrons and leaps space into the universe and fights out of the moment into non-conceptual time. Then ecology has a synonym which is ALL."

As Steinbeck himself noted while writing *Sea of Cortez,* "When this work is done I will have finished a cycle of work that has been biting me for many years and it is simply the careful statement of the thesis of work to be done in the future." (JS-PC, 6/9/41) And to his agents he wrote that the book was "a good clearing-out of a lot of ideas that have been working on me for a long time." [7] In its informal way, it is a record of Steinbeck's basic beliefs, and stands to his work very much as *Death in the Afternoon* and *Green Hills of Africa* stand to that of Hemingway.[8]

Sea of Cortez was published the month the United States entered the war, and although Steinbeck was shocked at this new evidence that wars are a biological trait of man, he was also eager to participate in the struggle. One of his efforts grew directly out of his knowledge of marine biology. Together with Ed Ricketts, Steinbeck compiled a list of papers written by Japanese zoologists, papers which gave minute information about "depth, tide, currents, reefs, nature of coast, etc." pertaining to Japanese-held islands of the Pacific—"all the information needed if we were to make beach landings." But the military were suspicious of this information and apparently nothing came of the suggestion. (LSC, lviii-lxii) Another scheme was actually approved by President Roosevelt. Early in the war, Steinbeck suggested that counterfeit money, properly "aged," be dropped behind enemy lines to cause inflation and disrupt financial traffic. According to Steinbeck, the idea was rejected by Secretary Morgenthau and Lord Halifax.[9] This "secret weapon" was later used with great effectiveness by the Germans.

Less spectacular, but perhaps more efficient, was Steinbeck's work on *Bombs Away*. The idea for this book grew out of a series of suggestions made by General "Hap" Arnold of the Army Air Force.[10] The purpose of the book was frankly propagandistic. In Steinbeck's words, ". . . mostly this book intends to tell the whole people of the kind and quality of our Air Force, of the caliber of its men and of the excellence of its equipment." (BA, 5) Accompanied by the photographer and flier John Swope, Steinbeck traveled from one training base to another gathering material for the new book. The Air Force could not have chosen a better man for the job. Steinbeck's prose is straightforward, simple, but retains some of the effectiveness of the intercalary chapters in *The Grapes of Wrath*. *Bombs Away* had a wide sale and was bought by Hollywood for $250,000, but Steinbeck turned over all royalties to the Air Forces Aid Society Trust Fund. Even in such a piece to journalism as this, Steinbeck refused to compromise his integrity. The book's last chapter was to depict the climax of that rigorous training which the book describes by giving an account of an actual bombing run. Steinbeck refused to write such a chapter because he had never been on a real bombing run and was afraid his description might be false. (JS-PC, *ca*, August, 1942) Instead, he ended the book very effectively with the bombers taking off for a raid: "The thundering ships took off one behind the other. At 5,000 feet they made their formation. The men sat quietly at their stations, their eyes fixed. And the deep growl of the engines shook the air, shook the world, shook the future." (BA, 185)

Not content with these contributions to the war effort, Steinbeck took a position as foreign correspondent for the New York *Herald Tribune,* and early in 1943 he left for Europe aboard a troopship. He stayed abroad until late October of that year.[11] For a while, he was stationed with a Flying Fortress unit in England. In August, he was reporting from North Africa; and early in September, after two weeks of silence, his communiqués came from the Italian front. Steinbeck had gone on the beaches with the American assault force. In his communiqués, Steinbeck wisely left specific military comment and analysis to more qualified observers. Instead, he stressed "human interest"—the hopes, fears, and activities of "G. I. Joes" under the various conditions of war. Occasionally, these communiqués are in the form of short stories, such as the ones about "Big Train Mulligan" (one of which is reprinted in *The Portable Steinbeck,* 1946). At times he describes the horrors of war—"a small Italian girl in the street with her stomach blown out." (New York *Herald Tribune,* Oct. 6, p. 25) Steinbeck's ability to mix with the ordinary man, an ability he had put to good use with the migrants, is everywhere evident in his dispatches. F. O. Mathiessen has remarked on the "freshness of observation" which some of these pieces have.[12] They reveal the same intimate, casual, yet shrewd observation that is apparent in the cartoons of Bill Mauldin.

Although most of Steinbeck's writing during the war was frankly journalistic, he did produce during this period his second play-novelette, *The Moon Is Down*.[13] Even this book, however, had its roots in Steinbeck's war effort. It was the result of several conversations he had with Colonel William J. Donovan (Office of Strategic Services) on ways of aiding resistance movements in Nazi-occupied countries.[14] Steinbeck began work on the book in the late summer of 1941, right after completing *Sea of Cortez*, and it was brought out in March of 1942.

Its publication was followed by a deluge of pro and con criticism which continued through the whole period of its career on the Broadway stage and motion-picture screen. The main issue was Steinbeck's apparently complacent, quietistic attitude toward a world catastrophe. James Thurber's all-out attack in the *New Republic* was countered by Lewis Gannett in the New York *Herald Tribune* as being "totalitarian" and "propaganda gone mad." The *New Republic* then offered its pages as an arena for the dispute and printed indignant letters from both camps. On April 20 *Newsweek*, itself a protagonist in the struggle, felt the battle had become so tangled that it needed clarification and so appointed itself referee and drew up an impartial list of the attacks and counterattacks delivered thus far.[15] A month later the *New Republic* felt it necessary to redefine these issues and named the two hostile camps the Blue and the Green armies, noting the re-enforcements and casualties on each side: "Clifton Fadiman has assumed command of the

Blue, or anti-Steinbeck forces. John Chamberlain has lately enlisted in the Green army, so called by its opponents because it is defending Steinbeck's moon, which they insist is really green cheese." [16]

The reading public joined in. An anonymous refugee from Poland wrote to the *New Republic* that Steinbeck was a fascist, that his book showed a criminal ignorance of what German occupations are really like.[17] This letter was countered by Mr. Frank G. Nelson, who was American guest professor of English at Oslo when the Nazis invaded Norway. He had lived under the occupation for fifteen months, seven of which were spent as a prisoner of the Gestapo in the famed jail at Møllergaten 19. Mr. Nelson found Steinbeck's book accurate: "If I did not know that Steinbeck has not been in Norway since the invasion, I should be tempted to name living models for all his characters." Another testimonial came from Mr. Hans Olav, Counselor for the Royal Norwegian Delegation in New York. Mr. Olav agreed that Steinbeck had been a little easy on the Nazis, but thought he had "protrayed the heroic resistance of a basically peace-loving people with great understanding." [18] In reply to one reader, who had called his unfavorable review "a slap in the face for all decent people who have been moved by the book's shining sincerity," Thurber wrote, "I am sorry about the slap in the face. I didn't realize my hand was open." [19]

It is now clear that the real critical issues were hopelessly entangled in the psychology of the war effort. But whether or not *The Moon Is Down* gave comfort and aid to the Nazis, it remains that the book was translated into many languages and became very popular among resistance movements throughout Nazi-occupied Europe.[20] The King of Norway thought enough of its effectiveness to decorate

Steinbeck for it,[21] and the book attained an apotheosis of sorts when "The Moon Is Down" became the title of a popular song somewhat on the order of "The White Cliffs of Dover."

Now that the din and dust of that paper war by home-front captains, "Park Avenue commandoes" as Steinbeck called them,[22] have been laid for well over a decade, the book's literary value can be disentangled from its topical implications, and its position in Steinbeck's work seems much clearer. For one thing, it seems inevitable that *The Moon Is Down*, following hard upon *Sea of Cortez*, should reflect the attitudes and ideas made explicit in that book.

Like the natives of Panama in *Cup of Gold*, the early California Mexicans and the "owners" of *In Dubious Battle* and *The Grapes of Wrath*, and the Incas mentioned in *Sea of Cortez*, the invaded people of *The Moon Is Down* exhibit that softness of moral fiber caused by habitual security, a softness which makes them fall easy prey to the invaders. Like the pirates of *Cup of Gold*, the early American settlers and the Okies of *The Grapes of Wrath*, and Pizarro of *Sea of Cortez*, the invaders of *The Moon Is Down* have energy and direction: "By ten-forty-five it was all over. The town was occupied, the defenders defeated, and the war finished."

Steinbeck's theory on war in *In Dubious Battle* and *Sea of Cortez*—that it is a phenomenon striking deep, unconscious roots in our species—is exemplified in *The Moon Is Down* by the invaders, none of whom is clear about the nature of the struggle in which he is participating. "Of them all, only Colonel Lanser knew what war really is in the long run. . . . treachery and hatred, the muddling of incompetent generals, the torture and killing and sickness, until at last it is over and nothing has changed except for new weariness and new hatreds." In the play version, Lanser is given some new lines which make the point even clearer: "I suffer from civilization. That means I can know one thing and do another. I know I have failed—I knew we would before we started. The thing the leader wanted to do cannot be done. . . . I can act quite apart from my knowledge. I will shoot the mayor. I will not break the rules. I will shoot the doctor, I will help tear and burn the world."

Finally, there is evident also in *The Moon Is Down* Steinbeck's concept that "over-integration in human groups might parallel the law in paleontology that over-armor or over-ornamentation are symptoms of decay and disappearance." (LSC, xlvi) The invaders must ultimately fail because the organization which gives them their immediate efficiency also prevents the "tendencies toward improvisation" and the "habit of creation" by which alone they can overcome new situations. (LSC, xlvi) Like all "herd men," they have a "capital" without whose direction and coordination they are helpless. As Doctor Winter observes in *The Moon Is Down,* "They know that ten heads lopped off will destroy them, but we are a free people; we have as many heads as we have people, and in a time of need leaders pop up among us like mushrooms." Steinbeck says the same thing in *The Log from Sea of Cortez:*

> A too greatly integrated system or society is in danger of destruction since the removal of one unit may cripple the whole.
>
> Consider the blundering anarchic system of the United States, the stupidity of some of its lawmakers, the violent reaction, the slowness of its ability to change. Twenty-five key men destroyed could make the Soviet Union stagger, but we could lose our congress, our president, and our general staff and nothing much would have happened. We would go right on. In fact we might be better for it. (LSC, xlvii)

The strength of the conquered people in *The Moon Is Down* is that of the pioneers in "The Leader of the People." Their leader is an expression of the body politic, one who happens to be going in the direction the people want to move. Colonel Lanser perceives this about the conquered people when he says, "Mayor Orden is more than a mayor. He is his people. He knows what they are doing, thinking, without asking, because he will think what they think."

While these attitudes and ideas had been Steinbeck's concern since his very first novel, there are several reasons why they are not effective in *The Moon Is Down*. One reason is that *Sea of Cortez* had given them final and abstract expression, so that *The Moon Is Down* lacks that nice tension which holds together *In Dubious Battle, Of Mice and Men,* and *The Grapes of Wrath,* a tension born of the author's struggles to strike a balance between his own ambivalent tendencies. The ideas in *The Moon Is Down* do not work themselves out; they are presented. It is this quality of static "presentation" which gives the effect of too little imagination, too complacent a vision. Another reason is that whereas in the earlier novels Steinbeck's group-man concept, his ecological orientation, and his non-teleological thinking had been qualified by actual observation and participation in his materials' particulars, in *The Moon Is Down* Steinbeck's abstractions are little less naked than they are in *Sea of Cortez.* In every other book since *Cup of Gold,* Steinbeck had been able to draw heavily on his own knowledge. There was nothing in his direct experience to provide material for *The Moon Is Down.*

Another kind of pitfall, though not an unavoidable one, lay in the very nature of his materials, and had been foreseen in *Sea of Cortez:*

Understandings of this sort [ecological, non-teleological,] can be reduced to this deep and significant summary: "It's so because it's so." But exactly the same words can also express the hasty or superficial attitude. There seems to be no explicit method for differentiating the deep and participating understanding, the "all-truth" which admits infinite change or expansion as added relations become apparent, from the shallow dismissal and implied lack of further interest which may be couched in the very same words.

As a matter of fact, whoever employs this type of thinking [non-teleological] . . . will be referred to as detached, hardhearted, or even cruel. Quite the opposite seems to be true. Non-teleological methods more than any other seem capable of great tenderness, of an all-embracingness which is rare otherwise.

These passages are directly applicable to the literary dilemma of *The Moon Is Down*. The author's conception may have been the "all-truth," but the result is a "superficial attitude," because this conception is not contained in a sufficiently concrete and particular context and not given a significant structure.

The defects of *The Moon Is Down* become even clearer when that book is compared to *Of Mice and Men*, Steinbeck's first play-novelette. There is first of all the problem of characterization. Whatever else George and Lennie may represent—mind and body, spirit and flesh, intelligence and will—they are first of all effective as credible human beings, doing and saying credible human things. The figures in *The Moon Is Down*, both invaded and invaders, are not real people who suggest certain qualities; they are qualities masquerading as human beings.

There is Doctor Winter, the scholarly, quiet, venerable family physician; there is the flighty, superficial, but devoted wife of the mayor; there is the mayor himself, who is a figure-head for his people in too many senses. He is made to rise from the triviality of the first scene, in which we see him getting the hair trimmed from his ears so he will look neat for the conquerors, to the greatness of the last scene, in which, as he is led out to be shot, he calmly quotes Socrates' last words.

The invading enemy are even more flatly typed. Their characters are set down in six consecutive pages, like the *dramatis personae* in a play:

> There was Major Hunter [the engineer], a haunted little man of figures, a little man who, being a dependable unit, considered all other men either as dependable units or as unfit to live. . . . Captain Bentick was a family man, a lover of dogs and pink children and Christmas. . . . Captain Loft was as much a captain as one can imagine. He lived and breathed his captaincy. He had no unmilitary moments. . . . Lieutenants Prackle and Tonder were snot-noses, undergraduates, lieutenants, trained in the politics of the day, believing the great new system invented by a genius so great that they never bothered to verify its results. They were sentimental young men given to tears and furies. . . . These were the men of the staff, each one playing war as children play "Run, Sheep, Run."

These descriptions might do as suggestions for the actors, but not as fiction. It is no wonder that in reviewing the book James Thurber said, "I could not believe that the people who enter Mayor Orden's living room come from the streets and houses of a little town. They come from their dressing rooms." [23]

The invaders' commanding officer fares a little better. Yet even he is a type of the disillusioned and cynical intellectual, who "tried not to think what he knew" and carries on his business of shooting hostages with thorough efficiency, salving his conscience by soul-revealing confessions to anyone who will listen. He is somewhat like Erfurt, the Nazi officer in Maxwell Anderson's *Candle in the Wind,* which Steinbeck had read. (JS-PC, 12/22/39) The difficulty with Lanser is the same as that with the other characters. After reading the first description of him, one knows as much about him as one does at the end of the book. His summary characterization precludes dramatic conflict.

Another difficulty with the book is that the background —the town, the people, the locale—is insufficiently particularized. There is not that sense of place which pervades *Of Mice and Men.* There are houses, streets, snow, rooms, and furniture; but they exist more as stage settings and props than as real things, because the novel moves alternately on two levels, the descriptive and the dramatic. In *Of Mice and Men* these two levels are fused by narrative.

It is quite probable that some of these "defects" were intended by Steinbeck. He was trying to avoid a realistic description of the Nazi invasion of Norway. The word "Nazi" does not occur in the book and the country is only vaguely "Scandinavian," as indicated by some of the names, the climate, and the occasional escapes across the sea to England. The play's stage directions are explicit on the point that the uniforms should not be identifiable as belonging "to any known nation." Steinbeck was concerned with dramatizing, in the abstract, the nature of a clash between democratic and "herd" men.

The difficulty is that the book is neither concrete nor universal—perhaps because the universal can be aesthetically apprehended only in the concrete and particular. The characters and situations in *The Moon Is Down* do not have that necessary credibility that they do in Steinbeck's other "pattern" novels—*In Dubious Battle, Of Mice and Men, The Grapes of Wrath, The Pearl,* and even *Burning Bright.*

This inadequacy may be observed in almost every scene. When Madame Orden is expecting the first arrival of Colonel Lanser, she asks her servant Joseph and Doctor Winter, "Should we offer them tea or a glass of wine? If we do, I don't know how many there will be, and if we don't, what are we to do?" This might be acceptable as a revelation of Madame's superficial character. But what are we to think when Doctor Winter replies, smiling, "I don't know. It's been so long since we conquered anybody or anybody conquered us. I don't know what is proper." Near the middle of the book, after Alex has killed a German officer and is to be tried for murder, the following conversation takes place between the two Orden servants, Annie and Joseph, the latter speaking first:

"They're going to try Alexander Morden."

"Molly Morden's husband?"

"Molly Morden's husband."

"For bashing that fellow with a pick?"

"That's right," said Joseph.

"But he's a nice man," Annie said. "They've got no right to try him. He gave Molly a big red dress for her birthday. What right have they got to try Alex?"

"Well," Joseph explained, "he killed this fellow."

"Suppose he did; the fellow ordered Alex around. I heard about it. Alex doesn't like to be ordered. Alex's been an alderman in his time, and his father, too. And Molly Morden makes a nice cake," Annie said charitably. "But her frosting gets too hard. What'll they do with Alex?"

"Shoot him," Joseph said gloomily.

"They can't do that."

Is this supposed to be comic relief? The scene is simply incredible. It is also incredible that when Annie scalds and bites some soldiers, Colonel Lanser "looked helpless" because although, as he says, he could have her shot, this would deprive them of her offices as cook.

The Moon Is Down does have some virtues. However otherwise typed, Colonel Lanser and his officers do avoid being prototypes of the brutal Nazi monomaniacs so often depicted in novels and motion pictures about the war. As Steinbeck stated twelve years later, "I had written of Germans as men, not supermen, and this was considered a very weak attitude to take. I couldn't make much sense out of this, and it seems absurd now that we know the Germans were men, and thus fallible, even defeatable." [24] Among those few critics who perceived what Steinbeck was getting at by making his "invaders" men rather than supermen, Harry Slochower is the most articulate: "What Steinbeck seems to be saying is that a change of the capital-situation makes possible at least a partial readjustment of their distorted humanity. To deny this is to invite as an alternative the necessity of exterminating all Germans or all deluded Nazi followers. Steinbeck's hope seems to lie in the people's aroused awareness that their capital is unrepresentative." [25]

Also, the conviction that it is always the "herd men, followers of a leader . . . who win battles and the free men who win wars" is stated without hysteria.[26] This is partly because, according to Steinbeck, when he wrote the play he was convinced that fascism had already lost the war.[27] As he noted some years later, he wrote the book "as a kind of celebration of democracy." [28] Part of the violent reaction was caused by the fact that it was three years too early for "celebration."

Finally, the book does contain some effective scenes. The scenes of quarreling among Colonel Lanser's staff are among the most real in the book, and the conversations between Dr. Winter and Mayor Orden suggest some of the true pathos, if not tragedy, inherent in the basic situation. The scene in which Molly Morden, widow of the executed Alex, hides a pair of long shears in her dress, blows out the lamp, and then goes to answer the gentle knocking of homesick Lieutenant Tonder, who has come to keep what he believes is a love tryst, is also effective. It moves both pity and terror. Also effective, in a strange way, is the scene just before Mayor Orden's death, in which he recites pertinent parts of Socrates' last speech, Colonel Lanser cooperating with Dr. Winter in prompting the Mayor to say correctly, "I prophesy to you who are my murderers that immediately after my—departure punishment far heavier than you have inflicted on me will surely await you."

The Moon Is Down is not nearly so good a play-novelette as *Of Mice and Men*, but it is a better play than it is a novel. In the play the abstract characters can be given particularity by the actors. The violations of taste perpetrated by the purely descriptive, sketchy, "filling-in" passages appear only in the actors' copies. And of course Steinbeck's theory that mass audiences have a different key of response from that of the lone individual reading in an armchair works as beautifully here as it does with *Waiting for Lefty*. As a novel, however, the main failure of *The Moon Is Down* is that it carries stylization beyond the limits where it emotionally concerns us, to the point of dehumanizing his materials. Looking back at *Tortilla Flat, In Dubious Battle, Of Mice and Men*, and *The Grapes of Wrath*, one realizes that Steinbeck had struggled with this problem of stylization before, and successfully. But the danger was always there.[29]

11 *Cannery Row*

Shorty after Steinbeck returned from his overseas assign-
ment in October of 1943 he had ready for publication a
book about his war experiences, but he was too disheartened
by what he had seen of the war to prolong the experience in
any way and decided not to publish it. Instead he set himself to work on a new novel and in six weeks produced
Cannery Row. Although the book was not published until
December of 1944, it is certain that it was finished eight
months earlier, in March of that year, just four months after
his return from Europe. (JS-PC, 3/22/44)

The appearance of this book, so different from the "social
protest" writing with which Steinbeck had become identified,
caused general consternation among reviewers and critics.
As F. O. Mathiessen put it, "It's a puzzler why Steinbeck
should have wanted to write or publish such a book at this

point in his career." [1] Edmund Wilson, in his review of the novel, confessed that of Steinbeck's books *Cannery Row* was the one he "most enjoyed reading," but went on to attack it for its sentimental and inadequate philosophy.[2] He had taken pretty much the same confusing attitude, as late as 1940, toward *Tortilla Flat*, which he attacked violently while at the same time asserting that "artistically" it was Steinbeck's "most successful production." [3] This split in critical attitude is also evident in Orville Prescott's comment that in *Cannery Row* Steinbeck "did not just write a trivial and seemingly meaningless and purposeless novel. He wrote, with all his usual professional felicity of expression, a sentimental glorification of weakness of mind and degeneration of character." [4] Similar views were expressed by many other critics.

Steinbeck's own statements about *Cannery Row* are contradictory. In a letter to his agents he described it as "a mixed-up book," with "a pretty general ribbing" in it.[5] To Pascal Covici he wrote, ". . . people are rushing to send it overseas to soldiers. Apparently they think of it as a relief from war." (JS-PC, 1/5/45) A week later, as reviewers continued to attack it, he wrote, "I *know Cannery Row* is a good book." A friend of Steinbeck reports that upon hearing Malcolm Cowley's theory that *Cannery Row* might be a "poisoned cream puff," [6] the author replied that if Cowley had read it yet again, "he would have found out how very poisoned it was." [7] In his most recent statements Steinbeck seems to contradict the tenor of his early remarks about the book. In October of 1953 he wrote that *Cannery Row* was "a kind of nostalgic thing written for a group of soldiers who had said to me 'Write something funny that isn't about the war. Write something for us to read—we're sick of war.' " [8] A few months later he said that he wrote *Cannery Row* as a relaxation from the war, which had depressed him, and that he wanted the troops to read it and enjoy it.[9]

There can be little doubt, however, that the author's early remarks, in a private letter addressed to his close friend and publisher shortly after writing the book, are more likely to be serious than are public statements made about the book nine years later, especially if these remarks are addressed to subscribers of a book club or an inquisitive critic. There is a parallel here to Steinbeck's statements about *Tortilla Flat,* of which he once said, "Curious that this second-rate book, written for relaxation, should cause this fuss. People are actually taking it seriously." [10] But, as has been demonstrated, Steinbeck's relaxed, humorous novel was quite serious in intention, and *Cannery Row* has many parallels to *Tortilla Flat.*

The structure of both novels is loose and episodic, but in a way very different from that of *The Pastures of Heaven,* which is frankly a collection of stories similar in theme and setting. Although there is a thin thread of plot in *Cannery Row* and in *Tortilla Flat*—Doc's party, The Pirate's candlestick—this plot is broken up by many interchapters. Also, both novels have as protagonists a tight little group with its own moral standards; and, although *Cannery Row* has a wider range of characters, in both novels this group is made up not so much of social outcasts as of individuals who have retreated from society. In both novels the structure and mores of this little group serve as commentaries on the structure and mores of that society which they have abandoned.

Despite these similarities, however, *Cannery Row* is not in any important sense a mere repetition of *Tortilla Flat.* In the intervening ten years Steinbeck had written *In Dubious Battle, Of Mice and Men, The Grapes of Wrath,* and *Sea of Cortez,* and had been abroad as war correspondent. The experience of these years is in *Cannery Row*, and it accounts for the difference in tone between the two books. Although Steinbeck had not considered the *paisanos* "quaint, dispossessed or under-doggish," neither had he considered them models of human conduct. They were people "who merge successfully with their habitat." [11] Ten years later, in *Cannery Row*, Steinbeck's detached, amused, tongue-in-cheek acceptance of such a group changes to an active championing of their way of life:

> Mack and the boys . . . are the Virtues, the Graces, the Beauties of the hurried mangled craziness of Monterey and the cosmic Monterey where men in fear and hunger destroy their stomachs in the fight to secure certain food, where men hungering for love destroy everything lovable about them. . . . In the world ruled by tigers with ulcers, rutted by strictured bulls, scavenged by blind jackals, Mack and the boys dine delicately with the tigers, fondle the frantic heifers, and wrap up the crumbs to feed the sea gulls of Cannery Row. What can it profit a man to gain the whole world and to come to his property with a gastric ulcer, a blown prostate, and bifocals? Mack and the boys avoid the trap, walk around the poison, step over the noose while a generation of trapped, poisoned, trussed-up men scream at them and call them no-goods, come-to-bad-ends, blots-on-the-town, thieves, rascals, bums.

In this sense Steinbeck's attitude toward his Virtues, Graces, and Beauties is very much like that of E. E. Cummings toward his "delectable mountains" as opposed to "officials." Steinbeck's heroes live in both "Monterey and the cosmic Monterey" as Cummings' heroes live in both the little room and *The Enormous Room*. Both authors stress the value of individual freedom and personal integrity as against regimentation.

This parallel to E. E. Cummings can also be seen in *Sea*

of Cortez, where Steinbeck speculates that "of the good we think always of wisdom, tolerance, kindliness, generosity, humility; and the qualities of cruelty, greed, self-interest, graspingness, and rapacity are universally considered undesirable. And yet in our structure of society, the so-called and considered good qualities are invariable concomitants of failure, while the bad ones are the cornerstones of success." (SC, 96) This sentiment is reiterated in almost the same words by Doc of *Cannery Row,* who also repeats, 120 pages later, Steinbeck's passage on the nature of Mack and the boys:

"There are your true philosophers. . . . I think they survive in this world better than other people. In a time when people tear themselves to pieces with ambition and nervousness and covetousness, they are relaxed. All of our so-called successful men are sick men, with bad stomachs, and bad souls, but Mack and the boys are healthy and curiously clean. They can do what they want. They can satisfy their appetites without calling them something else. . . . They could ruin their lives and get money. Mack has qualities of genius. They're all very clever if they want something. They just know the nature of things too well to be caught in that wanting."

These two statements, made by both Doc and Steinbeck, underlie the novel's basic "philosophic-moral system" and constitute the conceit out of which the novel's episodes are fabricated, episodes which comment on various aspects of civilized man—his business, his illusions, his sex drive, and his relations with his fellow man.

The businessman of the Cannery Row community is Lee Chong, in whose store it is possible to buy all commodities but one, and that one "could be had across the lot at Dora's." Lee Chong is successful in Cannery Row because he does not fight his environment, but adjusts his business to fit it. He is the opposite of Torrelli in *Tortilla Flat,* who attempts to survive Danny and the boys by cheating and chicanery, but is himself mercilessly cheated at every opportunity and driven to his wits' ends devising schemes of revenge which only boomerang. Lee Chong, on the other hand, takes things philosophically. When, by suggestions of possible arson and vandalism, he is subtly blackmailed into "renting" his warehouse to Mack and the boys, from whom he never even hopes to get any rent, he does not write off the transaction as a total loss.

> The windows were not broken. Fire did not break out, and while no rent was ever paid, if the tenants ever had any money . . . it never occurred to them to spend it any place except at Lee Chong's grocery. . . . If a drunk caused trouble in the grocery, if the kids swarmed down from New Monterey intent on plunder, Lee Chong had only to call and his tenants rushed to his aid. One further bond it established—you cannot steal from your benefactor. The saving to Lee Chong in cans of beans and tomatoes and milk and watermelons more than paid the rent.

In biological terms, Steinbeck might have said that Lee Chong succeeded in converting a parasitic into a commensal relationship.

This theme of mutual benevolence is also illustrated by the great frog hunt in chapters 13 and 15. When the "Captain" discovers Mack and the boys camping on his property, his first reaction is, "What the hell are you doing here? . . . . The land's posted. No fishing, hunting, fires, camping. Now you just pack up and put that fire out and get off this land." Mack's explanation that the frogs are needed for cancer research has no effect. It is only when Mack praises the Captain's dog and is solicitous of its welfare that the Captain remembers, "You know, I've got a pond up by the house that's so full of frogs I can't sleep nights. Why don't you look up there? They bellow all night. I'd be glad to get rid of them."

Another such commensal relationship is that of Doc and Frankie, who, like Tularecito, is "one of those whom God has not quite finished." (PH, 64) Although Frankie is not wanted either at school or at home, where numerous "uncles" give him nickels to leave them alone with his widowed mother, through Doc's acceptance and kindness the boy develops to the point where he can do little menial chores around the laboratory. In return, Doc provides him with food, shelter, and understanding, for which he receives virtual adoration.

This kind of adjustment through mutual understanding and acceptance is perhaps most evident in the position which Dora's sporting house holds in the community of Cannery Row. Dora's "decent, clean, honest, old-fashioned sporting house" is "no fly-by-night cheap clip-joint but a sturdy, virtuous club, built, maintained, and disciplined by Dora who, madam and girl for fifty years, has through the exercise of special gifts of tact and honesty, charity and a certain realism made herself respected by the intelligent, the learned, and the kind." Despite the accusations of "the twisted and lascivious sisterhood of married spinsters," Dora's establishment is not a parasite on society. Although her enterprise is officially illegal, it prospers under the gentle surveillance of an understanding police and chamber of commerce, who realize that it is no small factor in attracting annual conventions. In return for this peaceful existence, Dora finds she must be "twice as law abiding as anyone else" and much more generous in her contributions to organized charities and civic improvements.

Dora's contributions to the community are far in excess of the financial considerations expected of her. She also contributes a human value. When hard times strike Cannery Row, it is Dora who "paid grocery bills right and left for two years and very nearly went broke in the process." When an epidemic of influenza breaks out, the doctors find themselves too busy to attend to Cannery Row, which "was not considered a very good financial risk." But Dora keeps herself and her whole establishment busy ministering to the needy. They go in turns to sit with the sick families, taking them pots of homemade soup, and even buying medicines. Thus Dora not only provides an indispensable commodity, but makes her house a part of the stable ecological balance of Cannery Row.

Like the difference between the business ethics of Lee Chong and those of Torrelli, the difference between the function of Dora's girls and that of the "girls" of *Tortilla Flat* is an important one for understanding *Cannery Row*. With Sweets Ramirez and Cornelia Ruiz of *Tortilla Flat*, the nonprofessional nature of their "commodity" results in endless and frustrating consequences. They may covet material rewards (such as a vacuum cleaner), raise issues between friends, disrupt families, and arouse jealousies between competing lovers. Often, these situations result in violence, as in the stabbing of Cornelia's lover and the suicide of Old Man Ravanno. Sex in *Cannery Row* is assigned a role which avoids all these kinds of trouble. All relationships with Dora's girls terminate on paying the two dollars. The girls are so "well trained" that they "never speak to a man on the street although he may have been in the night before." The relationship is clean-cut, efficient, and simple.

This attitude toward prostitution, which is the same one fully depicted six years later in the sketch, "About Ed

Ricketts" (LSC, xxv-xxvii), and nine years later in *Sweet Thursday,* has been part of Steinbeck's materials since his very first book. Of course such an acceptance of prostitution is not singular, even in American literature. (Recently, James Jones's *From Here to Eternity* has given new life to this tradition.) But its calculated effect is usually farcical, naturalistic after the ash can school, or shocking. The closest thing to Steinbeck's treatment of the subject may be found in Maupassant's short story, "La Maison Tellier." The parallels are numerous and precise.[12] But although Steinbeck was familiar with Maupassant and has testified to the latter's effect on his early career,[13] it is unlikely that the French master had an important influence in this particular connection. Maupassant's story seems to be a tongue-in-cheek affair, while Steinbeck's attitude as shown in his works is consistently serious and an integral part of his world view as a novelist.

In *Sea of Cortez* Steinbeck declares that there is "a remarkable etiological similarity to be noted between cause in thinking and blame in feeling," and that if one can rid himself of strictly teleological thinking, the propensity to blame gives way to acceptive understanding. (SC, 148) Steinbeck's approach to prostitution stems more from this kind of inclusive understanding, this urge to accept man "as is," than from iconoclasm or proselytism. No major protagonist in his novels and stories goes to a whorehouse. Both Mac of *In Dubious Battle* and Doc of *Cannery Row* and *Sweet Thursday* (like his prototype, Ed Ricketts, in *The Log from the Sea of Cortez*), accept prostitution, but are explicit in expressing their personal dissatisfaction with this kind of sexual experience.

It is also significant that until *Burning Bright,* Steinbeck did not write a single novel or short story in which was depicted, to any extent, what might be called romantic love. Even among his later works, romantic love occupies a prominent place only in *Sweet Thursday*. In *East of Eden* the love affair of Cal and Abra is limited to the last section of the novel. The love of Joe Saul for Mordeen in *Burning Bright* is overshadowed, as is love in Shakespeare's sonnets, by the theme of immortality through biological propagation. In Steinbeck's work it is very seldom that boy meets girl; instead, man meets man. There are the very closely knit associations of Henry Morgan and Coeur de Gris in *Cup of Gold;* Mac and Jim in *In Dubious Battle;* Root and Dick in "The Raid"; Alex and the narrator in "Johnny Bear"; Junius Maltby and Jakob, Raymond Banks and the warden in *The Pastures of Heaven;* Danny and Pilon in *Tortilla Flat;* George and Lennie in *Of Mice and Men;* Tom and Casy in *The Grapes of Wrath;* Doc and Mack or the boys in *Cannery Row;* Juan Chicoy and Pimples Carson in *The Wayward Bus;* Charles and Adam, Caleb and Aaron in *East of Eden;* Doc and Mack or the boys in *Sweet Thursday;* Pippin and his uncle in *The Short Reign of Pippin IV.*

There are women in these novels, but their allurements are overshadowed by the more solid attractions of male companionship. As Mme. Claude-Edmonde Magny has observed, "One might say that for Steinbeck the normal, valid, durable couple can be formed only by two representatives of the male sex—and this without the least suggestion of homosexuality." Mme. Magny is also correct in observing that this couple is a union of two complementary natures, but she is incorrect in asserting that Steinbeck's maleism implies "the expulsion of Woman from the true human community." [14] Women in Steinbeck's work are not, as she suggests, prototypes for the Helen-Silene of the Trojan Wars or the *Giftmädchen* of Nordic sagas. There is only one Cathy in Steinbeck's work, but there are many noble women—Juana in *The Pearl,* Rama and Elizabeth in *To a God Unknown,* Mordeen in *Burning Bright,* Ma Joad in *The Grapes of Wrath,* and most of the women in *The Pastures of Heaven.* All of them are married.

As a matter of fact, in all of Steinbeck's work there are altogether only a half-dozen unmarried women who are not professional whores. Whatever Steinbeck's attitude may be as an individual, it is clear that for a long time part of his equipment as a novelist has been this classic emphasis on comradeship over love. In the world of his fiction women do have a place, but they seem compelled to choose between homemaking and whoredom. It is better to be a good whore than a bad wife, and better to be a good wife than a bad whore. Perfection is attainable in either field: there is Ma Joad and there is Dora Flood.

When Steinbeck's attitude toward man's sex drive in *Cannery Row* is seen in this context of his total work, it becomes clear that the book is not in any sense a new departure or "escape" literature. Rather, the disillusionment which Steinbeck suffered during the war impelled him to create a whole world in which the untouchables and misfits of the real world he had observed and previously depicted were given the major roles. "Its inhabitants are, as the man once said, whores, pimps, gamblers, and sons of bitches, by which he meant Everybody. Had the man looked through another peephole he might have said, Saints and angels and martyrs and holy men, and he would have meant the same thing." In *Cannery Row,* Steinbeck is looking through "another peephole."

Perhaps the greatest difficulty in discussing *Cannery Row* is its apparent lack of structure. That the book was intended to be more than a collection of anecdotes is indicated by one of the author's remarks to Pascal Covici, "No critic yet has stumbled on the design of the book." (JS-PC, 1/5/45) It is improbable that by "design" Steinbeck meant some detailed principle of unifying structure. The best description of the book's form still seems to be the analogy which Steinbeck proposes at the end of the introductory chapter:

> How can the poem and the stink and the grating noise—the quality of light, the tone, the habit and the dream—be set down alive? When you collect marine animals there are certain flat worms so delicate that they are almost impossible to capture whole, for they break and tatter under the touch. You must let them ooze and crawl of their own will onto a knife blade and then lift them into your bottle of sea water. And perhaps that might be the way to write this book—to open the page and to let the stories crawl in by themselves.

The arrangement of these flat worms in Steinbeck's bottle of sea water is not, however, entirely haphazard. The book has a unifying plot in the attempts of Mack and the boys to give Doc a party, an attempt which ends in disaster once and is successful only when they join forces with the girls of Dora's Bear Flag Restaurant. What makes this plot so tenuous as an organizing principle is the large number of digressions, which make up about fifteen of the book's thirty-two chapters. (They are sometimes difficult to distinguish.) Approximately six of these chapters have some very slight reference to the characters or events of the plot, but nine of them are entirely self-contained. Yet although these fifteen chapters are not directly involved in the book's plot, they are essential to its theme. As Steinbeck wrote to Pascal Covici, "No critic has discovered the reason for those little inner chapters in *Cannery Row*." (JS-PC, 1/15/45) For the most part, their function is the same as that of the interchapters in

Tortilla Flat. Each is an anecdote commenting on the book's central theme.

Sometimes these interchapters are placed so as to derive an added effect from following a contrasting chapter in the plot section. In chapter 18, Doc, while collecting octopi at low tide, notices a curious flash of whiteness under some floating weeds. Investigating further, he parts the brown weeds and finds himself looking straight into the open eyes of a beautiful, drowned woman, "and the hair washed gently about her head. . . . Just under water it was and the clear water made it very beautiful." [15] Doc gazes at this picture for many minutes and then goes back to the beach, where he sits in a daze while a "terrifying flute played in his brain." "Goose pimples came out on Doc's arms. He shivered and his eyes were wet the way they get in the focus of great beauty."

This reverie is interrupted by a stranger who, when told that Doc has been collecting octopi, remarks, "You mean devilfish? I didn't know there was any there. I've lived here all my life." And when Doc tells him about the body, all the man can think of is, "Say—You get a bounty for finding a body. I forget how much." His curiosity extends only a little further—"Rotten or eaten up?" Doc leaves the man, who promises to tell the authorities and collect the reward, and now "only the tiniest piping of the flute sounded in his head."

This is the last sentence of chapter 18, and the next chapter begins, "Probably nothing in the way of promotion Holman's Department Store ever did attracted so much favorable comment as the engagement of the flag-pole skater." The contrast between the attentive curiosity accorded the marathon skater and the lack of curiosity about the drowned girl is heightened by the revelation that most of the interest in the skater focuses on the problem of his toilet facilities: ". . . the most interesting question of all and the one that bothered the whole town was never spoken of." This kind of juxtaposition can also be seen in the chapter about the two soldiers and their girls, which follows the chapter in which the Captain invites Mack and the boys onto his property. If this patterning is systematic throughout the book, it escapes detection. But in most of the interchapters the general reference to the book's theme is clear enough.

There is another function which these interchapters serve. For although the events depicted in them are in contrast with the values of Mack and the boys, the people in these chapters, too, are residents of Cannery Row. Thus these chapters, with their suicides, physical mutilations, psychological maladjustments, and mental cruelties, serve as a built-in restraint on the tendency toward sentimentality. Steinbeck does not deny the presence of evil. In addition to that nameless kind of evil which is simply the result of multiple coincidences (as in *The Pastures of Heaven*), there is that kind of evil which people bring on themselves: Two little boys tease another about his father's suicide by means of rat poison; Mrs. Malloy is unhappy because she has no lace window curtains for the windowless boiler which is her home; William, the former bouncer at the Bear Flag Restaurant, commits suicide with an ice pick because he is not accepted by Mack and the boys, who find him too morose and self-pitying; Mary Talbot lives in a make-believe world because she cannot face the reality of her poverty. There is even the evil which comes from good intentions: It is because he is trying to do something nice for Doc, who has befriended him, that Frankie steals a seventy-five dollar clock and gets committed to an institution for the criminally insane. When Doc asks the boy why he did it, Frankie replies only, "I love you."

Another way in which some of these interchapters function can be illustrated by the last one of the book, which also serves to sum up the ideal values of this community. It is about a very healthy and attractive gopher, "in the prime of his life," who "took up residence in a thicket of mallow-weeds in the vacant lot on Cannery Row." This vacant lot was "a perfect place," with plenty of food and ideal soil, "black and soft and yet with a little clay in it so that it didn't crumble and the tunnels didn't cave in." He seems to lead an ideal existence. "There were no gardens about so no one would think of setting a trap for him. Cats there were, many of them, but they were so bloated with fish heads and guts from the canneries that they had long ago given up hunting." There are no "tigers with ulcers"; "strictured bulls" do not rut there; and it is not "scavenged by blind jackals." It is the same world in which live the Virtues, the Graces, and the Beauties—a gopher's equivalent of Cannery Row.

But the gopher is not content in his safe, comfortable place, because no female gopher comes to live with him. Finally, "in a sweat of impatience," he leaves his vacant lot and goes "across the track" and squeaks into a gopher hole there. Out of this hole there charges an old, battle-scarred gopher. The venturer from Cannery Row is mauled so badly that he loses two toes. It takes him three days to recover. "Again he waited and squeaked beside his beautiful burrow in the beautiful place but no female ever came and after a while he had to move away. He had to move two blocks up the hill to a dahlia garden where they put out traps every night."

At their best, these interchapters have this quality of parable, but there are a few whose function is obscure, such as the story about the embalming and re-burial of Josh Billings. Perhaps it is only intended to illustrate the great difference between the public's slight regard for a living literary figure and its disproportionate concern for the disposition of his dead body. In fact, the publishers felt that one of the original interchapters had so little relationship to the rest of the book that they did not wish to include it. This chapter was later published separately as "The Time the Wolves Ate the Vice-Principal."

Another obscure interchapter is that about the "old Chinaman," who every evening comes through a vacant lot, crosses the street, and disappears among the piles and steel posts which support the piers. No one sees him again until dawn, when he retraces his steps, carrying in his wicker basket something "heavy and wet and dripping." He is very ancient and, although he has been doing this for years, "no one ever got used to him." "Some people thought he was God and the very old people thought he was Death and children thought he was a very funny old Chinaman, as children always think anything old and strange is funny. But the children did not taunt him or shout at him as they should for he carried a little cloud of fear about him." Steinbeck may be indulging here in Hawthorne's technique of multiple suggestions, but it is likely that the "very old people" are right. When a stranger in Monterey, a young boy, chants a derisive jingle at the old man, he seems to find himself absorbed into the other's piercing eyes, where he sees a desolate landscape symbolic of death. Such an interpretation is reinforced by the fact that this chapter comes in the introductory part of the book, along with the description of the main protagonists—Mack and the boys, Dora and her girls, Lee Chong, and Doc.

Doc is an important figure in Cannery Row, because he completes the human community by serving as its local deity. Although, like the Greek deities, he mixes freely with ordinary mortals, his home is in his laboratory, and he is essentially set apart. "In spite of his friendliness and his friends Doc was a lonely and a set-apart man. . . . In a group Doc seemed always alone. . . . Even in the dear close contact with a girl Mack felt that Doc would be lonely." In addition to his scientific discipline, he takes great pleasure in fine music, especially the contrapuntal, religious music of Palestrina, Byrd, and Bach. He reads widely in the great books of both occidental and oriental culture, and the walls of his room are covered with reproductions of great art. Although he is a good friend and counselor of Dora and her girls, he has no business with their commodity. "His sex life was too complicated for that." (LSC, xxvi) Although he associates freely with Mack and the boys and enjoys his beer, he does not drink the communal mixture which Eddie brings home from La Ida Bar. As Mack says, "Doc wouldn't like this stuff from the winin' jug. . . . No—you couldn't offer him none of this." Doc's character, like his bearded face, suggests a strange mixture, "half Christ and half satyr." At one point his face is compared to that of a statue of St. George killing the dragon. Even his sex life is bound up with this religious motif. When the shades of Doc's laboratory are drawn and the great phonograph is playing a Byrd mass or Gregorian chants, everyone in Cannery Row knows that Doc is with a girl.

The extent to which Doc is modeled on Steinbeck's good friend, Ed Ricketts, is clear from the biographical sketch which Steinbeck published in *The Log from the Sea of Cortez* after Ricketts' death. Almost every detail about Doc has its parallel in the actual life and personality of Ed Ricketts. *Cannery Row* is itself dedicated to Ed Ricketts—"For Ed Ricketts who knows why or should." After reading the novel in manuscript, Ricketts expressed concern that it would make him a popular figure; and it did. *Life* wanted to print photographs and a story about him and his laboratory, which

Ricketts did not allow. Tourists began to drive slowly by the Pacific Biological Laboratories at 800 Oceanview Avenue. Frequently they would stop and ask if they could come in and look around. Two results of this publicity, however, gave Ricketts much pleasure. As he himself put it, "Some of the callers were women and some of the women were nice looking." (LSC, lviii) Also, a soldier stationed nearby visited him and asked, "Are you the guy who likes early music?" The soldier turned out to be a fine musician and proceeded to form a vocal group in Monterey devoted exclusively to performing the early church music Ricketts loved so well.

It is a similar impulse to "do something nice for Doc" which gives rise to *Cannery Row's* tenuous plot. And it is this impulse which best reveals the relationship between Doc and the inhabitants of Cannery Row. "Everyone who knew him was indebted to him," and looks up to him for advice and help. These he is always willing and able to give. If the cause is evidently just, the help is immediate. When his people come to him for small favors of questionable virtue, the deity nods and grants their "prayer" only if its ingenuity gives evidence of earnest effort. As he is quick to reward, so is he quick to punish, and in the same ambiguous manner as the deity. When Mack presents himself to Doc the morning after wrecking his laboratory in a drunken brawl, the deity's eyes shine "with a red animal rage." He breaks the suppliant's mouth with his fists and then hands him a glass of beer. The culprit is properly penitent and accepts his just deserts; Doc realizes that the intention was good and forgives.

The effort of Cannery Row's inhabitants to throw a party for their deity finally succeeds because he foresees this effort and provides for it. The celebration is more like a bacchanalia than a solemn mass, but it has its somber moments when

Doc plays the "ethereal, disembodied" music of Byrd and Palestrina on his great phonograph and when he reads aloud half a hundred lines from "Black Marigolds," at which Dora and her girls weep. Even such traditional enemies as the police join in the celebration, and the deity looks down on his children from a Buddha-like pose: "Doc sitting cross-legged on the table smiled and tapped his fingers gently on his knee."

The apotheosis of Doc is inevitable, when it is considered that he embodies all the qualities which Steinbeck finds admirable. In him all opposites are reconciled. He is both scientist and mystic, both calculating and tender, both learned and common, both intellectual and emotional, both classicist and romanticist. He can kill twenty cats in an afternoon and stuff their veins and arteries with color mass for dissection, but he can also beat up a much bigger man for mistreating a dog. He can write learned papers in his field of marine biology, but he can also get drunk with Mack and the boys. He can be completely enthralled with the mathematical, polyphonic music he loves best, but if the mood is on him he can listen to *Pavanne for a Dead Princess* and follow that with *Daphnis and Chloe*. As he puts it to himself, "I can play anything I want. I can play *Claire de Lune* or *The Maiden with Flaxen Hair*. I'm a free man."

The climax of *Cannery Row* is the great party in chapter 30, surely one of the most riotous in American literature. Of the remaining two chapters, the first is devoted to the parable of the gopher and the last to a final glimpse of Doc as he clears up the party's debris. While working, he plays one of his albums of Gregorian music, a *Pater Noster* and an *Agnus Dei*. Then, while the dishes are soaking in the sink, he picks up the volume containing "Black Marigolds" and continues reading:

Even now
I mind the coming and talking of wise men from towers
Where they had thought away their youth. And I, listening,
Found not the salt of the whispers of my girl,
Murmur of confused colors, as we lay near sleep;
Little wise words and little witty words,
Wanton as water, honied with eagerness.

Even now
I mind that I loved cypress and roses, dear,
The great blue mountains and the small gray hills,
The sounding of the sea. Upon a day
I saw strange eyes and hands like butterflies;
For me at morning larks flew from the thyme
And children came to bathe in little streams.

Out of context, these stanzas from the Sanskrit poem (translated by E. Powys Mathers) perhaps seem unwarrantably
tender and sentimental. They are made incisive, however, by
their immediate context. For as Doc reads his poetry, "in
the sink the high white foam cooled and ticked as the bubbles
burst. Under the piers it was very high tide and the waves
splashed on rocks they had not reached in a long time." Doc
closes the book, and he "could hear the waves beat under
the piles . . . the scampering of white rats against the wire."
The last stanza, he recites to "the sink and the white rats
and to himself."

Even now
I know that I have savored the hot taste of life
Lifting green cups and gold at the great feast.
Just for a small and a forgotten time
I have had full in my eyes from off my girl
The whitest pouring of eternal light—

The book ends with, "And the white rats scampered and scrambled in their cages. And behind the glass the rattlesnakes lay still and stared into space with their dusty frowning eyes." Ricketts once referred to the novel as being, among other things, "an essay in loneliness." It is this context of loneliness in the face of mutability, time, and death which makes the three stanzas of poetry an adequate statement of the "reverence for life" which pervades *Cannery Row* and the frame of mind into which Steinbeck retreated following his experience of war.

12 } *The Pearl*

By the time that *Cannery Row* appeared, in December of 1944, eight months after it was completed, Steinbeck was well into a novelette which while still in progress was called "The Pearl of La Paz." (JS-PC, 11/25/44; 11/30/44) Although the story was finished by early February of 1945 (JS-PC, 2/?/45), it did not appear until ten months later, in the December issue of *Woman's Home Companion,* under the title of "The Pearl of the World." It was first published in book form two years later, in December of 1947, to coincide with the RKO release of the motion picture Steinbeck had adapted from it, and was called simply *The Pearl.*

The essential story had been in Steinbeck's mind since before the war. In *Sea of Cortez,* while remarking on the role of La Paz in providing the conquistadores with pearls, Steinbeck tells of an event "which happened at La Paz in recent years." (SC, 102)

An Indian boy by accident found a pearl of great size, an unbelievable pearl. He knew its value was so great that he need never work again. . . . In his great pearl lay salvation, for he could in advance purchase masses sufficient to pop him out of Purgatory like a squeezed watermelon seed. . . . He took his pearl to a broker and was offered so little that he grew angry for he knew he was cheated. Then he carried his pearl to another broker and was offered the same amount. After a few more visits he came to know that the brokers were only the many hands of one head and that he could not sell his pearl for more. He took it to the beach and hid it under a stone, and that night he was clubbed into unconsciousness and his clothing was searched. The next night he slept at the house of a friend and his friend and he were injured and bound and the whole house searched. Then he went inland to lose his pursuers and he was waylaid and tortured. But he was very angry now and he knew what he must do. Hurt as he was he crept back to La Paz in the night and he skulked like a hunted fox to the beach and took out his pearl from under the stone. Then he cursed it and threw it as far as he could into the channel. He was a free man again with his soul in danger and his food and shelter insecure. And he laughed a great deal about it. (SC, 102–103)

When Steinbeck came to write "The Pearl of the World" four years later, he kept the basic pattern of this story—the discovery of the pearl, the persecution, and the renunciation —but he introduced certain important changes. The Indian boy becomes the man Kino, husband of Juana and father to Coyotito. The pearl is to provide not "the ability to be drunk as long as he wished," but an education for Coyotito: "My son will read and open books, and my son will write and will know writing. And my son will make numbers, and these things will make us free because he will know—he will know and through him we will know." The pearl is returned to the sea, but not before it has brought strife between husband and wife, destroyed their home, and caused the violent death of their child. Steinbeck also added several minor figures—a greedy doctor, a kind and understanding brother.

These changes were intended to amplify and make more complex those qualities of parable which Steinbeck perceived in the original: "This seems to be a true story, but it is so much like a parable that it almost can't be. This Indian boy is too heroic, too wise. He knows too much and acts on his knowledge. In every way, he goes contrary to human direction. The story is probably true, but we don't believe it; it is far too reasonable to be true." (SC, 103) Similarly, in his introductory remarks to *The Pearl* Steinbeck wrote, "and because the story has been told so often, it has taken root in every man's mind. And, as with all retold tales that are in people's hearts, there are only·good and bad things and black and white things . . . and no in-between anywhere." Five years later, he said of the novelette, "I tried to write it as folklore, to give it that set-aside, raised-up feeling that all folk stories have." [1]

Part of Steinbeck's success in creating this feeling in *The Pearl* lies in the theme itself. The action is simple, but, as in all parables, suggestive of underlying planes of meaning. The surface story is told in a manner which urges the reader to look beyond the physical events into their spiritual significance. Alex Comfort has remarked that "with the advent of an intelligent insight into symbolism, realism as we knew it before the new psychology must be reconsidered, because we now know that any imaginative narration exists both as a direct statement of events and as a reflection of conscious or unconscious forces dictating the imagery in which it is presented." [2] All of Steinbeck's statements about *The Pearl* point in this direction.

In the story itself there are several details which suggest the symbolic nature of this pattern of events. When Kino first finds the pearl, it is described as "the greatest pearl in the world," and two pages later as "the Pearl of the World," a phrase which is often repeated. After the first attack on Kino by unknown assailants, his wife Juana says of the pearl, "This thing is evil. This pearl is like sin! It will destroy us. Throw it away, Kino. Let us break it between stones. Let us bury it and forget the place. Let us throw it back in the sea. It has brought evil. Kino, my husband, it will destroy us." But Kino's "face is set." The pearl has "cozened his brain with its beauty." The people of the village are suspicious. "That good wife Juana," they say, "and the beautiful baby Coyotito, and the others to come. What a pity it would be if the pearl should destroy them all." After Kino has insulted the agents who told him that the pearl was of no great value, his brother, Juan Thomás, says to him, "You have defied not the pearl buyers, but the whole structure, the whole way of life, and I am afraid for you." After the second attack on him, Kino still refuses to give up the pearl and says, "This pearl has become my soul. If I give it up I shall lose my soul."

This aura of suggestion extends not only to the pearl itself, but to the characters and setting as well. Kino's assailants come at night and are never actually seen except as vague shadows. After the first attack, Kino answers his wife's cries with, "I am all right. The thing has gone." After their hut has been ransacked and burned down, Kino asks Juana, "Who?" and she replies, "I don't know. The dark ones." The two Indians, "people from the inland," who guide the vague "dark man" on horseback in the pursuit of Kino and his family are described in animal terms. They "whined a little, like excited dogs on a warming trail," and are referred to only as "the dark trackers." Kino is named after a late seventeenth-century

Jesuit, Eusebius Kino, who was a great missionary in the Gulf region and a great explorer, the first to prove that lower California was a peninsula, not an island.[3] The name of Kino's wife, Juana, means simply "woman." The doctor and the pearl buyers are obvious symbols of greed.

The setting of *The Pearl* is just as suggestive as the theme, the characters, and the pearl itself: "The uncertain air that magnified some things and blotted out others hung over the whole Gulf so that all sights were unreal and vision could not be trusted; so that sea and land had the sharp clarities and the vagueness of a dream. . . . Part of the far shore disappeared into a shimmer that looked like water. There was no certainty in seeing, no proof that what you saw was there or was not there."

When Kino and Juana escape from their coastal village, they "go out into the world." At one point in their flight, the landscape, though realistically described, has the same symbolic suggestiveness that the landscape has in "Flight" and "The Great Mountains":

> The land was waterless, furred with the cacti which could store water and with the great-rooted brush which could reach deep into the earth for a little moisture and get along on very little. And underfoot was not soil but broken rock, split into cubes, great slabs, but none of it water-rounded. Little tufts of sad dry grass grew between the stones, grass that had sprouted with a single rain and headed, dropped its seed, and died. Horned toads watched the family go by and turned their little pivoting dragon heads. . . . The stinging heat lay over this desert country, and ahead the stone mountains looked cool and welcoming.

The direction of these symbolic details suggests that although the Mexican incident "of recent years" which Steinbeck first heard of in La Paz provided him with the bare essentials of plot, the meaning with which he chose to invest this incident may have had a different origin. In the gnostic fragment called the "Acts of Thomas," there is a passage, often edited separately, usually known as "The Song of the Pearl," a phrase which in several modifications is often repeated in the text of *The Pearl:* "the Song of the Pearl That Might Be" and "the music of the pearl," for example. This passage, which seems to be an allegory of the soul's redemption from bondage, is also known as "The Hymn of the Soul," a title which is alluded to in Kino's statement, "This pearl has become my soul. If I give it up I shall lose my soul." [4]

That Steinbeck may have been familiar with this apocryphal fragment is not surprising. His interest in oriental and early Christian literature goes back as far as *To a God Unknown*, whose theme and title refer to both the Vedic Hymns and the Acts of the Apostles, and whose kindly priest reads *La Vida del San Bartolomeo*. *Sea of Cortez* demonstrates an intimate knowledge of the works of several Spanish Jesuits who wrote about *Baja California*, and *The Wayward Bus* shows a familiarity with St. John of the Cross. While he was working on *The Pearl*, he wrote to Pascal Covici about the *Arabian Nights*, "strange how you can find the roots of practically all western stories there." (JS-PC, 1/15/45) In his letters and fiction there are occasional references to the *Bhagavad-Gita*, Buddhism, and Oriental concepts of Being. Doc of *Cannery Row* quotes from "Black Marigolds" and reads Li Po. Ricketts once referred to *The Golden Bough* as "Steinbeck's *vade mecum*."

But although Steinbeck may have brought together a Mexican folk tale and a passage from the "Acts of Thomas" to create a pattern of man's search for his soul, that search takes place in a context which gives it also a materialistic and a practical meaning, one related to Steinbeck's concepts of non-teleological thinking and ecology. This meaning has its roots in the same attitude which produced *Tortilla Flat*, and, in the same year as *The Pearl*, *Cannery Row*.

As his brother, Juan Thomás, points out, Kino is not engaged in a private struggle, and he is not defying just the pearl buyers, "but the whole structure, the whole way of life." Also, Kino is not the first one who has attempted to redeem his pearl for a greater price. All those who tried in the past have never been heard of again, and the local priest takes this for a text at least once a year. As Kino sums up this sermon, "The loss of the pearl was a punishment visited on those who tried to leave their station. And the father made it clear that each man and woman is like a soldier sent by God to guard some part of the castle of the universe. And some are in the ramparts and some far deep in the darkness of the walls. But each one must remain faithful to his post and must not go running about, else the castle is in danger from the assaults of Hell."

In *Tortilla Flat* Steinbeck had treated with tongue in cheek a withdrawal from social competition, and in *Cannery Row* he had written of the Virtues, Graces, and Beauties with sincere though humorous approval of their acceptance of the position assigned them in "the castle of the universe": "Our Father who art in nature, who has given the gift of survival to the coyote, the common brown rat, the English sparrow, the house fly and the moth, must have a great and overwhelming love for no-goods and blots-on-the-town and bums, and Mack and the boys. Virtues and graces and laziness and zest. Our Father who art in nature." (CR, 10) The retreat from competition in these books is an accomplished fact. Both Danny and his *paisanos* and Mack and the boys have thrown the jewel of great price back into the sea before their stories begin. In *The Pearl* Steinbeck shows one man's struggles to redeem his pearl, despite the "blind jackals" (pearl buyers), the "strictured bulls" (the doctor), and the "tigers with ulcers" (the pursuing horseman).

However meaningful the parable of the pearl may be in the abstract, Steinbeck's success in fleshing out this parable to the dimensions of a credible, forceful human adventure ultimately rests on his prose style, which is flexible to the extent that here as in most of his other novels it becomes technique as well as medium. It is capable not only of creating an aura of symbolic suggestion (as in the descriptions of landscape cited above), but also of rendering details in terms of a camera—as when Kino, in hiding, peers at his pursuers:

> Kino could see only their legs and only the legs of the horse from under the fallen branch. He saw the dark horny feet of the men and their ragged white clothes, and he heard the creak of leather of the saddle and the clink of spurs. The trackers stopped at the swept place and studied it, and the horseman stopped. The horse flung his head up against the bit and the bit-roller clicked under his tongue and the horse snorted. Then the dark trackers turned and studied the horse and watched his ears.

The more panoramic descriptions have this same reality and authenticity, which create a firm foundation for the abstract pattern:

> The beach was yellow sand, but at the water's edge a rubble of shell and algae took its place. Fiddler crabs bubbled and sputtered in their holes in the sand, and in the shallows little lobsters popped in and out of their tiny homes in the rubble and sand. The sea bottom was rich with crawling and swimming and growing things. The brown algae waved in the

gentle currents and the green eel grass swayed and little sea horses clung to its stems. Spotted botete, the poison fish, lay on the bottom in the eel-grass beds, and the bright-colored swimming crabs scampered over them.

The objectivity of the prose style in these descriptive passages is paralleled by Steinbeck's objectivity in portraying his characters' inner feelings. The pearl buyer's nervousness while he is waiting for Kino to walk up the street and into his office is conveyed by a nervous tic which is at the same time a perfect visual symbol of his legerdemain activities as a pearl buyer: "He rolled a coin back and forth over his knuckles and made it appear and disappear, made it spin and sparkle. The coin winked into sight and as quickly slipped out of sight, and the man did not even watch his own performance. The fingers did it all mechanically, precisely, while the man hummed to himself and peered out the door. Then he heard the tramp of feet of the approaching crowd, and the fingers of his right hand worked faster and faster until, as the figure of Kino filled the doorway, the coin flashed and disappeared." As Kino talks to him about his pearl, the agent's fingers "worked furiously with the coin." When Kino places the magnificent pearl on the velvet pad, he quickly glances up at the agent's face. "But there was no sign, no movement, the face did not change, but the secret hand behind the desk missed in its precision. The coin stumbled over a knuckle and slipped silently into the dealer's lap."

A more complex example of this substitution of symbolic action for omniscient narration is the action with which the novel ends. After Coyotito is killed, Kino and Juana come back to their village and walk wordlessly through the crowded streets. "The sun was behind them and their long shadows stalked ahead, and they seemed to carry two towers of darkness with them." They do not pause until they come to the shore.

> And then Kino laid the rifle down, and he dug among his clothes, and then he held the great pearl in his hand. . . . Kino's hand shook a little, and he turned slowly to Juana and held the pearl out to her. She stood beside him, still holding her dead bundle over her shoulder. She looked at the pearl in his hand for a moment and then she looked into Kino's eyes and said softly, "No, you."
> And Kino drew back his arm and flung the pearl with all his might. Kino and Juana watched it go, winking and glimmering under the setting sun. They saw the little splash in the distance, and they stood side by side watching the place for a long time.

For the reader who has been following the story, these bare details are rich with unstated meaning. He knows that when Kino first offers the pearl to Juana he is admitting that she has been right about the evil of the pearl, and he, the leader of the family, wrong. The reader recalls how Kino once struck Juana brutally when she had tried to throw the pearl into the sea, and knows that they are both remembering the same incident. The reader also understands that in Kino's simple gesture Juana recognizes her triumph and the humility of her man. By her refusal to throw the pearl she gives dignity and pride once more to her husband, whose position it is to do such final things. And all this is under·stood by Kino as he accepts again his rightful role and throws the pearl into the sea.

In addition to using completely objective and visual images to reveal his characters' inner feelings, Steinbeck also makes use of partly subjective and auditory images— when Kino is working the oyster beds, for example: "And as he filled his basket the song was in Kino, and the beat of the song was his pounding heart as it ate the oxygen from his held breath, and the melody of the song was the gray-green water and the little scuttling animals and the clouds of fish that flitted by and were gone. But in the song there was a secret little inner song, hardly perceptible, but always there, sweet and secret and clinging, almost hiding in the counter-melody, and this was the Song of the Pearl That Might Be, for every shell thrown in the basket might contain a pearl." There are similar passages which depict Kino's feelings of love, hate, anger, and fear. They would never do to describe the emotions of a Jamesian character, but they are adequate for the relatively simple materials and parable structure of *The Pearl.*

Steinbeck had used this same technique once in *Cannery Row* to depict Doc's emotions when he sees the drowned girl: "Music sounded in Doc's ears, a high thin piercingly sweet flute carrying a melody he could never remember, and against this a pounding surf-like wood-wind section. The flute went up into regions beyond the hearing range and even there it carried its unbelievable melody. . . . the flute climbed and plucked cellos sounded below and the sea crept in and in toward the beach." (CR, 100-101) This device is not a retreat before the problems of a writer, but an experiment in attempting to render undefined and partly subliminal emotions in terms of an objective correlative.

The Pearl brings together several more of Steinbeck's techniques and preoccupations as a writer. His tendency to think of groups as unit animals is revealed in his description of the "nerve lines" and "units" of a small town. His non-teleological thinking and his unwillingness to assign absolute blame and create "villains" is evident here as in *In Dubious Battle, The Grapes of Wrath, The Moon Is*

Down, and *Sea of Cortez.* The pearl buyers' motives in attempting to cheat Kino are understood. Like the "owners" of *In Dubious Battle* and *The Grapes of Wrath,* they are but part of a system, "and if it be a man's function to break down a price, then he must take joy and satisfaction in breaking it as far down as possible. For every man in the world functions to the best of his ability, and no one does less than his best, no matter what he may think about it,"

There is also in *The Pearl* Steinbeck's technique of interrupting the action to insert a passage illustrating predatory nature as an implicit comment on that action. After the doctor has learned of Kino's great pearl and has come on a professional visit he has previously refused to make, there occurs the following description, set off as a separate paragraph: "Out in the estuary a tight woven school of small fishes glittered and broke water to escape a school of great fishes that drove in to eat them. And in the houses the people could hear the swish of the small ones and the bouncing splash of the great ones as the slaughter went on. . . . And the night mice crept about on the ground and the little night hawks hunted them silently." This and similar passages throughout Steinbeck's works serve not to suggest that nature is evil, but to remind man of his continuity with nature, and to reveal the predatory drive which, beneath his civilized mask, he shares with other living creatures.

It would be a mistake, however, to say that in these passages Steinbeck is equating human and animal activity. For although his work shows a persistent interest in man's biological heritage, such novels as *The Pearl* demonstrate his equally persistent interest in man's mythopoeic heritage as well. It is to this aspect of his work that Harry Slochower refers when he groups Steinbeck with André Malraux and Thomas Mann, among others, and says of them, ". . . they look back to history and myth for the prototypes of human fate. But they reach back not out of love for the dark night, as is the case with anti-intellectualism, but because with Freud and Marx, they seek the categories which on a higher level chart a liberating future. . . . they are for these men the promises of continuity and recurrence. Their work reclaims our faith in the rationality of man's natural history. It is a kind of moral-esthetic counterpoint to the physical disorder of our day. Their art is the contemporary secular equivalent of man's divinity."[5]

13 } *The Wayward Bus*

Steinbeck's third book of this postwar period, *The Wayward Bus,* appeared early in 1947, two years after "The Pearl of La Paz" was written but almost a whole year before that story was published in book form as *The Pearl. The Wayward Bus* had been in Steinbeck's mind for a long time, possibly since his trip to Mexico in 1940, but it was not actually written until the summer of 1946. By July of 1945, he had sketched out the book's structure and theme; as originally conceived, it was to have a Mexican background. (JS-PC, 7/12/45)

Although each of Steinbeck's books up to *The Wayward Bus* had seemed a new departure at the time, by 1947 critics had begun to classify them into three main areas: social protest (*In Dubious Battle, Of Mice and Men, The Grapes of Wrath, The Forgotten Village*); quaint and picturesque comedy (*Tortilla Flat, Cannery Row*); and simple rural life (*The Pastures of Heaven, The Long Valley, The Pearl, The Red Pony*). *Cup of Gold* and *To a God Unknown* were conveniently forgotten. Because *The Wayward Bus* did not seem to fit into any of these areas, for which clichés of Steinbeck criticism were readily available, most critics seemed confused about the book. Bernard De Voto, for example, found that "as narrative, it is superb—a fine craftsman working at his most expert—as comedy it is excellent; as novel it is satisfying and no more." [1]

The Wayward Bus may be taken with the first two books Steinbeck published after the war (*Cannery Row* and *The Pearl*) as forming a triptych which, while varying widely in materials and techniques, is dedicated to one purpose—an examination of the underlying assumptions of modern civilization. *Cannery Row* had dealt with this civilization's "no-goods and blots-on-the-town and bums"—actually "the Virtues, the Graces, the Beauties," if seen through "another peephole." *The Pearl*, like the chapter on the gopher in *Cannery Row*, depicted the individual struggling to survive in that civilization. *The Wayward Bus* is pitiless examination of the civilization which Mack and the boys reject, to which the gopher succumbs, and over which Kino and Juana gain a tragic victory. This is the book's most obvious meaning.

There is, however, another, more complex, level of meaning which is a part of the book's structure and technique. Steinbeck had great ambitions for the story of his wayward bus. Its driver, Juan Chicoy, was to be "all the god the fathers you ever saw driving a six cylinder, broken down battered world through time and space." (JS-PC, 7/12/45) The frame story of the wayward bus taking its assorted passengers cross-country from one main highway to another, coming to washed-out bridges, traveling the forgotten back road, and finally arriving at San Juan de la Cruz, becomes itself part of the novel's meaning. There are two main "plots": the gathering of the characters and their interaction with each other; the actual journey of the allegorical bus.

On the level of character, the plot is held together by a play of tensions which are resolved in a series of incidents during the space of a few hours when Juan Chicoy temporarily abandons his passengers in a deep rut of the muddy back road to San Juan de la Cruz. Responsible for most of these incidents, directly or indirectly, is a blond stripper who calls herself Camille Oaks. She is introduced in a separate action on another bus, and by the time she joins the main group at Rebel Corners her future role as *femme fatale* is clear and the individuals of the main group have been defined by a series of little actions among themselves.

Because *The Wayward Bus*, unlike most Steinbeck novels, is more concerned with action on the level of character than on the physical level of events, it is necessary here to sketch in some detail the main personalities. They seem to be arranged in three main groups: the damned, those in purgatory, and the saved or elect. The damned are Mr. Elliot Pritchard, Mrs. Bernice Pritchard, Alice Chicoy, Louie (the first bus driver), and Norma.

Mr. Pritchard is a slight variation on Sinclair Lewis' businessman, and his description seems to come right out of *Babbitt*. "He was never alone. His business was conducted by groups of men who worked alike, thought alike, and even looked alike. His lunches were with men like himself who joined together in clubs so that no foreign element or idea could enter. . . . One night a week he played poker with men so exactly like himself that the game was fairly even." He conducts both his business and personal life according to all the clichés of boosterism, service, ambition, and progress.

Mr. Pritchard's role as a business unit is paralleled by his attitude toward sex. At the age of twenty he had made one drunken visit to a parlor house. He now goes to occasional stags, "but five hundred Mr. Pritchards were there with him."

Mr. Pritchard's wife, Bernice, is also recognizable as a type. "She was feminine and dainty and she dressed always with a hint of a passed period. . . . She met the ideas of other people with a quiet smile, almost as though she forgave them for having ideas. . . . Women of lusty appetites she spoke of as 'that kind of woman,' and she was a little sorry for them as she was for dope fiends and alcoholics. Her husband's beginning libido she had accepted and then gradually by faint but constant reluctance had first molded and then gradually strangled, so that his impulses for her became fewer and fewer until he himself believed that he was reaching an age when such things did not matter." In addition to this sexual power over her husband, Mrs. Pritchard resorts to sudden, violent headaches, which can be brought on whenever the occasion requires. "Having few actual perceptions, she lived by rules. Education is good. Self-control is necessary. Everything in its time and place. Travel is broadening."

Although Elliot and Bernice Pritchard are damned in part for being hypocritical prudes, Juan Chicoy's wife, Alice, despite her lusty appetites, is also among the damned. "All relations and all situations to Alice were person-to-person things in which she and the other were huge and all others were removed from the world. There was no shading." "Alice was not very aware of things or people if they did not in some way either augment or take away from her immediate life." Her lack of an ecological orientation is aptly and grotesquely symbolized by her attitude toward the common housefly, which she regards as a trespasser in her private world. There are several incidents illustrating this. The most amusing occurs during her prodigious drunk in the closed lunchroom after Juan has driven off with the passengers. At the height of her debauchery she sees a fly dipping into a spot of wine on the table and her flesh "crawled with hatred. All her unhappiness, all her resentments, centered in the fly." In her drunken attempts to kill this fly, she reduces the world of the lunchroom to a shambles. After she has collapsed on the floor, "the fly moved to the edge of the drying pool of wine. . . . and then deliberately he dipped his flat proboscis in the sweet, sticky wine."

Norma, the Chicoys' hired waitress, is another of the damned. Her spiritual flaw is a combination of the weak qualities exemplified by the elder Pritchards and Alice Chicoy. Her soul is an odd combination of sexual frustration, illusions, and clichés. "The actual love-making in her life had been a series of wrestling matches, the aim of which was to keep her clothes on in the back seat of a car. So far she had won by simple concentration." Her insight into life is that provided by motion-picture magazines. She writes long, intimate letters to Clark Gable, with whom she is in love, and is waiting for the day when he will walk into the lunchroom, recognize "this was his woman," and take her away from it all. She keeps his picture on her dresser and at night wears a gold wedding ring to bed. The rest of her soul is concocted of clichés about personal appearance— "you could always find some little bit of beauty even on the wash dresses." She brushes her hair "ten strokes on one side and ten on the other. And while she brushed she raised and flexed the muscles of one leg and then the other to develop the calves."

While not involved in the central action of the book,

Louie, the bus driver who brings Camille to Rebel Corners, is an important character because he clarifies the sexual attitudes of Juan Chicoy, Ernest Horton, and Camille Oaks. His attitude is cheap and vulgar. He has read somewhere that if you "looked directly into a girl's eyes and smiled it had an effect," and that if it bothered you to look into people's eyes you could stare them down by looking "at a point on the bridge of the nose." He has also read in a magazine that wide-set eyes mean sexiness. His masculinity is false and sterile. "Nearly all his waking hours Louie thought about girls. He liked to outrage them. He liked to have them fall in love with him and then walk away. He called them pigs. 'I'll get a pig,' he would say, 'and you get a pig, and we'll go out on the town.'" Camille Oaks sees through Louie's cheapness; her parrying of his "slick" advances provides some of the book's finest comedy.

The saved characters, the elect, are Juan Chicoy, Ernest Horton, and Camille Oaks. Juan Chicoy has all the characteristics of a Steinbeck hero. He is a skilled mechanic. He is self-reliant and self-contained. In contrast to Mr. Pritchard, who is always toying with a nail clipper, "his movements were sure even when he was not doing anything that required sureness. . . . His hands moved with speed and precision and never fiddled with matches or nails." Unlike his wife, Alice, in his dealings with other people he can "look at each thing in relation to the other. . . . He could see and judge and consider and enjoy." His relations with women are particularly successful, because his sexuality is open and honest.

Like Juan, Ernest Horton is able to accept people as they are, is self-sufficient and honest. He immediately sees through Norma's dream world; but, unlike Alice, he does not make fun of her. Instead he plays along, even volunteering to deliver a letter to Clark Gable, and he tries to protect Norma when she has her final quarrel with Alice. Although Ernest Horton makes a living by selling comical gadgets (artificial sore toes, a shot glass in the shape of a toilet bowl), unlike Mr. Pritchard he is not taken in by his own salesmanship. And he does not fool himself about the morality of business. He is perfectly willing to go into a scheme which would force clothing companies to buy his patent in order to suppress it. But again unlike Mr. Pritchard, who wants to become his partner in the venture, he is able to face reality and admit that such a scheme is really a legal and safe form of blackmail, not "service." His sexual desires are as honest and straightforward as Juan's, and, like Juan, he finds the trip successful in this respect.

Finally, there is Camille Oaks, the blond stripper. "She knew she was different from other girls, but she didn't quite know how. . . . Men couldn't keep their hands off her. . . . All men wanted the same thing from her. . . ." Like Juan and Ernest Horton, she has the ecological view—"that was just the way it was. She took it for granted and it was true." Camille cannot help having this effect on men. For a time she tried to counteract it. "She tried wearing severe clothes, but that didn't help much. She couldn't keep an ordinary job. She learned to type, but offices went to pieces when she was hired." As one young doctor tells her, "You just put it out in the air. . . . Some women are like that." [2] Although she would like nothing better than "a nice house in a nice town, two children, and a stairway to stand on," she accepts the fact that this is impossible for her. "She didn't understand stags or what satisfaction the men got out of them, but there they were, and she made fifty dollars for taking off her clothes and that was better than having them torn off in an office."

These saved characters, no matter how different their surface lives seem, have four important traits in common: honesty with themselves and others, an ecological view of things, ability in their respective fields, and sexual attractiveness. They are also set apart from the damned by a common physical characteristic. Each has on his or her body some mark or scar caused by the world. Juan Chicoy has one joint missing from the third finger of his left hand, a scar alongside his nose, and a scar on his lip. Camille Oaks has deep forceps marks along her jaws. Ernest Horton's scars are not visible, but they are implied by the Congressional Medal of Honor ribbon which he wears in his lapel.

There are two other passengers who have physical disfigurements—Pimples (suffering from acne), and Mildred Pritchard (almost blind without her glasses). Unlike the scars of the saved characters, both these disfigurements are natural, not caused by the world. Pimples and Mildred are souls in Purgatory who progress upward several circles during the bus trip.

Mildred is a sexually attractive though slightly masculine woman of twenty-one, who is slowly but successfully overcoming the effects of her home environment. In this struggle she has been helped by a college education and certain "dangerous companions," as her father considers them, "professors and certain people considered Red." Before the war she picketed a scrap-iron ship bound for Japan. Unlike her mother, she possesses a normal sexual appetite, and ". . . she had experienced two consummated love affairs which gave her great satisfaction and a steady longing for a relationship that would be constant." Mildred is immediately attracted to Juan Chicoy, but has not yet progressed to the cardinal virtues shared by the saved characters. There are definite indications, however, that she is well on the road. One doctor has told her that her weak eyes "had to do with puberty" and that they may become strengthened when she has her first baby.

Pimples Carson, like Mildred Pritchard, is in a state of Becoming. As is the case with Norma, the elder Pritchards, and the first bus driver (Louie), a good part of his soul is made up of advertising slogans and clichés of the "You too can be successful" type. He eats prodigious amounts of sweets because they are " 'rich in food energy. . . . Fellow's going to work, he needs food energy. Take about three o'clock in the afternoon when you get a let-down. Why, you need something rich in food energy.' " He is planning to take a course in radar engineering, by mail. "Pimples took most of his ideas from moving pictures and the rest from the radio." Like Mildred, however, Pimples has possibilities. His skin condition may clear up after adolescence. He has a genuine interest in mechanical things and, under Juan's tutorship, is actually a good apprentice. Juan trusts him to make preparations for the trip. Only Pimples knows enough about driving to realize that Juan has stuck the bus on purpose, and when Juan abandons it he leaves Pimples in charge.

The last member of the group of passengers is Mr. Van Brunt, an old man of over sixty who does not clearly belong in any of the three categories. He may be intended to suggest the ultimate stage of the damned. His physical disfigurements are not caused by the world, but neither are they, like those of Pimples and Mildred, the temporary ones of youth. They are the ills of an old and decaying body. "He had his head bent permanently forward on the arthritic stalk of his neck so that the tip of his nose pointed straight at the ground. . . . His long, deeply channeled upper lip was raised over his teeth like the little trunk of a tapir. The point over his teeth seemed to be almost prehensile." His twisted body is the sign of a twisted soul. His self-righteousness masks an essentially malicious and dirty mind, as Mildred points out. "Physical hatred of everyone around him crowded in his throat."

These are the passengers of Steinbeck's allegorical bus. With the exception of the saved characters, and possibly Alice Chicoy, each of them has surrendered a large portion of his soul to the superficial conventions of a society ruled by business and advertising. This surrender is signaled by the clichés which rule their lives. But although Steinbeck examines these characters with the pitiless eye of a biologist, he does not withhold human understanding and even, perhaps, sympathy, for as author he endows each of them with the seed of some virtue.

In his youth, before succumbing to his society, Mr. Pritchard had voted for Eugene Debs. And even now, as his daughter observes, "when she had him catalogued rather smugly as a caricature of a businessman, grasping, slavish, and cruel, he ruined her peace of conception by an act or a thought of kindliness and perception." Despite his cheapness and vulgarity, Louie has that Steinbeck virtue of skill in his work: "Louie was a good driver with a perfect record." Pimples, too, is good at his work and will develop into a fine mechanic. Norma has been mixed-up all her life, but she is not stupid, and she learns quickly from Camille Oaks. Even Mrs. Pritchard receives a measure of understanding. Her frigidity and consequent inhumanity is probably caused by a hidden physical defect. "She . . . was handicapped by what is known as a nun's hood, which prevented her experiencing any sexual elation from her marriage; and she suffered from an acid condition which kept her from conceiving children without first artificially neutralizing her body acids." Van Brunt, too, has been in part shaped by forces beyond his control. Like his father, whom he watched lie like a "gray, helpless worm in a bed for eleven months," he is subject to strokes. He has already had two, "and he waited, waited for another one, the one that would flash in his mind, would flash through his body, and if it didn't kill him, it would numb out all feeling. Knowing it had made him angry, angry at everyone."

None of these characters actually changes during the trip, but in a chain reaction of events culminating during Juan Chicoy's temporary desertion of his six-cylinder world, each of these characters bound for San Juan de la Cruz undergoes some dark night of the soul in which he achieves a measure of self-knowledge.

Under the Socratic examination of Ernest Horton, Mr. Pritchard is made to realize the fact that his business ethics and ideal of "service" are really "high-class blackmail." When Camille begins to tire of his persistent "fatherly" interest in getting her a job in his office, she reveals herself to him as the stripper he ogled during a stag for businessmen in Chicago. And when he is holding a stick in Van Brunt's mouth to keep him from swallowing his tongue, "he found that he hated this man because he was dying. He inspected his hatred in amazement . . . 'What kind of a thing am I?' he cried. 'What makes these horrible things in me?'"

Mrs. Pritchard's illusion that her family is far removed from the vulgarity of other people is shattered when her daughter deserts her and runs after the Mexican Juan Chicoy. A short time later her·husband, smarting under the two quick blows given him by Ernest Horton and Camille, assaults Mrs. Pritchard on the dirt floor of the cave and commits conjugal rape. When he leaves, Mrs. Pritchard gouges her cheeks and throat with her nails, bites her lips, and rubs dirt over her face.

Van Brunt tries to make Mildred Pritchard uncomfortable by pointing out that her slip is showing and then prolonging the conversation—"I don't care to hear about your underwear. . . . I don't want you to think I had any other motive. . . . Too many girls get self-conscious on their legs. They think everybody is looking at them." Remembering that Van Brunt had "never missed any show of legs," Mildred looks deliberately at him and says, "You see, there are two straps on each shoulder. One is for the slip and the other supports the brassiere and the brassiere holds the breasts up firmly. There isn't anything below that until the panties, if I wore panties, which I don't." Van Brunt is uncomfortable for the rest of the trip.

Under the influence of Camille's sympathy and interest, Norma seems to be becoming eligible for a place in purgatory along with Pimples and Mildred. But her attitude toward sex is still that "Mr. Gable not only would not do things like that, but wouldn't like them if he heard about them." She is brought up short when her expression of sympathy for Pimples results in his crude attempt to seduce her.

Mildred becomes disgusted with her parents and deserts them. She finds Juan in an old, abandoned barn and is forced to admit to him, "I don't want you to think it's you. It's me. I know what I want. I don't even like you." She is even forced to make the advances. "You don't give me any pride. You don't give me any violence to fall back on later."

As these tensions work themselves out among the passengers, most of them in the shadow of a stone cliff on which some inspired man of God has painted the one word REPENT, the physical journey of the busload of people becomes itself a part of this vision of humanity. Although the journey from Rebel Corners to San Juan de la Cruz is described in realistic terms, most of the book's geography and toponymy is fictitious, and there is an underlying suggestiveness in almost every detail. That *The Wayward Bus* is intended as more than a realistic narrative is also pointed out by its epigraph.

I pray you all gyve audyence,
And here this mater with reverence,
By fygure a morall playe;
The somonynge of Everyman called it is,
That of our lyves and endynge showes
How transytory we be all daye.

Juan Chicoy (whose initials, like those of Jim Casy, are significant) has inherited his bus from a previous owner. One of the changes he has made in his "six cylinder world" is painting out its previous inscription, which is "still barely readable"—*el gran Poder de Jesus.* "Now the simple word 'Sweetheart' was boldly lettered on front and rear bumpers." At various stages of the journey the pilgrims see such signs as "Come to Jesus," "Sinner, come to God," and "It is late" painted on rocks and cliffs and interspersed with advertisements for patent medicines.

Although Juan carries on the bus's dashboard "a small metal Virgin of Guadalupe painted in brilliant colors," its powers are not entirely trusted, and there are false gods before it. "Hanging from the top of the windshield were the penates: a baby's shoe—that's for protection, for the stumbling feet of a baby require constant caution and aid of God; and a tiny boxing glove—and that's for power, the power of the fist on the driving forearm, the drive of the piston pushing its connecting rod. . . . a little plastic kewpie doll with a cerise and green ostrich-feather headdress and a provocative sarong. And this was for the pleasures of the flesh. . . . When the bus was in motion these hanging items spun and jerked and swayed in front of the driver's eye." Juan Chicoy, not "a believer in an orthodox sense, now he was fifty," keeps the *Guadalupana* only because he would be "uneasy" without it. The penates and the Virgin are supported by a revolver, a roll of bandage, a bottle of iodine, smelling salts, and a pint of whiskey. "His religion was practical."

Juan Chicoy's role as conductor of this six-cylinder world is paralleled by that of the old man, Van Brunt, in his capacity as prophet. He foresees and tells of the raging San Ysidro River, the washed-out bridge, and the impassable back road, but his efforts are bent toward frustrating any positive action in the face of these difficulties. In this sense, as incarnating the everlasting nay, he is the Satan of this world on wheels. As Juan Chicoy is always in the driver's seat, so Van Brunt is always seen in the last seat back, watching the passengers with a baleful eye. Van Brunt is, however, a prophet without honor, for Juan Chicoy (in his capacity as "all the god the fathers") does not finally desert the "battered broken down world."

The events of the journey are also allegorical. The first adventure which is encountered after the bus leaves the crossroads significantly called Rebel Corners is the problem of crossing the San Ysidro River. This river, named after a patron saint of agriculture, is in flood and is destroying the farmers' property—tearing down fences, washing away topsoil, and drowning livestock. The bridge over the river is unsafe because, as Van Brunt points out, it has been built by a crooked politician. It may be passable, but the passengers don't want to risk it. (They fear death by water.) The only alternatives are going back to Rebel Corners or leaving the paved highway and taking the old dirt road which was used by the stagecoaches of their pioneer ancestors. Juan offers to let the passengers decide upon the course of action, and this they seem willing to do until Van Brunt (a lawyer) points out that by making a decision they are shifting responsibility from Juan Chicoy onto themselves. When Juan chooses the long way around, the old back road, Van Brunt is the first to object, though he is also against crossing the bridge or going back.

When Juan abandons the bus and walks off in the rain, it becomes clear that the passengers are unable to provide for themselves in any way, and they must resort to caves for shelter and to a crate of "Mother Mahoney's Home-Baked Pies" for food. As Ernest Horton forces Mr. Pritchard to admit, the successful and enterprising businessman knows nothing about gasoline engines, cannot keep from getting pneumonia under the circumstances, and cannot even "kill a cow. . . . cut it up and cook it."

While the passengers are quarreling among themselves, Juan and Mildred Pritchard have found each other and are consummating their love affair in an old barn. When they return to the bus, Juan digs it out of the mud and continues to drive it along the old back road to San Juan de la Cruz without incident. "Far ahead and a little to the left a cluster of lights came into view—little lights winking with distance, lost and lonely in the night, remote and cold and winking, strung on chains. Juan looked at them and called, 'That's San Juan up ahead.'"

The novel ends on this positive note. The allegorical bus has been on a wayward pilgrimage, but it does arrive at Saint John of the Cross. The prophet Van Brunt has not really foreseen all. Steinbeck seems to be saying that despite the artificial and dishonest Pritchards, the deluded Normas, the cynical Van Brunts, the self-centered Alices and the vulgar Louies, there are also realistic and objective people like Juan Chicoy, without whom the world would founder, who always return to dig it out of the mud.

The novel's energy derives from this tension between the plot on the level of character and the plot on the level of journey. The action of the novel can be plotted as an ascending spiral, the characters providing its circular and the journey its vertical motion. Perhaps the parallel to the *Divine Comedy* is not accidental.

The Wayward Bus is one of Steinbeck's "well-made" novels from the point of view not only of structure, but of prose style as well. For here again Steinbeck has tailored a distinct prose which serves him as both medium and technique. Of Steinbeck's previous novels, only *In Dubious Battle* approaches the complete scientific objectivity of *The Wayward Bus,* which carries the catalogue-like prose of the earlier novel to an even greater extreme.

> The electric lantern, with a flat downward reflector, lighted sharply only legs and feet and tires and tree trunks near the ground. It bobbed and·swung, and the little incandescent bulb was blindingly blue-white. Juan Chicoy carried his lantern to the garage, took a bunch of keys from his overalls pocket, found the one that unlocked the padlock, and opened the wide doors. He switched on the overhead light and turned off his lantern.
>
> Juan picked a striped mechanic's cap from his workbench. He wore Headlight overalls with big brass buttons on bib and side latches, and over this he wore a black horsehide jacket with black knitted wristlets and neck.

This kind of writing keeps the reader as close to purely visual perception as possible. It is exactly as if one were watching a realistic motion picture—without background music. Furthermore, this film is completely uncensored: "He [Juan] went into the bedroom. He slipped the shoulder straps of his overalls and let the pants fall down around his shoes. He had on shorts with narrow blue stripes. He peeled his blue chambray shirt over his head and kicked off his moccasins and stepped out of the overalls, leaving shoes and socks and overalls in a pile on the floor."

This kind of "camera eye" realism is used throughout, except for brief passages of omniscient narration in which the author fills in the historical background of his characters. And even these passages sound like cards in an FBI file. The lunchroom, the bus, the passengers, the ladies' room—all are subjected to this harsh, glaring light. Steinbeck renders physical details so immediate that the reader often feels his nose is willfully being rubbed in man's biological functions. The effect is sometimes similar to that of Swift's close-up descriptions in "A Voyage to Brobdingnag," which has a similar intention—to expose man in all his meanness. But whereas Swift leaves the reader with his nose in the human mire, Steinbeck lifts his head somewhat painfully by the hair, and points to the cliff, whereon is written REPENT. It may be, however, that Steinbeck's realistic materials and objective prose have done their work all too well, so that the sign on the cliff lacks sufficient reality. One might feel toward this affirmation as Juan Chicoy feels toward the *Guadalupana* on the dashboard—it's nice to have it there, but the revolver, the pint of whiskey, the roll of bandages, and the smelling salts in the glove compartment are more convincing.

In *The Wayward Bus* Steinbeck reveals himself at a point of stasis between the rejections of *Cannery Row* and *The Pearl* and the affirmations of *Burning Bright* and *East of Eden*.

14 } *Burning Bright*

The new emphasis in Steinbeck's work indicated by the affirmations of *The Wayward Bus* was sustained in his next two books of fiction (*Burning Bright* and *East of Eden*), the first of which appeared in 1950, almost four years after *The Wayward Bus*.

These intervening years were busy ones for Steinbeck. In the summer of 1947, just a few months after the publication of *The Wayward Bus,* Steinbeck went to Russia with Robert Capa, the photographer, and on his return he published *A Russian Journal* (April, 1948). During this period he also wrote a motion-picture script from *The Red Pony* (Republic, 1948), and in the fall of 1948 he began writing both the story and script for *Viva Zapata* (Twentieth Century-Fox, 1952), which occupied him until May of 1950.[1] Both these ventures turned out well. Steinbeck was pleased that Hollywood followed carefully his script for *The Red Pony* (JS-PC, 1/5/49), and he worked conscientiously on *Viva Zapata*. He even wrote a special introduction to the shooting script so that the producer, director, and cameraman would understand what it was about, and he went on location with Twentieth Century-Fox to supervise the actual filming. (JS-PC, 12/6/48; 4/7/50) Two short stories also date from this period: "The Miracle of Tepayac" (December, 1948) and "His Father" (September, 1949). It was during this period, too, that he suffered the loss of his great friend, Ed Ricketts, and wrote his memorial sketch, "About Ed Ricketts," which introduced *The Log from the Sea of Cortez* (1951). (JS-PC, 4/1/50) In addition, Steinbeck was doing research in the files of Salinas Valley newspapers, particularly the *Salinas Index*, and wrote a good part of the material which went into *East of Eden,* at that time called "Salinas Valley." (JS-PC, 2/24/48; 2/22/49)

Although there is little of literary value in this period, some of the work is interesting, especially the motion picture *Viva Zapata,* whose materials are similar to those of *The Grapes of Wrath* and *In Dubious Battle*. Like the Okies, the Mexicans are deprived of their farms by absentee landlords. But whereas the struggle in the strike novel remains dubious, both in its merits and its outcome, Zapata wins his revolution—only to become gradually aware that power corrupts. Steinbeck treats this theme in terms of tragedy. Zapata realizes what has happened to him and dies in an attempt to rectify his errors. His death becomes a myth from which his oppressed people can take strength.

Another interesting figure in this motion picture is Fernando. He is Jim of *In Dubious Battle* carried to an extreme of ruthless efficiency. Even more than the organizers in the strike novel, Fernando puts his job as revolutionary ahead of the people he is supposed to serve. In the end his love for power becomes stronger than his love for the people, and he chooses to keep his power even though it means becoming a counter-revolutionary and setting the fatal trap for his idealistic leader, Emilio Zapata. If there was doubt as to Steinbeck's attitude toward revolutionaries in 1937 and 1939, there could be none in 1952.

Steinbeck once remarked that he did not like motion-picture writing because whereas the camera functions in "literal" terms, "most of my work depends on suggestion." (JS-PC, 7/10/45) But, as motion pictures, *Viva Zapata* and *The Pearl* are very moving and, like many passages in his novels, attest to his great power of communicating complex ideas and feelings in purely visual terms.

A Russian Journal is an interesting piece of reporting and, despite its controversial subject, was well received by reviewers. It appeared just before the beginning of the cold war, while our national attitude toward Russia was still one of watchful cooperation. But because Steinbeck and Capa were interested in the people and avoided "politics and the larger issues" (RJ, 4) the book is still interesting reading. Anyone who had followed Steinbeck's career up to this time was not surprised to learn that while Steinbeck found the common people of Russia as human as people anywhere, he was depressed by the regimentation, bureaucracy, and lack of individual freedom. What he saw in Russia seemed to confirm the suspicions about a highly cooperative society which he had expressed in *Sea of Cortez* seven years earlier. The situation was even worse, for in *Sea of Cortez* he thought that the "elimination of the swift, the clever, and the intelligent" was the price paid for "mediocre efficiency." But in *A Russian Journal* he presents a great deal of proof that the stifling of individual initiative actually resulted in gross in-efficiency. Steinbeck was also depressed by the subjection of the artist to the state. He remarked that no great art had yet come from such a relationship and that the purpose of the artist was to be not an "architect" of society, but a "watchdog of society." (RJ, 164)

While working on his biographical piece called "About Ed Ricketts," which prefaces *The Log from the Sea of Cortez*, Steinbeck wrote to Pascal Covici that this essay was "no thing to be dashed off in a week end," and that the effect was to be neither "careful nor contrived"; it was "to flow out with great speed and turbulence almost draining the uncon-sciousness." (JS-PC, 4/1/50) The biography not only makes clear that Ricketts was the original for Doc of *Cannery Row*, it also hints at the importance of Ricketts in Steinbeck's de-velopment as a writer, a relationship which will be explored in connection with *Sweet Thursday*.

The two short stories of this period do not add to Stein-beck's stature. "The Miracle of Tepayac" is nothing more than the story of the Virgin of Guadalupe, whose image Juan Chicoy carried with him in his wayward bus. All the facts are there—the poor Juan Diego, the vision, the miracle, the bishop, the sick uncle. Steinbeck merely invents a dialogue between Juan Diego and the Virgin and between Juan Diego and the Bishop. The other short story, "His Father," com-prises only two and a half short pages and is of interest for two reasons. It is written in a stream-of-consciousness tech-nique from the boy's point of view, something new for Stein-beck, and its subject (the grief felt by a boy who has lost his father) is indicative of the frame of mind which prompted Steinbeck's next book—*Burning Bright*.

Burning Bright is Steinbeck's third attempt at a play-novelette, a form the rationale of which is cogently explained in a "Foreword" repeating many of the concepts he had elucidated in a similar piece about *Of Mice and Men,* discussed above. From late in 1949 until its completion in the summer of 1950, the book underwent several thorough revisions and changes of title. It was called "In the Forests of the Night," "Tiger, Tiger," and finally *Burning Bright.* (JS-PC, 2/24/50; 5/29/50. PC-JS, 7/26/50) The final title was decided upon after Steinbeck had read the proof sheets, which bear the title "In the Forests of the Night." The fact that these various titles are all taken from Blake's poem testifies to the affinity which Steinbeck saw between that poem and his play-novelette.

Unlike his previous experiments in this form (*Of Mice and Men, The Moon Is Down*), *Burning Bright* was put on Broadway before being published in book form, one month later (November). Also unlike his previous two experiments, *Burning Bright* was a miserable failure, running less than two weeks. Critics seemed to vie with one another in heaping abuse upon the play, especially upon its form and language. As Steinbeck himself summed it up in an article called "Critics, Critics Burning Bright," "We had favorable reviews from two critics, a mixed review from one, and the rest gave the play a series of negatives—from a decisive no through a contemptuous no to an hysterical no, no, no." [2] This article, a kind of post-mortem of the play by its author, is interesting because it contains an *apologia* for *Burning Bright* in terms of the author's intentions concerning theme, structure, and language.

Of the book's theme Steinbeck wrote, "I can find no play, poem, essay, or novel which uses sterility as its theme. . . . In working with this theme I began to fear that if the subject had not been used, it might be that it was too terrible and secret a thing to be brought into discussion." This impression was fortified by the experiences of the dramatic company when they took the play on the road, before putting it on Broadway. Steinbeck had believed that "any basic human problem [was] . . . a fit subject for literature," but he found that "to the average audience the whole subject of sex is funny if . . . permitted to find it so." He also found that sentences which were clean to individuals were dirty to an audience, that "pregnancy was a matter for laughter and in some cases for great distaste," and that it was impossible to use "the slightest image indicating the act of sex without drawing a curious self-conscious laughter." [3]

Actually, no critic objected to the play on these grounds, and, insofar as content can be separated from form, there can be no such objection. The theme of *Burning Bright* has a modern analogue in O'Neill's *Strange Interlude,* and especially in Federico García Lorca's *Yerma,* in which the potent man, the friend of the husband, is called Victor, as in *Burning Bright.* Norman Cousins praised Steinbeck's theme because it "demolishes the supposed importance of a continuing biological immortality, revealing the blazing truth that so long as human beings exist anywhere every man is immortal." [4]

The effectiveness of this theme, as theme, is to some extent vitiated by the treatment accorded Victor, who is denied the fellowship of man which the book preaches. It is true that at the beginning of the book he embodies those qualities for which Steinbeck damned Alice Chicoy and the bus driver, Louie, in *The Wayward Bus.* Victor's intellectual equipment is a "poolhall, locker-room, jokebook wisdom," and his orientation is not ecological. "His was the self-centered chaos of childhood. All looks and thoughts, loves and hatreds, were directed at him. . . . He was full

colored and brilliant—all outside of him was pale." But it is
not even *this* Victor who is murdered, for Steinbeck takes
great pains to demonstrate by Victor's lines in the last two
Acts of the book that his character has changed because of
his contact with Mordeen. His speech progresses from "jokebook wisdom" to the most poetic language in the book, as
when he considers Mordeen's suggestion that he go away:
"I can say with my mind that I will go—but I would refuse
it. That I know. For I think of the summer ending now and
the stubble on the ground and the hay brushing the ridge
pole in the barn and windfall apples on the orchard earth.
And you—a swelling below your breasts and my child kicking
against the soft wall, and turning, and I not able to put my
hand there and feel its moving life." It is *this* Victor, whom
Mordeen has used as a stud and now wishes to put away,
the Victor who really tries "to stand by like a cuckolded goat
and see my woman and my child in Joe Saul's arms," who is
given a "crunching blow" on the head by Friend Ed and
dumped overboard to drown, an end which seems satisfactory
to all the other characters. In the play, an attempt is made
to mitigate these ethics by having Victor carried onto an
outbound ship after being knocked unconscious. Also, in the
play it is he who villainously suggests the physical examination which proves Joe Saul's sterility. These are makeshift
improvements on a basically inadequate idea. In *Burning
Bright* the brotherhood of man is asserted by denying both
his physical and spiritual fatherhood.

Steinbeck tells us that he tried to give his theme "a universality of experience" by placing the story "in the hands of
three professions which have long and continuing traditions,
namely the Circus, the Farm and the Sea." [5] Each of the
three Acts has a different setting, in the above order, and
that setting is particularized by the characters' changing

occupations and by the references in their speech. These three Acts are tied together by the story, which progresses unbroken, and the numerous references are all in terms of the current Act. Thus Uncle Will is mentioned as being killed by a fall from the high-wire in Act One and by a tractor in Act Two; in Act Three he is presumably lost at sea. The huge Christmas tree which is brought in at the end of Act Two becomes the little tree on the mantel in the opening of Act Three. But while this device is well handled and does not seem awkward, it does seem an unnecessary bit of stage conjuring. It is too superficial a device to give the desired effect of universality. There was more universality in the simple bunkhouse of *Of Mice and Men*. The order of the scenes (air-land-sea) may have been intended to retrace the course of man's evolution, underlining his unity as a species, but while this may be perceived on scrutiny it is not a functioning part of the actual work.

This expressionistic handling of the structure of *Burning Bright* has a parallel in the handling of time. After learning that Mordeen is pregnant, early in Act Two, Joe Saul and Friend Ed leave for town to get things for a party. There follows a long conversation between Mordeen and Victor (twelve pages). By means of dialogue and description (the latter translatable as stage effects), the last three pages of this conversation are made to span a time of about eight months, at the end of which Joe Saul and Friend Ed re-enter with a huge Christmas tree, which has now become the object of their last exit. This time is telescoped by references to the changing weather in the author's narration and a picking up of these details in the characters' lines. This scene had to be completely rewritten for the play because too much weight was carried by the author's narration. In fact, the essential failure of *Burning Bright* as a play-novelette is indicated here as everywhere by the extensive revisions which were necessary for the stage. Steinbeck's previous play-novelettes, *Of Mice and Men* and even *The Moon Is Down,* were played right from the book with very little revision. In *Burning Bright,* however, the elements of drama make the book awkward as a novelette and the elements of the novel-ette make it unfeasible as drama.

There is another reason for the failure of *Burning Bright,* one which goes much deeper and is a particularly puzzling one to find in Steinbeck. It is the failure of language. For an author who had in the past wielded this instrument with such versatility and power, making it the most distinguishing mark of his genius, this is a very serious sign of weakness. Stein-beck intended the language of *Burning Bright* to be "a kind of universal language not geared to the individual actors or their supposed crafts but rather the best I could produce." He thought that dramatic practice from Aeschylus through O'Neill had sanctioned this kind of language. It was not to sound like "ordinary speech, but rather by rhythm, sound, and image to give the clearest and best expression. . . . the attempt was to lift the story to the parable expression of the morality play." [6]

The real difficulty is not that the characters speak "a kind of universal language," as Steinbeck puts it (and whatever that may mean), but that this language is a kind of incredible hash of realism, coined archaisms, and poetic rhetoric. The closest thing to it in Steinbeck's works is found in the lan-guage of his first book, *Cup of Gold,* and indeed some of the images are taken right out of that early book—"the black-birds flocked nervously a week and now they are gone"; "the steel winter lay on the land and crept to the doors and win-dows and peered whitely in." The passages of simple conversation about daily affairs are studded with such synthetic gems as "wife-loss," "friend-right," "Friend Ed," and "very yes," which make the characters sound like nothing so much as members of an isolated and inbred religious group. Friend Ed remarks that Joe Saul's story of his grandfather would be "a strange telling for the children" and that his ancestors were "the only gay in that laughter-starving time [the Middle Ages]." Joe Saul wants to get Mordeen a present which will make her say, "Who would have thought that I would have a beauty thing like this." Joe Saul and Friend Ed (first and last names are always used) go out to "get the partiness—all cooked and carved and poured," along with "some little twist of a present." In the course of the play, Mordeen's "hard self-corners are smoothed."

These Gongorisms, arresting as they are, take on an added luster in their context, as when Mordeen confides to Victor that she is a good lover. "I know the tricks, techniques of duration, of position, games, perverse games to drive the nerves into a kind of hysterical laughter. . . . I've wondered how it is that one act can be ugly and mean and enervating, like a punishing drug, and also most beautiful and filled with energy, like milk." There is some bad prose in every Steinbeck novel, but in *Burning Bright* it is rampant.

Since *Burning Bright*, like *Yerma*, has sexual sterility for its theme, it is instructive to quote some of Lorca's "universal language" as a contrast. Yerma, wife of the sterile Juan, speaks of her desire for children. "For I'm hurt and humiliated beyond endurance, seeing the wheat ripening, the fountains never ceasing to give water, the sheep bearing hundreds of lambs, the she-dogs; until it seems the whole countryside rises to show me its tender sleeping young, while I feel two hammer-blows here, instead of the mouth of my child." [7]

Steinbeck does attempt this kind of expression, and sometimes it is successful, as when Joe Saul says of his unborn child, ". . . it will be a piece of me, and more, of all I came from—the blood stream, the pattern of me, of us, like a shining filament of spider silk hanging down from the incredible ages." This attempt is also evident when Joe Saul is trying to think of a suitable present for his pregnant wife—". . . something like a golden sacrament, some pearl like a prayer or a red flaring ruby of thanks. Some hard, tangible humility of mine that she can hold in the palm of her hand or wear dangling from a ribbon at her throat." But these passages are rare, and their effect is marred by their context. At one point Friend Ed, hearing that the child has moved in Mordeen's womb, says to Joe Saul, "and if you want to feel a real rumpus, you have twins sometime. I think they play volley ball." Later, Mordeen tells Joe Saul that her child has shifted in the womb and that "he will sleep until he has to make the big fight." These and other laugh-getters were cut from the stage version. It is this kind of insensitivity to texture which is the main reason for the failure of *Burning Bright.*

Although at first Steinbeck was puzzled by the failure of his play-novelette, he came to see the deficiencies of the book, and he did not include it in *The Short Novels of John Steinbeck* (October, 1953). Four years after the book's failure, he admitted in a private conversation that the play was a failure in writing, that it was too abstract, that it preached too much, and that the audience was always a step ahead of it.[8] At the time he wrote *Burning Bright* Steinbeck was very busy with *Viva Zapata*, with his piece "About Ed Ricketts," and, especially, with work on his new novel, *East of Eden.* It is doubtful that *Burning Bright* represented the best work he could do.

While not aesthetically significant, *Burning Bright* is an

interesting Steinbeck novel because it reveals in positive terms his mystic conception of the unity of all life in the group animal, especially as this conception was presented in *To a God Unknown, The Grapes of Wrath,* and *Sea of Cortez.* This is the awareness to which Joe Saul is brought in the last scene of *Burning Bright:* "It is the race, the species that must go staggering on. Mordeen, our ugly little species, weak and ugly, torn with insanities, violent and quarrelsome, sensing evil—the only species that knows evil and practices it—the only one that senses cleanliness and is dirty, that knows about cruelty and is unbearably cruel."

The new tone of *Burning Bright,* which was to be maintained in *East of Eden,* had been hinted at in the affirmative journey of *The Wayward Bus.* That these two books initiated a new departure for the author is explicit in his correspondence with Pascal Covici and the entries in the journal he started keeping while working on these books. To a suggestion that he make a play out of *Cannery Row,* Steinbeck replied, "I'm not going to do it. . . . I have finished that whole phase." (JS-PC, 8/2/50) About this time also, he wrote in his journal a new manifesto for himself as a writer.

The writers of today, even I, have a tendency to celebrate the destruction of the spirit and God knows it is destroyed often enough. It is the duty of the writer to lift up, to extend, to encourage. If the written word has contributed anything at all to our developing species and our half developed culture, it is this—great writing has been a staff to lean on, a mother to consult, a wisdom to pick up stumbling folly, a strength in weakness and a courage to support weak cowardice. And how any despairing or negative approach can pretend to be literature, I do not know. It is true that we are weak and sick and ugly and quarrelsome but if that is all we ever were, we would, millenniums ago have disappeared from the face of the earth and a few remnants of fossilized jawbones, a few teeth in strata of limestone would be the only mark our species would have left on the earth.[9]

It was in this spirit that Steinbeck was writing his next book—*East of Eden.*

15 ⎰ East of Eden

Having asserted in *The Wayward Bus* his belief that despite the "weak and sick and ugly and quarrelsome" nature of man, this six-cylinder world does go on, and having made the point in *Burning Bright* that "so long as human beings exist anywhere every man is immortal," Steinbeck went on in *East of Eden* to insist at great length that every man has the power to choose between good and evil.

As the title suggests ("And Cain went out from the presence of the Lord, and dwelt in the land of Nod, on the east of Eden."), the vehicle for this theme is a reworking of the Cain and Abel story, told through three generations of the Trask family. Steinbeck sees this story in Genesis as a true account of man's condition, especially as made clear in the Lord's words to Cain after rejecting his sacrifice: "If thou doest well, shalt thou not be accepted? and if thou doest not well, sin lieth at the door. And unto thee shall be his desire, and thou shalt rule over him." Steinbeck grounds his interpretation of the story on a new translation of the Hebrew word *timshel,* which the King James version renders as "thou shalt." He proposes that the word is more meaningfully and truly rendered as "thou *mayest,*" for this gives man responsible moral choice, the dignity of free will—"thou mayest rule over him [sin]."

Although the story of Cain and Abel is the novel's main theme, what it is intended to be essentially *about,* a great deal of the book is taken up with an accurate, factual account of Steinbeck's own maternal family, the Hamiltons, and the author himself appears sporadically in the novel as the narrator "I," as "me," and as "John." The explanation for this agglutination of materials, and the book's essential failure, lies in the history of the novel's composition.

Steinbeck's original plan for *East of Eden* was "to set down in story form for his two small sons the full record of their ancestors from the time they moved westward to Salinas Valley just after the Civil War." [1] Thus the first draft of *East of Eden* begins, "Dear Tom and John: You are little boys now, when I am writing this," and many passages are addressed directly to his children as readers. In a short introduction to this first draft, which Steinbeck intended for Pascal Covici, his editor at Viking, he further explains that "Salinas Valley," as the book was first called, "will be two books—the story of my country and the story of me." Part of Steinbeck's preparations for this family saga set against the Salinas Valley background consisted of extensive research in the files of Salinas Valley newspapers, particularly the *Salinas Index,* and conversations with old-timers in the area. (JS-PC, 2/24/48)

Somewhere in the early stages of this family saga, how

ever, Steinbeck introduced a fictional family, the Trasks, and he soon found himself at the mercy of his materials. The importance of the Trask family in the novel grew until the author realized that he had a far different book on his hands from what he had originally conceived, one which centered on the Trasks and not on the Hamiltons, Steinbeck's maternal family. By this time, however, the two families were inextricably entangled, and the author decided to keep them that way, but reduced the story of his own family to its vestigial elements and struck out all the special passages written to his sons.[2]

Steinbeck began work on his book in 1947, and as late as March of 1949 he was still thinking of it in terms of "Salinas Valley." (JS-PC, 3/23/49) It was not until two years later that the book's new theme was acknowledged by a change in title—to *East of Eden*. (JS-PC, 6/22/51) Other indications that the book's change in emphasis from the personal family saga to the biblical theme took place at this time are evident in Pascal Covici's letter to the author acknowledging receipt of the chapter on Adam and Cathy (PC-JS, 7/10/51), and also in Steinbeck's frequent requests during this period for materials on the Bible. Part Four of *East of Eden* was begun in August of 1951, when Steinbeck wrote to his editor, "It is a book in itself and could be set alone except of course for background. It will have its own pace and tone." [3] The final draft was ready in the spring of 1952, and *East of Eden* was published in September of that year.

Steinbeck's attempts to impose an order on his diverse materials proved unsuccessful, and many reviewers pointed out that because he tried to say too many things at once, Steinbeck failed to achieve fictional concentration. As the reviewer for *Time* so succinctly put it, "perhaps Steinbeck should have stuck to his original idea of telling just the family history. As it stands, *East of Eden* is a huge grab bag. . . ." [4]

The dissenting voices were few, but they included the French critic Claude-Edmonde Magny, Mark Schorer, and Joseph Wood Krutch. Mme. Magny found in the book a "special type of coherence, which is not in the least novelistic," [5] and Mr. Krutch thought that never, "not even in *The Grapes of Wrath*," had Steinbeck "exhibited such a grasp upon himself and upon his materials." [6] Mark Schorer, like Mme. Magny, found a new kind of unity in *East of Eden*: ". . . yet the tone of this book, the bold ease with which the 'I' takes over at the outset and appears and disappears and reappears throughout, both holds it together and gives it its originality, the relaxations of its freedom." [7]

It is instructive to examine the reviews of Mark Schorer and Joseph Wood Krutch in a little more detail, for they contain a certain ambivalance which is an accurate index to the peculiar effect of Steinbeck's novel, one of both greatness and failure. For example, although both critics praise the author's grasp on his materials, they also admit doubts about the book's structure. At the end of the review Mr. Krutch poses an unanswered question which might well have been the basis of his discussion: "On the highest level the question is this: Does the fable really carry the thesis; is the moral implicit in or merely imposed upon the story: has the author created a myth or merely moralized a tale?" Mr. Schorer not only remarks on "the gap between speculative statement and novelistic presentation," but points out elements of "sentimentalism" and "melodrama." At times this critic's remarks convey the impression that he is trying to talk himself into something: "This account of the book's style and themes may suggest a kind of eclectic irresolution of view which is, in fact, not at all the quality of the book. . . . I am trying to praise the audaciousness with which this novelist asserts his temperament. . . ." Comparing the novel with other Steinbeck works, Mr. Schorer admits that *East of Eden* is, "in a sense, more amorphous, less intent on singleness of theme and effect," while at the same time he asserts that it is "the best of John Steinbeck's novels." It is interesting that three years later Mr. Schorer refused to allow his review to be reprinted in Tedlock and Wicker's collection of Steinbeck criticism (*Steinbeck and His Critics*), saying that, after rereading the novel, he found the review totally mistaken in judgment and regretted its publication.[8] The paradox in this kind of criticism is a close approximation of what Steinbeck himself wrote to his editor while *East of Eden* was in progress: "It's a kind of sloppy sounding book, but it is not sloppy really." (JS-PC, 3/15/51)

Even a casual reading, however, will reveal just how sloppy, or to use Mr. Schorer's terms, how "audacious" is Steinbeck's "eclectic irresolution of view." Of the Hamilton family, only Samuel and Will, Steinbeck's maternal grandfather and uncle, respectively, become in any way involved with the Trasks. Samuel first meets Adam Trask on page 140, and dies halfway through the novel. He sees the Trasks only four times. Will's only contacts with the Trasks consist of three short scenes. In one of these he sells them a Ford, in another he has a short and unimportant conversation with Adam in a lunch wagon, and in the third he accepts Caleb Trask as a short-term partner in a bean-growing venture. Except for these contacts and a brief visit by Liza, Samuel's wife, the Trasks and the Hamiltons pursue separate courses, and nothing *results* from their juxtaposition. There is not the organic relationship between these parts of the novel that there is between the scenic and panoramic sections of *The Grapes of Wrath*, or even the parallels and contrasts which exist among the separate sections of *Cannery Row, Tortilla Flat,* and *The Pastures of Heaven.* Steinbeck simply shifts back and forth between the Trasks and the Hamiltons with no apparent purpose or method, and his efforts to keep the two stories abreast result in many awkward flashbacks and lacunae. After delivering the Trask twins, Samuel does not see the family again until a year later, when he names the boys. The next time he visits Adam Trask the boys are eleven years old.

The domestic problems of the Hamiltons and their eight children—George, Will, Tom, Joe, Una, Lizzie, Dessie, Mollie, Olive (Steinbeck's mother)—are given in detail. Some of these anecdotes, such as the death of Dessie, the suicide of Tom, and Olive's airplane ride, are interesting in themselves, but at no point do they contribute to some greater purpose, and they remain essentially distracting and unintegrated fragments.

In addition to this peripheral contact between the two families, as a device for pulling the book together, Steinbeck also makes use of the narrator "I" to interlard the objectively rendered details of plot with moral essays in the manner of Thackeray. What makes this device particularly unsuccessful is that whereas Thackeray wisely kept himself and his family out of the action, remaining a detached commentator on a moral tale, the narrator "I" in *East of Eden* is confused with the "me" and the "John" and the "my" and the "we" of the actual narrative. By far the greater part of the book is not told by the autobiographical "I" at all, since it concerns events which he not only could not have witnessed, but could not even have heard about. This "I" is plainly a vestigial element from the first draft of the book as a family saga addressed to his children, and is ill-mated to the "I" as narrator. Finally, this "I" (whether narrative or autobiographical) comes up so infrequently (about twenty times in six hundred pages) and so briefly that no permanent association with the story is created. Each time it appears it effects a momentary shock of intrusion. The novel is in no sense dominated or given form by its narrator, and the narrator is in no sense defined by the novel. He is merely the third major fragment.

The moral philosophy of the narrator is no more convincing than its structural function, and at times seems to be in direct variance with the action. While Samuel and the Chinese servant, Lee, explicate the Cain and Abel story, and thus the Trask story, as giving evidence of man's free will in choosing between good and evil, Lee later denies free will to Adam Trask: "He couldn't help it, Cal. That's his nature. It was the only way he knew. He didn't have any choice." The author himself denies free will to the novel's most wicked character—Cathy: "And just as there are physical monsters, can there not be mental or psychic monsters born? The face and body may be perfect, but if a twisted gene or a malformed egg can produce physical monsters, may not the same process produce a malformed soul? . . . . It is my belief that Cathy was born with the tendencies, or lack of them, which drove and forced her all her life. Some balance wheel was misweighted, some gear out of ratio. She was not like other people, never was from birth."

That the author is truly confused on this question of free will is evident in other moral essays scattered throughout the book and in the fact that the reader learns, quite suddenly near the end of the novel, that the monster, Cathy, has become a religious penitent (Episcopal) and has committed suicide because of moral loneliness, leaving a great fortune to her "Abel" son, Aaron. This fortune amounts to over a hundred thousand dollars, the same sum that Cyrus left his sons and that Charles left Adam.

The Cain and Abel theme fares much better as it is worked out in Caleb, who inherits both good and evil and in whom a genuine moral struggle takes place. As Steinbeck wrote to Pascal Covici while working on the last section of the book, "He is the everyman, the battleground between good and evil, the most human of all, the sorry man. . . . In that battle the survivor is both." (JS-PC, 8/?/51) Unfortunately, Caleb's story takes up only a small part of the book.

Furthermore, Steinbeck is so anxious to make his theme evident that he badgers it into an uninteresting obviousness. All the Cain characters in the novel are identified by names beginning with "C" (Cyrus, Charles, Cathy, Caleb) and the Abel characters by names beginning with "A" (Alice, Adam, Aaron, Abra). The weighty paraphernalia of the "C" and "A" initials is made still more ponderous by the fact that both Cathy and Charles have livid scars on their foreheads. The mark on Cathy's forehead looks like "a huge thumbprint, even to whorls of wrinkled skin." The rejection of Cain's offering is presented twice, once in terms of a pocketknife and once in terms of fifteen thousand dollars. The crime of Cain is presented five times in the novel, once with Cathy and her parents (whose surname is Ames), twice with Charles and Adam, once with Cathy and Adam, and again with Caleb and Aaron. Although Adam rejects Samuel's suggestion that he name his twin sons Cain and Abel, which, as Samuel himself admits, "would be tempting whatever fate there is," it is supposed to be a coincidence that the names Caleb and Aaron are chosen instead. Cathy is so often described in terms of a serpent, from the shape of her features and her flickering tongue to her dislike of the light, that one suspects Steinbeck had been reading *Elsie Venner*. Charles explains to Adam, and to the reader, "I ought to be wandering around the world instead of sitting here on a good farm . . . ," and another time says of his scar, "It just seems like I was marked. And when I go into town, like to the inn, why, people are always looking at it. I can hear them talking about it. . . ." Both Charles and Caleb find occasion to ask, "Am I my brother's keeper?" There are possibly hundreds of such allusions to the details of those sixteen verses in Genesis which contain the story of Cain and Abel.

If a dozing reader should miss these hints, there are several longer passages in the book in which both the author and his characters discuss the Cain and Abel theme. Even four elderly Chinese (the youngest is over ninety) investigate the problem, spending two years learning Hebrew to translate one word. In fact, the sixteen verses of Genesis are read aloud by Samuel and interpreted by Lee just before Caleb and Aaron are named. Adam is not only fully aware of the significance of his name, but is consciously trying to make a new garden of Eden in a valley which, as Samuel discovers while drilling, lies over the remnant of "another world" which casts its shadow on the present one. Samuel also associates the buried meteorite (falling star, hence Lucifer) which wrecks his well drill with Cathy, who bites his hand while he is helping her give birth to her twin sons, on the same day he discovers the meteorite. Steinbeck keeps worrying his theme until there is nothing left for his or the reader's imagination.

To these faults of structure and theme must be added one other fault which, except for Steinbeck's first novel, had not been evident until *Burning Bright*—the failure of language. This difficulty is introduced into the novel by Samuel Hamilton: "I'll tell you now, quiet. In a bitter night, a mustard night that was last night, a good thought came and the dark was sweetened when the day sat down. And this thought went from evening star to the late dipper on the edge of the first light—that our betters spoke of. So I must invite myself." This blarney may be excused as coming from an old Irishman, but it seems to be a contagious language which infects the other characters—especially the Chinese Lee, who has attended the university at Berkeley for several years, smokes opium, and drinks wormwood, as well as quoting from "*The Meditations of Marcus Aurelius* in English translation." Even the author speaks in a kind of blarney reminiscent of *Burning Bright,* as when he says of a conversation between Charles and Adam, "All around the main subject the brothers beat." The scrambled syntax and awkward expression are evident everywhere. "He worked inhumanly, only to lose in effort his crushing impulses." "The wrinkles around them [his eyes] were drawn in radial lines inward by laughter." "But he didn't seem to care whether we caught trout or not. He needed not to triumph over animals." "Abra was a strong fine-breasted woman, developed and ready and waiting to take her sacrament—but waiting." "Oh, strawberries don't taste as they used to and the thighs of women have lost their clutch!" (given twice, pp. 129, 130).

Often, the author's language and tone are such as might be heard in a small-town post office: "Another man, but he was crazy, said that someday there'd be a way, maybe ice, maybe some other way, to get a peach like this here I got in my hand clear to Philadelphia." (Three hundred pages later the author decides to let Adam Trask undertake this venture.) At other times the author sounds like Charlie Chan's Number One Son: "In human affairs of danger and delicacy successful conclusion is sharply limited by hurry. So often men trip by being in a rush. If one were properly to perform a difficult and subtle act, he should first inspect the end to be achieved and then, once he had accepted the end as desirable, he should forget it completely and concentrate solely on the means. By this method he would not be moved to false action by anxiety or hurry or fear. Very few people learn this."

There are few passages of pure description in the six hundred odd pages of *East of Eden,* relatively fewer than in any other of his novels; but in these, too, which are usually among the best pieces of writing in Steinbeck's books, it is possible to see the failure of his language, as in this passage from the opening description:

> I remember that the Gabilan Mountains to the east of the valley were light gay mountains, full of sun and loveliness and a kind of invitation, so that you wanted to climb into their warm foothills almost as you want to climb into the lap of a beloved mother. They were beckoning with a brown grass love. . . . The whole valley floor, and the foothills too, would be carpeted with lupins and poppies. Once a woman told me that colored flowers would seem more bright if you added a few white flowers to give the colors definition. Every petal of blue lupin is edged with white, so that a field of lupins is more blue than you can imagine. And mixed with these were splashes of California poppies. These too are of a burning color—not orange, not gold, but if pure gold were liquid and could raise a cream, that golden cream might be like the color of the poppies.

It is not necessary to go back to *The Grapes of Wrath, Of Mice and Men, The Long Valley,* and other works of the thirties to find the antithesis of this baroque language. It is there in *The Pearl* and even in *The Wayward Bus,* where the color of poppies is not like the cream raised by gold (if it were a liquid and if it could raise a cream), but where after a rain the petals "lay on the ground like gold coins" (WB, 33), and "the lupins and poppies made a splendid blue and gold earth, when the great trees awakened in yellow-green young leaves. . . ." (WB, 12) Even the few descriptions of animal life in *East of Eden* suffer from this artificiality. "The coyotes nuzzled along the slopes and, torn with sorrow-joy, raised their heads and shouted their feelings, half keen, half laughter, at their goddess moon." Steinbeck's prose is not so much casual or careless as affected.

This affectation is the result of his attempt to exploit an aspect of prose style which, after his first novel, he had avoided until *Burning Bright*. Previous to this play-novelette, his mastery of prose styles could be attributed to his keen ear for the idioms and rhythms of speech (whether those of the *paisanos* of *Tortilla Flat*, the laborers of *In Dubious Battle*, or the folk of *The Pastures of Heaven*) and a fine sense of appropriate narrative style (the cold prose of *In Dubious Battle*, the poetic realism of the Jody stories and *The Pearl*, or the elevated periods and American rhythms of the interchapters in *The Grapes of Wrath*). In *East of Eden*, as in *Burning Bright*, Steinbeck's exploration of language as technique concerns itself almost exclusively with figurative language, and the result is disastrous: "The ranch was a relative, and when he left he plunged a knife into a darling." ". . . Tom got into a book, crawled and groveled between the covers, tunneled like a mole among the thoughts, and came up with the book all over his face and hands." "Tom raged crazily through the hills like a lion in horrible pain." "Liza Hamilton, her cheeks flaming red, moved like a caged leopard in front of the stove when Samuel came into the kitchen in the morning." For the most part, the prose of *East of Eden* alternates between this kind of pseudo-poetry and an abandoned, unstudied carelessness incapable of organizing the sprawling materials, and, because the narrator himself is so ambiguously defined, incapable of emphasizing them.

As the failure of prose style is allied to the failure of structure, so both are allied to the new emphasis on character. In *East of Eden,* for the first time since *Cup of Gold,* Steinbeck is concerned with his characters primarily as individuals who exist and have importance apart from the materials of his novel, for it is through them rather than through structure and language that he tries to establish his theme. While lesser novelists have succeeded with this method, Steinbeck fails because his characters are neither credible as individuals nor effective as types but are an incongruous mixture of both. Samuel is too much like the Old Testament prophets for one of whom he was named to be effective as a human being, and too much of a human being to be convincing as an Old Testament prophet. Lee is too much of a scholar to be a Chinese servant, and too much the stereotype of a Chinese servant to be the learned man he is. Cathy is too much like Satan to be a credible human being, and too much like a weak, pitiful human being to be properly Satanic. The same sort of ambivalence can be discerned in most of Steinbeck's cast—Cyrus, Charles, Caleb, Adam, and Abra.

Where Steinbeck does succeed is with the portraits of minor characters and of his maternal family—excepting Samuel Hamilton, who is nevertheless more credible and effective than any of the other major characters. These are successful because they are drawn from memory, with no attempt to make them fit into a myth or illustrate a type. Unfortunately, these warm, credible human beings are in no way involved in the novel's narrative. The element of greatness which both Joseph Wood Krutch and Mark Schorer noted in their reviews might have been brought to fulfillment in a subtle fusion of *East of Eden*'s imposing theme and its more credible human beings and events—a fusion which is not accomplished in the novel.

The generally favorable reception of *East of Eden* is an amazing phenomenon in Steinbeck criticism, because whereas commentators had gone to ridiculous extremes in finding highly technical faults with his earlier well-made novels, they now bent over backward to celebrate the excellence of his latest book by avoiding all technical considerations and exulting over its great moral theme. While in the early stages of the novel, Steinbeck had feared that the critics would be "very angry with the *Salinas Valley* because it will be even more unlike *Of Mice and Men*. They catch up very late." (JS-PC, 3/23/49) Ironically, it is an approval of this change which underlies not only the favorable reviews of Schorer and Krutch, but even those reviews which were otherwise unfavorable. "In this novel," wrote one critic, "John Steinbeck wrestles with a moral theme for the first time in his career. . . ." [9] Another critic thought he observed in the novel "a definite advance in Steinbeck's thinking which has been defined by Edmund Wilson as too barely naturalistic." [10] Joseph Henry Jackson believed that "*East of Eden* reflects a Steinbeck who has now put past him something [his biological view of man] which once . . . threatened to close him in, to narrow him as a creative writer. . . . he has been thinking more deeply than ever before about life and the human beings who live it." [11]

The only important dissenting voice in this chorus exalting moral theme over art was that of Arthur Mizener who, also perceiving the new departure in *East of Eden*, went directly to the heart of the matter. Far from seeing hope in Steinbeck's overt concern with moral theme, Mizener advised that the author return again to the world of *The Long Valley* and *The Red Pony*: "There is evidence even in *East of Eden* of what is quite clear from Steinbeck's earlier work, that so long as he sticks to animals and children and to situations he can see to some purpose from the point of view of his almost biological feeling for the continuity of life he can release the considerable talent and sensitivity which are naturally his. As soon as he tries to see adult experience in the usual way and to find the familiar kind of moral in it, the insight and talent cease to work and he writes like the author of any third-rate best seller." [12]

This shift in emphasis, which was noted by most reviewers, whether favorably or unfavorably, and which actually began with *The Wayward Bus,* is undoubtedly the most important change in Steinbeck's work since the beginning of his career twenty-three years earlier. It is impossible to agree with the author when he says of *East of Eden,* "I think everything else I have written has been, in a sense, practice for this. . . . If *East of Eden* isn't good, then I've been wasting my time. It has in it everything I have been able to learn about my art or craft or profession in all these years." [13] Actually, there is very little in *East of Eden* which goes back further than *Burning Bright.* Mr. Mizener's suggestion that Steinbeck return to *The Long Valley* and *The Red Pony* may be extreme, but it is certain that the new direction of *Burning Bright* and *East of Eden* had disastrous consequences for his art.

16 ⎱ *Sweet Thursday*
   ⎰ *The Short Reign of Pippin IV*
     Some Conclusions

Just a year and a half after his pontifical sermon on the theme of Cain and Abel, extended to six hundred pages by reminiscences of his maternal family, Steinbeck published *Sweet Thursday*, on which was based the libretto for a musical comedy. This change of pace, which disconcerted those critics who saw in *East of Eden* a moral rebirth, had been in Steinbeck's mind.while he was still a year from completing *East of Eden*, when he wrote to his editor that he wanted to do a comedy next, possibly in play form. (JS-PC, 7/17/51) In an interview shortly after the publication of *East of Eden*, Steinbeck remarked, "I'm so fascinated by everything about the theatre I don't really care if the show's a flop." [1] A year later it was reported that Steinbeck was well into a new short novel, which would be converted into a musical for the sponsors of *Guys and Dolls*. *Sweet Thurs-*

day's origin as a musical comedy is also attested by the fact that the title was decided upon after Pascal Covici informed the author that Rodgers and Hammerstein were already writing a song by that name. (PC-JS, 2/?/54) Earlier the book had been announced variously as "The Palace Flophouse" and "The Bear Flag Restaurant," two institutions made famous by *Cannery Row*. (JS-PC, 1/15/54; 1/25/54) The Rodgers and Hammerstein adaptation of *Sweet Thursday* was called *Pipe Dream* and opened at the Sam S. Shubert Theatre on December 19, 1955, with Helen Traubel in the role of Fauna, the new madam of the Bear Flag Restaurant. It was an instant popular success.

That *Sweet Thursday* is a sequel to *Cannery Row* is made evident by the first two sentences of the "Prologue": "One night Mack lay back on his bed in the Palace Flophouse and he said, 'I ain't never been satisfied with that book *Cannery Row*. I would have went about it different.'" The first chapter, "What Happened In Between," brings the reader up to date. Lee Chong has been replaced by Joseph and Mary Rivas; Dora Flood has died, and her place as madam of the Bear Flag has been taken by an older sister, Fauna. Gay, too, is dead, killed by anti-aircraft fallback in London. The remaining characters—Doc, Mack, Hazel, Whitey—have been augmented by Old Jingleballicks, Whitey No. 2, and Joe Elegant, the writer.

Although *Sweet Thursday* is a return to the characters and locale of *Cannery Row* and utilizes the same basic plot of that community's efforts to throw a party for Doc, it is as essentially different from *Cannery Row* as that novel was from the earlier *Tortilla Flat*. For one thing, whereas the plots of the two earlier novels are tenuous and the principle of structure is primarily tonal and thematic, the plot of *Sweet Thursday* is strong and organizes most of the material.

This dependence on plot, however, results in the comparative isolation of the relatively few interchapters (two of them clearly marked as "Hooptedoodle") because the strategy of theme is not adequate for making them part of the total material.

Because *Sweet Thursday* was written in the spirit of modern musical comedy, it is unrewarding to subject it to those criteria of formal analysis applied to major literature. Some of the unintegrated episodes, such as the refusal of Whitey No. 2 to take a mass loyalty oath with some country club members for whom he caddies, Joe Elegant's struggles with his very symbolic novel, *The Pi Root of Oedipus* (in which the grandmother stands for guilt, the reality below the reality), and Joseph and Mary Rivas' cultivation of marijuana in the public gardens which he tended, have a genuine satiric thrust. The chapters called "The Great Roque War," "There's a Hole in Reality. . . ." and "Hooptedoodle (2) . . ." recapture that sense of parable which informed so much of *Cannery Row* and *Tortilla Flat.* But for the real significance of *Sweet Thursday* and its relationship to Steinbeck's work nothing is so instructive as examining in detail the great changes which the book effects in one of the author's most constant and important symbols—Doc, the marine biologist.

Doc first appeared in Steinbeck's work in a short story called "The Snake" (1935), but he was not clearly defined until his appearance as Doc Burton in *In Dubious Battle* (1936), where he expresses his philosophy of disinterested observation and his theory that biological and sociological phenomena are subject to the same immutable laws. The detailed reiteration of these views in Steinbeck's letters, in *Sea of Cortez,* and in "About Ed Ricketts" leaves no doubt that for the author Doc was a mask, a *persona,* through whom he expressed his own attitudes and beliefs. It was the implicit assumption of this *persona* by Steinbeck in *In Dubious Battle, Of Mice and Men,* and *The Grapes of Wrath* which enabled him to deal so effectively with material which might easily have lent itself to sentimental or propagandistic treatment.

Although Doc was not created as a character until 1935, Steinbeck had met Ed Ricketts in 1930, and it was his assumption of the biologist's personality as early as 1933 that had enabled Steinbeck to balance so neatly the multiple suggestions concerning man's relationship to nature which were embodied by the various characters in *To a God Unknown.* It was this same objective approach which two years later enabled him to pose his essentially sentimental approval of the *paisanos* in *Tortilla Flat* against a sustaining mock-epic tone. Insofar as *The Moon Is Down* (1942) was a failure, the reason lay in the fact that in this work Steinbeck carried scientific objectivity too far, as he almost did again in *The Wayward Bus* (1947).

In *Cannery Row* (1945), which for obvious reasons was dedicated to Ed Ricketts, Doc received further definition. To his love of science was added a love of mankind, but a love which was in perfect accord with his ecological and non-teleological thinking. He enjoyed the antics of Mack and the boys and could think of them as "your true philosophers," but he did not identify himself with them. "In spite of his friendliness and his friends Doc was a lonely man. . . . In a group, Doc seemed always alone." (CR, 91) He was indulgent of his friends' tastes, but did not share their pleasures—whether social, sexual, literary, or alcoholic. As a *persona* for the author, Doc retained his distance. *The Pearl,* written in the same year, owed its success to this same equipoise between sentiment and objectivity.

In *Sweet Thursday* all this is changed, a fact which Steinbeck calls to our attention in Chapter 3, "Hooptedoodle (1)": "Doc was changing in spite of himself, in spite of the prayers of his friends, in spite of his own knowledge." ". . . now the worm of discontent was gnawing at him." "And so Doc threw himself into his work, hoping, the way a man will, to smother the unease with weariness." Doc's efforts to lose himself in work do not succeed. "And sometimes, starting to turn over a big rock in the Great Tide Pool—a rock under which he knew there would be a community of frantic animals—he would drop the rock back in place and stand, hands on hips, looking off to sea. . . ." He begins a scientific paper called "Symptoms in Some Cephalopods Approximating Apoplexy," but cannot sustain his scientific attention. While peering through his microscope or observing his octopi in the aquarium, he is always conscious of a voice "from his marrow" saying, "Lonesome! Lonesome! What good is it? Who benefits? Thought is the evasion of feeling."

On one level, *Sweet Thursday* is a definition of this change in Doc and an account of how his happiness is restored. The first analysis of Doc's difficulties is made by Mack: "Doc acts like a guy that needs a dame. . . . He needs a dame around. He needs a dame to fight with." The reader familiar with *Cannery Row* is inclined to think this a very poor analysis indeed, but Mack's suggestion is supported by Fauna, the "seer," the author, and finally Doc himself. The remaining two hundred and fifty pages of the book are devoted to a grotesque intrigue for uniting Doc with Suzy (a young hustler from Fauna's whorehouse) and to Doc's gradual realization that this is exactly what he wanted and needed most. In the process of coming to this realization he takes her boxes of chocolates, hangs around in the shadows at night to get a glimpse of her, worries about not having a proper necktie, engages in mortal combat with a man he suspects of being a rival, and gets an arm broken by a softball bat. And while these musical comedy antics are going on, the author leaves no doubt that he intends the reader to take this love affair as seriously as does Doc:

> "What did Bach have that I am hungry for to the point of starvation? Wasn't it gallantry? And isn't gallantry the great art of the soul? Is there any more noble quality in the human than gallantry?" He stopped and then suddenly he seemed to be wracked with inner tears. "Why didn't I know before?" he asked. "I, who admire it so, didn't even recognize it when I saw it. Old Bach had his talent and his family and his friends. Everyone has something. And what has Suzy got? Absolutely nothing in the world but guts. She's taken on an atomic world with a slingshot, and, by God, she's going to win! If she doesn't win there's no point in living any more. . . . I'm warming myself at her gallantry. Let me face this clearly, please! I need her to save myself. I can be whole only with Suzy."

By the end of the novel Doc is not only saved and made whole by being united with Suzy, the reformed whore who is going to be his inspiration and help, he is also awarded a research grant to work at the California Institute of Technology, given an opportunity to read his paper before a learned society, and presented with a telescope (*sic*) by Mack and the boys. Musical comedy could go no further.

On another level, what makes all of this so interesting to the student of Steinbeck is that in Doc's surrender to romantic love it is possible to see Steinbeck's own capitulation to his materials, as suggested by the fact that the personality of Doc had been the author's mask in every book from *The Pastures of Heaven* up to *Burning Bright*. Even more specifically, this capitulation is suggested by Doc's attitude toward *his* materials—marine biology. He is no longer capable of the sustained attention required for his work. He takes every excuse to malinger and is genuinely relieved when his specimens die. "He had worn thin the excuse of his lack of a proper microscope. When the last octopus died he leaped on this as his excuse. . . . 'you see, I can't go on without specimens, and I can't get any more until the spring tides. As soon as I have specimens and a new microscope I can whip the paper right off.' "

It is difficult not to see these changes in Doc's attitude toward life and toward his work as corresponding to shifts in Steinbeck's own attitude. The relationship of Doc and marine biology is just as significant and symbolic to Steinbeck as that of the bullfighter and the art of bullfighting or the fisherman and his fish is to Hemingway. At the present point in Steinbeck's career it is difficult to see clearly just what the degradation of Doc signifies, though certain speculations are interesting. It may well be that in *Sweet Thursday* Steinbeck is purposefully trying to destroy or depreciate his former mask because he now feels that he has (as a writer, at least) exhausted the possibilities of that mask. On the other hand, Steinbeck may be merely modifying that mask to make it a closer expression of his present attitudes, attitudes which would have been disapproved of by the original Doc, Ed Ricketts. Finally, it is also possible, though hardly probable, that Steinbeck has truly lost contact with the original, vital purpose of his mask or *persona* and is unaware of the violence done to the figure of Doc. Whichever of these explanations be correct, and there is evidence for each in Steinbeck's last four novels, it is certain that the destruction of Doc symbolizes a new period in Steinbeck's art, a period which began with *Burning Bright* and was intimated in *The Wayward Bus*.

The capitulation of Doc to the manners of a musical comedy is reflected in the changes undergone by certain other standard characters. It is discovered that all his life Lee Chong had "wanted to go trading in the South Seas," and that one day he had bought a schooner, loaded the entire stock of his store in the hold, and set sail. "And the last anyone saw of him, he was waving his blue naval cap from the flying bridge of his dream ship as he passed the whistle buoy at Point Pinos into the sunset." Although the new owner of Chong's store has a long police record and is congenitally incapable of entertaining even the notion of honesty or altruism, he is so free with his beer, whiskey, and cash that only his illegal activities keep him solvent. In *To a God Unknown*, Steinbeck described an old man who lived by the sea and who offered sacrifices to the setting sun as a way of relating himself to nature. "In the moment, I am the sun. Do you see? I, through the beast, am the sun. I burn in his death." (TGU, 266) In *Sweet Thursday*, this old man appears as a crackpot seer who has visions of mermaids and steals candy bars from grocery stores. He retains some of his ritual feeling for the sun, but it seems motivated by adjustment psychology. "I've come to the point where I don't think it can go down without me. That makes me seem needed." And his metaphysics have shifted their ground from mystic concepts of the unity of all life to the doctrine of romantic love, which he prescribes for Doc. In *Cannery Row*, Steinbeck used Mrs. Malloy's desire to glue a pair of white curtains on the walls of the windowless boiler in which she lived as a parable of the senseless frustration avoided by Mack and the boys. In *Sweet Thursday*, Suzy, who now occupies the same boiler, is obviously approved of by both Steinbeck and Doc for gluing to the walls a pair of pink cottage curtains with blue flowers—". . . what a brave thing is the human!"

The important thing about *Sweet Thursday* is not that it is an inferior novel, as almost all reviewers noted,[2] but that through the treatment of certain personal symbols Steinbeck seems to confirm that relaxation of attention, that surrender, which first became evident in *Burning Bright*, where it resulted in an irresponsible sentimentality, and in *East of Eden*, where it resulted in a disintegration of form.

Beginning in 1943 with his dispatches from the European War Theater, an increasing proportion of Steinbeck's energies have been devoted to journalism—and a journalism far removed from such terse, hard-hitting, informed writing of the 1930's as "The Harvest Gypsies" and "Dubious Battle in California." Whereas these earlier pieces seemed to spring from a deep inner conviction, Steinbeck's recent journalism seems motivated by the necessity to make a living.

Out of his trips to the Continent have come such articles as "How to Fish in French" (*Punch*); "Vegetable War," a criticism of the way the English cook Brussels sprouts; "Yank in Europe," a defense of the manners of American tourists in Paris; and many similar items. For such periodicals as *Holiday, Collier's, Saturday Review,* and *Ford Times,* he has written "Trust Your Luck," on the need for instilling optimism in children; "Mail I've Seen," a discussion of his fan letters; "Random Thoughts on Random Dogs," noting the similarity usually found between the physical appearance of a dog and his master; "Jalopies I Cursed and Loved"; "A Model T Named 'It'"; and "My War with the Ospreys," an account of his attempts to revenge himself on two birds for not building a nest near his summer home at Sag Harbor.

The intellectual level of this recent journalism can be

gauged by the following quotation from "Yank in Europe": "I, myself, have had to learn not to blame all American tourists for the ugliness of one. I know some pretty bad Frenchmen, some Italians of outrageous conduct, and some ugly British but this does not cause me to hold the French and Italians and British in contempt. A wormy peach does not make me hate the peach tree." [3] It is to this level of expression that Steinbeck's sympathies have descended, that of a third-rate popular journalist.

Evidence of this surrender of artistic integrity is everywhere. In his "Introduction" to *The World of Li'l Abner* (1953), Steinbeck found it necessary to say, "I get interviewed by lean and hungry Yurrpeens [sic] now and then and they always want me to say who is the best writer in America today and I can't think of any name but Capp." On the next page he thinks that Al Capp "may very possibly be the best writer in the world today. I am sure he is the best satirist since Laurence Sterne." A little further on, Capp is compared favorably with Cervantes and Rabelais, and his "high-faluting, shimmering, gorgeous prose" is admired.

Many of Steinbeck's recent articles have been of a political nature—"Madison Avenue and the Election," "How to Tell Good Guys from Bad Guys," "The Death of a Racket" —and this interest, combined with his firsthand knowledge of France, has resulted in *The Short Reign of Pippin IV* (1957), the last of Steinbeck's works to be considered in this study. This novelette, subtitled "A Fabrication," is, as the dust jacket announces, the story of "what happens to a retiring middle-aged astronomer suddenly drafted to rule the unruly French; of his teen-age, glamour-struck daughter and her American swain, son of the Egg King of Petaluma, California; and of sundry members of the ancient nobility, art dealers, nuns, guards, gardeners, politicians, and plain people." Here at last Steinbeck has come full circle, back to the topical satire of his juvenilia—the short stories and poems published in *The Stanford Spectator* and the *Stanford Lit* while he was an undergraduate, and the eight poems published in the *Monterey Beacon* in 1935.

Unlike *Tortilla Flat*, *Cannery Row*, and *Sweet Thursday*, this new "Fabrication" came as no shock to those readers who had been following Steinbeck's career since *Burning Bright*. A serious writer who turns to the kind of journalism exemplified by "How to Fish in French" and "Vegetable War," has either lost the distinction between literature and cheap journalism or has willingly embraced the latter. The difficulty is not that there is very little of the old Steinbeck in *The Short Reign of Pippin IV*, but that it is anybody's potboiler.

Actually, almost every Steinbeck theme, character, and attitude reappears in this "frothy extravaganza," as the publishers call it. But they are there as old props and gimmicks rather than as the novelist's materials. His casual attitude toward sex is presented through Sister Hyacinthe, who used to dance in the nude at the Folies Bergère but had to take holy orders because her feet hurt. It is she who discourses on the value of laziness. Steinbeck's group-man theory is exemplified by the citizens' fickleness and mob spirit. His concept of "physical memory" comes up in the parable of the city-bred pointer's reactions when first let loose in the country. The idea that "it is the misfortune of men to want to do a thing well, even a thing they do not want to do at all" is presented by Pippin himself, who is a scientist of sorts—an amateur astronomer. Such shrewd shopkeepers as Torrelli and Lee Chong are present in Uncle Charlie, who runs an art shop. Doc's willingness to be fooled as long as he knows about it is ascribed to the Egg King of Petaluma. The various wise hermits and seers are present in the lonely old man who pulls statuary out of the moat and who answers Pippin's question of "Good or bad?" as did Casy in *The Grapes of Wrath*—"I don't understand. There's just people —just what people do."

More important than what is present of the earlier Steinbeck in *The Short Reign of Pippin IV*, though in terms of clichés, is what is not present. There is none of the concern with technique and form. The materials are fragmentary, and the prose is that of a conventional storyteller. The humor is not that burlesque humor of *Tortilla Flat*, that Rabelaisian humor of "St. Katy the Virgin," that folk humor of *The Grapes of Wrath*, that tender humor of *Cannery Row*, that terrible Swiftian humor of *The Wayward Bus;* and it is nothing as good. It is a sophomoric humor of grotesque improbability and wordplay.

Pippin's royal robes are too large and must be fastened up the back with safety pins; the crotch of his breeches hangs down to his knees. During the coronation one company makes a small fortune selling miniature guillotines; part of the procession is made up of peasants in nylon country dress. An American newspaper carries the headline "FROGS CROWN PIP." The Lafayette Fund collects money from American school children to make possible the refurbishing of the royal quarters at Versailles. Pippin inspects his country incognito, riding a motor scooter and wearing a crash helmet. Among the place names are Chateau Vieilleculotte (Oldrump), Patisserie Pasmouches (Bakery Without-flies), and Café des Trois Puces (Three Fleas). One of the newspapers is called *Monde Dieu* (*Mon Dieu, Nom de Dieu*). The names of the minor characters are in the same vein: M. Rumorgue, Duc des Troisfronts (Three-faces), Senator Veauvache (Lazy-cow), Comte des Quatre Chats (Four Cats), and many more. The only previous examples of this level of humor in Steinbeck's mature fiction are in *Sweet Thursday,* with its chapters titled "Tinder Is as Tinder Does," "Whom the Gods Love They Drive Nuts," "Where Alfred the Sacred River Ran," etc. There is very little humor in *The Short Reign of Pippin IV* which rises above this level. And it is significant that the burlesque of scholarly and scientific interests—Professor Rumorgue's Separate entitled *Tendencies and Symptoms of Hysteria in Red Clover* and his article, "Inherited Schizophrenia in Legumes"—finds its parallel also in *Sweet Thursday*—Doc's paper on "Symptoms in Some Cephalopods Approximating Apoplexy."

It may be objected that *The Short Reign of Pippin IV* should not be taken so seriously. Steinbeck himself purports to have been amused and "greatly surprised when the Book-of-the-Month Club selected it," since he had thought of it as "a very special book that would have an extremely limited audience." (JS-CVW, 1/16/57) But as one reviewer noted, "though *The Short Reign of Pippin IV* is a fable that makes no claims for itself beyond the desire to please, its author waters Aesop with Alsop, mixes persiflage with prescriptions for the ills of modern France. The satiric lapses into the pontifical." [4] And there is no flesh on the bare bones of his tenuous plot. Steinbeck had written humorous books before—*Tortilla Flat, Cannery Row*—but each of these, at various times, was chosen as being in some ways his best by no less a critic than Edmund Wilson. It is certain that the only interest in Steinbeck's last two books—*Sweet Thursday* and *The Short Reign of Pippin IV*—lies in their evidence of the author's present state of decline.

This rapid decline of Steinbeck's work after *The Wayward Bus* (1947), as the ecologically minded Steinbeck would be the first to admit, cannot be an isolated fact. And although, with one exception, it would be hazardous to sort out cause and effect, it remains that this decline has been accompanied by certain changes in the author's personal and public life. Steinbeck's move from his "long valley" of California to the fashionable East Side of New York City, with its concomitant change of personal contacts—from plain people, bums, and *paisanos* to Broadway, Hollywood, and international celebrities—must figure in the total picture. In the late 1930's and early 1940's, when Steinbeck was writing at his best, he showed a deep distrust of publicity and book-club success, claiming that "if the public makes him [the writer] think he is somebody, it destroys him. He pontificates, and that's the end of him." [5] Also, he resisted all attempts to lure him into journalism, suspicious of what deadline pressures would do to his writing, and saying, "I wouldn't give a hoot if it [a story] were printed in Captain Billy's Whiz Bang. . . . I swear I'd sell a story to be printed in the Sunday supplement, but I wouldn't write for a Sunday supplement." (JS-MO, 3/19/37) Before the success of *The Grapes of Wrath* he had even hoped that he would never write a best-seller, for it could "ruin a writer forever." [6] On one of the handwritten drafts of *In Dubious Battle* he had expressed his shock at the personal intimacy of Lincoln Steffens' *Autobiography:* "I could see him lying in his bed." Even when he could afford first-class accommodations, his trips to Europe and even to New York were made as secretly as possible via freighters. Now Steinbeck not only writes for Sunday supplements, but for the dailies. His trips abroad are public affairs whose progress he reports at frequent intervals in syndicated columns across the nation—his stateroom aboard ship, the excavations under the dome of St. Peter, the fine Parisian restaurants. In other pieces of journalism, he has revealed not only personal biographical details, but the size and location of his summer home and the name and horsepower of his motor launch. He has pontificated on topics from juvenile delinquency to cookery.

It is all part of a pattern of change, like that which overcomes Doc in *Sweet Thursday*. And perhaps, like Doc, Steinbeck is changing "in spite of himself, in spite of the prayers of his friends, in spite of his own knowledge." That this change has been accompanied by a decline in the quality of Steinbeck's writing has been apparent since *Burning Bright* (1950) and *East of Eden* (1952); it has been made painfully obvious in *Sweet Thursday* and *The Short Reign of Pippin IV*.

The one important fact in this pattern of change that can with certainty be distinguished as a cause is the death of Edward F. Ricketts—in May of 1948. Steinbeck's great debt to this marine biologist with whom he had been the closest of friends since 1930 has been frequently pointed out in the preceding chapters, and particularly in the discussion of *Sweet Thursday*. Most of the facts are in the biographical sketch "About Ed Ricketts," which Steinbeck wrote to preface *The Log from the Sea of Cortez* (1951). As the author said to Pascal Covici, this sketch is not only about Ed Ricketts, "but about many other things." (JS-PC, 4/1/50) One of these things is the nature of Steinbeck's attachment to this incredible, real, wonderful person, who provided him with a mature biological view of life and a *persona* or mask to project that view.

In addition, Ricketts' intellectual companionship also provided Steinbeck with at least the means of arriving at some of his most central tenets as a writer. The extent to which he helped shape these tenets is suggested by the fact that the essay on non-teleological thinking in *Sea of Cortez*, though put in its final form by Steinbeck, was, as Ricketts himself noted, "99³⁴⁄₁₀₀%" his own. Also, he said that the book contained "excerpts here and there from other unpublished essays of mine." Ricketts had been working on this essay since the early 1930's, and there exists a completed draft dated 1937. He had made several attempts to have it published (*Harper's, Atlantic*), and it had circulated freely among his many friends—including Paul de Kruif, Joseph Campbell, and Henry Miller. That Ricketts also had a hand in formulating Steinbeck's group-man theories is evident from a folder of notes for a study of "phalanx literature." The titles of other unpublished essays by Ricketts are just as suggestive—"Ecology and Sociology," for example. Another essay, "The Philosophy of Breaking Through," is on the need for transcending the barriers of individual personality and perception and achieving a universal acceptance and understanding of the whole picture. It is precisely this kind of thinking which underlies the classification of characters in *The Wayward Bus*. Still other unpublished essays include "A Spiritual Morphology of Poetry" and "A Study of Genius," as well as notes toward "A Systematic Study of Sex."

That Ricketts took an active interest in Steinbeck's work is obvious from the fact that he read most of the novels in manuscript; sometimes Steinbeck would read them to him aloud. Ricketts must have occasionally taken exception. For in addition to praising *The Wayward Bus* ("a novel of some significance") and *The Grapes of Wrath* (parts of which moved him to tears), he disagreed enough with *The Forgotten Village* to write in final form a fourteen-page "Thesis and Materials for a Script on Mexico, which shall be motivated oppositely to John's 'Forgotten Village.'" Ricketts had accompanied Steinbeck to Mexico in 1940, when *The Forgotten Village* was being filmed. Although only *Cannery*

Row was dedicated to Ricketts, it is probable that beginning in the mid-1930's Ricketts was the ideal audience for whom Steinbeck wrote and also his artistic conscience.

After the death of Ricketts in 1948, Steinbeck has found it increasingly difficult to keep up that nice tension between mind and heart, science and poetry, which underlies all his successful fiction. And with the resolving of this tension, the mind, the science, emerges as the instrument of a heart, a poetry, which seems inclined toward the sentimental.

It is altogether possible, even probable, that if Ricketts had lived, Steinbeck would have found in him and his Pacific Biological Laboratories, of which Steinbeck was part owner and in which he was a working partner, an attachment strong enough to resist those attractions which have drawn him to a new, busier, more comfortable, but less creative career.

Although the quality of Steinbeck's work has been declining rapidly since 1947, it is not possible either to announce with any certainty his demise as a writer who should be taken seriously or to predict that he will not be able to equal or surpass his best achievements. In his mid-fifties, Steinbeck is still very much alive both to the great literature of the past and to the political and social currents of his day— as he always has been. Whether the important changes in key symbols effected by *Sweet Thursday* truly comprise a capitulation to romantic sentimentality or whether, like the changes in Hemingway's *Across the River and Into the Trees*, they constitute a purposeful destruction heralding a new period in his art, is a question which the next few years will answer. It seems certain only that Steinbeck is in the process of abandoning his informing biological view of man and reviving an interest in character *per se,* an interest which, until *Burning Bright* and especially *East of Eden,* had not been evident except in *Cup of Gold* and such early stories as "The Chrysanthemums," "The White Quail," and "Vigilante." If Steinbeck can recapture the concentration and discipline with which he handled character in these short stories twenty-some years ago, and if he can subject this aspect of his art to a vital though different informing view of life, then it is quite possible that he will once more resume writing on the level of major fiction. That he has to some extent retained this ability to depict character is evident from the minor figures in *East of Eden;* that he is groping toward some new informing view of life is evident in that novel's theme—every man's ability to choose between good and evil.

Even if Steinbeck should not succeed again in writing major literature, the sixteen volumes of fiction he has thus far published make up a substantial body of work which, despite unevenness of texture, remains viable and suggests an enduring value.

Paradoxically, this value has been obscured by the very richness and variety of that work, which has resisted all attempts at classification and filing. Steinbeck once said, "My experience in writing has followed an almost invariable pattern. Since by the process of writing a book I have outgrown that book, and since I like to write, I have not written two books alike." For "if a writer likes to write," continued Steinbeck, "he will find satisfaction in endless experimentation with his medium. . . . techniques, arrangements of scenes, rhythms of words, rhythms of thought." [7]

Although this endless experimentation has occasionally led him to materials and techniques he could not fully control, it has for the most part resulted in work which is remarkable for the range of its achievements: achievements in prose style as different as *In Dubious Battle* and *Tortilla*

Flat; in structure as different as *The Pearl* and *The Grapes of Wrath;* in symbolism as different as *To a God Unknown* and *Of Mice and Men;* in materials as different as *The Pastures of Heaven* and *Cannery Row;* in sentiment as different as *The Red Pony* and *The Wayward Bus.* But the grounds of comparison can be interchanged. *In Dubious Battle* and *Tortilla Flat,* for example, are different not only in prose style, but in structure, symbolism, materials, and sentiment; *The Pearl* and *The Grapes of Wrath* are different not only in structure, but in prose style and sentiment. For Steinbeck's constant experimentation with form and materials has resulted largely in their fusion. His prose style not only presents the materials, but evaluates them; his structure not only orders materials, but gives them meaning.

It is this craftsmanship which has enabled Steinbeck, almost alone among the writers of his generation, to give permanent aesthetic values to the materials of the Great Depression: in *Of Mice and Men* a symbolic construct of man's psychological and spiritual as well as his social condition; in *In Dubious Battle* an impartial, cold, but powerful analysis of the struggle between labor and capital; in *The Grapes of Wrath* what constitutes, in theme, purpose, scope, and language—an American epic.

Perhaps Steinbeck's most significant accomplishment has been the new dimensions he has given to the materials of literary naturalism. For whereas these materials have in aesthetics led writers (from Frank Norris to James T. Farrell) to abandon form, and in ethics either to celebrate man as the superior predator or to pity him as the product of forces beyond his control, these same materials have led Steinbeck not only to experiment with all aspects of form, but to assert man's divinity. "Why do we dread to think of our species as a species?" asks Steinbeck. "Can it be that we are afraid of what we may find? That human self-love would suffer too much and that the image of God might prove to be a mask? This could be only partly true, for if we could cease to wear the image of a kindly, bearded interstellar dictator, we might find ourselves true images of his kingdom, our eyes the nebulae, and universes in our cells." (SC, 264–265)

But Steinbeck does not pause here, for his study of nature through the discipline of marine biology led him to a reverence for life in all its forms. "All that lives is holy," says Jim Casy in *The Grapes of Wrath*. And in *Cannery Row* the author prays to "Our Father who art in nature"—the same Father whom Pilon of *Tortilla Flat* perceives in the calmness of the evening, and the same Father to whom Joseph sacrifices himself in *To a God Unknown*. Steinbeck's close observation of "the relationships of animal to animal" results in the conclusion that ". . . species are only commas in a sentence, that each species is at once the point and base of a pyramid . . . . groups melt into ecological groups until the time when what we know as life meets and enters what we think of as non-life. . . . all things are one thing and that one thing is all things—plankton, a shimmering phosphorescence on the sea and the spinning planets and an expanding universe, all bound together by the elastic string of time." (SC, 216–217)

NOTES

CHAPTER 1

1 "Proletarian Writing and John Steinbeck," *Sewanee Review*, 48 (October-December, 1940), p. 452.
2 "John Steinbeck and the Coming Literature," *Sewanee Review*, 50 (April-June, 1942), p. 146.
3 *Ibid.*, p. 148.
4 "Repent," *Time*, 49 (February 24, 1947), p. 119.
5 "John Dos Passos and John Steinbeck, Contrasting Notions of the Communal Personality," *Byrdcliffe Afternoons* (Woodstock, New York, January, 1940), pp. 21, 11.
6 "Toward a Bibliography of John Steinbeck," *Colophon*, 3 (Autumn, 1938), p. 558.
7 "Careers at Crossroads," *Virginia Quarterly Review*, 15 (October, 1939), p. 632.
8 *The Patterns of English and American Fiction* (Boston, 1942), p. 490.
9 "Steinbeck: Through a Glass, Though Brightly," *The New Republic*, 96 (October 12, 1938), p. 274.
10 "Writers in the Wilderness," *The Nation*, 149 (November 25, 1939), p. 578.
11 "The End of a Literary Decade," *The American Mercury*, 48 (December, 1939), pp. 413, 414.
12 "The Californians: Storm and Steinbeck," *The New Republic*, 103 (December 9, 1940), pp. 784–787.

13   *The Novel and Society* (Chapel Hill, 1941), p. 18.
14   *On Native Grounds* (New York, 1942), p. 394.
15   "Some Notes on John Steinbeck," *Antioch Review*, 2 (Summer, 1942), p. 194.
16   "John Steinbeck-Geneviève Tabouis," *The American Mercury*, 54 (June, 1942), p. 754.
17   "John Steinbeck: Earth and Stars," *University of Missouri Studies in Honor of A. H. R. Fairchild*, (XXI), ed. by Charles T. Prouty (Columbia, 1946), p. 185.
18   "Fable Retold," *Saturday Review of Literature*, 30 (November 22, 1947), p. 14.
19   *This World, San Francisco Chronicle*, February 16, 1947, p. 17.
20   "John Steinbeck, Californian," *Antioch Review*, 7 (Fall, 1947), p. 359.
21   *The Modern Novel in America* (Chicago, 1951), p. 150.
22   "John Steinbeck: Life Affirmed and Dissolved," *Fifty Years of the American Novel*, ed. by H. C. Gardiner (New York, 1951), p. 227.
23   "Out of the New-born Sun," *Saturday Review*, 35 (September 20, 1952), p. 11.
24   "John Steinbeck: American Dreamer," *Southwest Review*, 26 (July, 1941), pp. 454, 466.
25   "Some Notes on John Steinbeck," p. 190.
26   *Writers in Crisis* (Cambridge, 1942), p. 266.
27   "Jeffersonian Agrarianism in *The Grapes of Wrath*," *University of Kansas City Review*, 14 (Winter, 1947), pp. 149–154.
28   Frederick I. Carpenter, "The Philosophical Joads," *College English*, 2 (January, 1941), pp. 315–325.
29   *American Idealism* (Norman, Oklahoma, 1943), pp. 159–166.
30   *American Fiction 1920–1940* (New York, 1942), p. 327.
31   "John Steinbeck and the Coming Literature," p. 153.
32   *On Native Grounds*, pp. 393–394.
33   W. M. Frohock, "John Steinbeck's Men of Wrath," *Southwest Review*, 31 (Spring, 1946), pp. 152, 146, 148.
34   "Who Are the Real People?" *Saturday Review of Literature*, 28 (March 17, 1945), p. 14.
35   "Steinbeck Against Steinbeck," *The Pacific Spectator*, 1 (Autumn, 1947), p. 454.
36   "The Case of John Steinbeck," *The American Mercury*, 64 (May, 1947), pp. 624–630.
37   "Bankrupt Realism," *Saturday Review of Literature*, 30 (March 8, 1947), p. 22.
38   "John Steinbeck, Californian," p. 362.
39   "Fable Retold," p. 15.
40   "Steinbeck: One Aspect," *The Pacific Spectator*, 3 (Summer, 1949), pp. 302–310.
41   *The Novel and the World's Dilemma* (New York, 1947), pp. 272–291.
42   *The Modern Novel in America*, p. 148.
43   *In My Opinion* (Indianapolis, 1952), p. 59.
44   *The Shapers of American Fiction* (New York, 1947), pp. 194, 193.
45   *Cavalcade of the American Novel* (New York, 1952), p. 448.
46   "John Steinbeck: Life Affirmed and Dissolved," p. 225.

47 "Steinbeck at the Top of His Form," *The New York Times Book Review*, November 30, 1947, pp. 4, 52.
48 "Mr. Steinbeck's Cross-Section," *The New York Times Book Review*, February 16, 1947, pp. 1, 31.
49 "Steinbeck of California," *Delphian Quarterly*, 23 (April, 1940), pp. 40–44.
50 "*In Dubious Battle* Revalued," *The New York Times Book Review*, July 25, 1943, pp. 4, 16.
51 "Steinbeck and the Biological View of Man," *The Pacific Spectator*, 2 (Winter, 1948), p. 29.
52 "John Steinbeck: Naturalism's Priest," *College English*, 10 (May, 1949), pp. 437–438.
53 Bernard Bowron, "*The Grapes of Wrath*: A 'Wagons West' Romance," *Colorado Quarterly*, 3 (Summer, 1954), pp. 84–91. Mr. Bowron's article was countered in the Winter issue by Warren G. French, "Another Look at *The Grapes of Wrath*," pp. 337–343.
54 Martin Staples Shockley, "Christian Symbolism in *The Grapes of Wrath*," *College English*, 18 (November, 1956), pp. 87–90.
55 *The Modern Novel in America*, p. 153.
56 *Writers in Crisis*, p. 262.

CHAPTER 2

1 For a fuller account of Steinbeck's reading and literary references, see the biographical sketch in Harry Thornton Moore's *The Novels of John Steinbeck* (Chicago, 1939), pp. 73–96. I am indebted to Mr. Moore for several details of biography.
2 Moore (*The Novels of John Steinbeck*, pp. 76, 77, 78) states that Steinbeck graduated from Salinas high school in 1918, entered Stanford in 1919, left in the spring of 1920, returned briefly in the autumn of 1921, attended during 1922–1923, and left for good in 1925. Lewis Gannett, "Introduction," *The Portable Steinbeck*, (New York, 1946) states that Steinbeck was a high school senior in 1919. Seeking to solve this problem, the present writer asked the registrar at Stanford directly and received the following cryptic reply: "I can tell you that Mr. Steinbeck attended Stanford during three quarters during the academic year 1920–21, during the academic year 1922–23, 1923–24, and during the year 1924–25."
3 John Bennett, *The Wrath of John Steinbeck or St. John Goes to Church* (Los Angeles, 1949).
4 "Making of a New Yorker," *The New York Times Magazine*, February 1, 1953, Part II, pp. 26–27.
5 Moore, *The Novels of John Steinbeck*, p. 12.
6 See William Bysshe Stein, *Hawthorne's Faust* (Gainesville, Florida, 1953).

CHAPTER 3

1 Harry Thornton Moore, *The Novels of John Steinbeck* (Chicago, 1939), p. 30.

2 Moore states that there was "a forty-year hiatus" in the earlier version called "The Green Lady."

3 See the biographical sketches in *Wilson Library Bulletin*, 11 (March, 1937), p. 456; *Cosmopolitan*, 122 (April, 1947), p. 18; Moore, *The Novels of John Steinbeck*, pp. 92–94.

4 Concerning this matter of influence, it is only fair to point out that in a note to me Mr. Steinbeck takes issue with me on this point, stating that he "didn't read him [Hemingway] until about 1940." He generously suggests, however, that critics have their rights, and I let the evidence stand.

5 See, for example, pp. 14, 66, 105, 231, 284.

CHAPTER 4

1 *The Novels of John Steinbeck* (Chicago, 1939), p. 30.

2 Frederick I. Carpenter, "John Steinbeck, American Dreamer," *Southwest Review*, 21 (Summer, 1941), pp. 458–459.

3 Blake Nevius, "Steinbeck: One Aspect," *The Pacific Spectator*, 3 (Summer, 1949), p. 302.

4 Albert Gerard, *A la recontre de John Steinbeck* (Liége, Belgium, 1947), pp. 34–35.

5 *Nothing So Monstrous* (New York, 1936), p. 30.

CHAPTER 5

1 Harry Thornton Moore, *The Novels of John Steinbeck* (Chicago, 1939), p. 30.

2 This information I obtained through conversations with Ben Abramson and Pascal Covici. Moore, *The Novels of John Steinbeck*, pp. 82–83, gives the same account.

3 "My Short Novels," *Wings*, October, 1953, p. 6.

4 Carlos Baker, for example, has said that "to call *Tortilla Flat* a novel insults literary genres. . . . [it] is little more than a sketch-book." "Steinbeck of California," *Delphian Quarterly*, 23 (Spring, 1940), p. 42.

5 Mr. Covici informs me that when he received the typescript it contained the "Preface" and chapter headings as published.

6 Lewis Gannett, "Introduction," *The Portable Steinbeck* (New York, 1946).

7 *E.g.*, Stanley Edgar Hyman, "Some Notes on John Steinbeck," *Antioch Review*, 2 (Summer, 1942); Woodburn Ross, "John Steinbeck: Earth and Stars," *University of Missouri Studies in Honor of A. H. R. Fairchild*, (XXI), ed. by Charles T. Prouty (Columbia, Missouri, 1946).

8 "The Californians: Storm and Steinbeck," *The New Republic*, 103 (December 9, 1940), p. 787.

9 "John Steinbeck, Californian," *Antioch Review*, 7 (Fall, 1947), 355.

10 *Best Film Plays, 1945*, ed. by John Gassner and Dudley Nichols (New York, 1945), p. 640.

CHAPTER 6

1 "The Snake" appeared in *The Monterey Beacon* on June 22, 1935. In January of that year, under the pseudonym of Amnesia Glasscock, he had also contributed a number of poems to this periodical. See Checklist.

2 Harry Thornton Moore, *The Novels of John Steinbeck* (Chicago, 1939), p. 92.

3 *The Journals of André Gide*, trans. by Justin O'Brien (New York, 1951), 29 July 1941.

4 "Steinbeck: Through a Glass, Though Brightly," *The New Republic*, 96 (October 12, 1938), p. 274.

CHAPTER 7

1 "John Steinbeck, Californian," *Antioch Review*, 7 (Fall, 1947), 345–362.

2 Quoted by Harry Thornton Moore in *The Novels of John Steinbeck* (Chicago, 1939), p. 102.

3 *Ibid.*, p. 47.

4 Joseph Henry Jackson, "Introduction," Limited Edition of *The Grapes of Wrath* (New York, 1940).

5 Carey McWilliams, "What's Being Done About the Joads?" *The New Republic*, 100 (September 20, 1939), pp. 178–180.

6 *The Journals of André Gide*, trans. by Justin O'Brien (New York, 1951), 27 September 1940.

7 Moore, *The Novels of John Steinbeck*, p. 41.

8 *Ibid.*, p. 84.

9 CF-JS, 6/10/35; MO-Miss Otis (telegram), 5/10/35; JS-MO, 5/13/35; Bobbs-Merrill-MO, 5/8/35: CF-MO, 5/14/35. For further details of Steinbeck's association with Covici-Friede, see Donald Friede's autobiography, *The Mechanical Angel* (New York, 1948), especially pp. 126–132.

10 The person here addressed is probably George Albee, a minor novelist (*Not in a Day, Young Robert, Girl on the Beach, Three Young Kings*) with whom Steinbeck was intimate. There are several characters called George in Steinbeck's early work, and Professor George Hand of the University of California recalls meeting Steinbeck and Albee together in 1929 or 1930.

11 Moore, *The Novels of John Steinbeck*, p. 41.

12 This statement is repeated in a letter to Ben Abramson early in the spring of 1936.

13 *The Journals of André Gide*, 27 September 1940.

14 Moore, *The Novels of John Steinbeck*, pp. 48–49, 85.

15 *Ibid.*, pp. 40, 46.

16 For a similar analogy, see *Sea of Cortez*, p. 165.

17 For a full discussion of this point, see Claude-Edmonde Magny, *L'âge du roman américain* (Paris, 1948), pp. 183–184, 189. Mme. Magny's chapter on Steinbeck has been translated and is now available in *Steinbeck and his Critics*, ed. by E. W. Tedlock, Jr., and C. V. Wicker (Albuquerque, 1957), pp. 216–227.

18   *The Journals of André Gide,* 27 September 1940.
19   "Some Thoughts on Juvenile Delinquency," *The Saturday Review,* 38 (May 28, 1955), 22.

CHAPTER 8

1   Harry Thornton Moore, *The Novels of John Steinbeck* (Chicago, 1939), p. 86, states that this incident did not occur "until after type had been set and proofs corrected," but this letter is explicit about there being "no other draft" and there being "two month's work to do over again." Moore's contention is disproved also by Steinbeck's letter of February 12, quoted below. Some twenty years later, Steinbeck repeated the story about the pup and added, "I don't know how close the first and second versions would prove to be." ("My Short Novels," *Wings,* October, 1953, p. 6.)
2   John Steinbeck, "the novel might benefit by the discipline, the terseness . . . ," *Stage* (January, 1938), pp. 50–51. Although this article was published while *Of Mice and Men* was on Broadway, the editors inform us that it had been submitted earlier.
3   Mark Van Doren, "Wrong Number," *The Nation,* 144 (March 6, 1937), p. 275; also, Joseph Wood Krutch, *American Drama Since 1918* (New York, 1939), p. 396.
4   Stark Young, "Drama Critics Circle Award," *The New Republic,* 94 (May 4, 1938), p. 396; also, Frank H. O'Hara, *Today in American Drama* (Chicago, 1939), p. 181.
5   "How Do You Like It Now, Gentlemen?" *Sewanee Review,* 59 (Spring, 1951), pp. 311–328.
6   "Introduction," *The Portable Hemingway* (New York, 1944).
7   Carlos Baker, "Steinbeck of California," *Delphian Quarterly,* 23 (April, 1940), 42.
8   Toni Jackson Ricketts [Antonia Seixas], "John Steinbeck and the Non-Teleological Bus," *What's Doing on the Monterey Peninsula,* 1 (March, 1947). This article is now available in *Steinbeck and His Critics,* ed. by E. W. Tedlock, Jr., and C. V. Wicker (Albuquerque, 1957).
9   Stark Young, "Drama Critics Circle Award," p. 396.

CHAPTER 9

1   This series of articles is more widely known as "Their Blood Is Strong," the title given them when, with an epilogue, they were reprinted in pamphlet form under the auspices of the Simon J. Lubin Society of California in the spring of 1938.
2   Lawrence Clark Powell, "Toward a Bibliography of John Steinbeck," *Colophon,* 3 (Autumn, 1938), pp. 562–563.
3   *Occident* (Fall, 1936), p. 5.
4   Lewis Gannett, "Introduction," *The Portable Steinbeck* (New York, 1946), pp. xx–xxi.
5   *Ibid.,* p. xxiv.
6   Marshal V. Hartranft, *Grapes of Gladness: California's Refreshing and Inspiring Answer to John Steinbeck's "The Grapes of Wrath"* (Los Angeles, 1939).

7 George Thomas Miron, *The Truth About John Steinbeck and the Migrants* (Los Angeles, 1939), p. 5.

8 For details, see Martin Staples Shockley, "The Reception of *The Grapes of Wrath* in Oklahoma," *American Literature*, 15 (January, 1954), 351–361.

9 Margaret Marshall, "Writers in the Wilderness," *The Nation*, 149 (November 25, 1939), p. 579.

10 Shockley, "The Reception of *The Grapes of Wrath* in Oklahoma," p. 357. The reader interested in pursuing this topic further may find useful, in addition to items already cited, the following: Carey McWilliams, "California Pastoral," *Antioch Review*, 2 (March, 1942), 103–121; *The La Follette Committee Transcript*, vol. 51; *Wilson Library Bulletin*, 14 (October, 1939), pp. 102, 165, and vol. 13 (May, 1939), p. 640; Carey McWilliams, "What's Being Done About the Joads?" *The New Republic*, 100 (September 20, 1939), pp. 178–180; Frank J. Taylor, "California's 'Grapes of Wrath,'" *Forum and Century*, 102 (November, 1939), pp. 232–238; *Look* (January 16, 1940); Leon Whipple, "Novels on Social Themes," *Survey Graphic*, 28 June, 1939), p. 401; Richard Neuberger, "Who Are the Associated Farmers?" *Survey Graphic*, 28 (September, 1939), 517–521, 555–557; the Nazi Bund's *Deutscher Weckruf und Beobachter*, edited by Fritz Kuhn; Carey McWilliams, *Factories in the Field* (Boston, 1939). Others are listed by Shockley.

11 Miron, *The Truth About John Steinbeck and the Migrants*, p. 7. See also Elizabeth N. Monroe, *The Novel and Society* (Chapel Hill, 1941), p. 272, and Earle Birney, review of *The Grapes of Wrath* in *The Canadian Forum*, 19 (June, 1939), p. 94.

12 "Some Notes on John Steinbeck," *Antioch Review*, 2 (Summer, 1942), p. 195.

13 "The Harvest Gypsies," *San Francisco News*, October 5, 1936, p. 3.

14 "Dubious Battle in California," *The Nation*, 143 (September 12, 1936), p. 304.

15 "The Harvest Gypsies," *San Francisco News*, October 7, 1936, p. 6.

16 "The Harvest Gypsies," *San Francisco News*, October 12, 1936, p. 8.

17 "The Philosophical Joads," *College English*, 2 (January, 1941), pp. 324–325. The resemblance of Casy to Emerson is also noted by Floyd Stovall in his *American Idealism* (Norman, Oklahoma, 1943), p. 164.

18 "Jeffersonian Agrarianism in *The Grapes of Wrath*," *University of Kansas City Review*, 14 (Winter, 1947), p. 150.

19 "The Harvest Gypsies," *San Francisco News*, October 8, 1936, p. 16.

20 *The Novel and Our Time* (Letchworth, Hertfordshire, England, 1948), p. 8.

21 *The Craft of Fiction* (New York, 1945), p. 33.

22 For an excellent discussion of this point, see Joseph Warren Beach, *American Fiction, 1920–1940* (New York, 1942), pp. 337–338.

23 Joseph Henry Jackson, "Introduction," Limited Edition of *The Grapes of Wrath* (New York, 1940), pp. viii–ix.

24 *The River* (New York, 1938), unpaginated. According to the "Preface," the text for this book was taken verbatim from the motion picture of the same name.

25 *The Craft of Fiction*, p. 40.

26 Harry Thornton Moore, for example, refers to Steinbeck's failure to provide *The Grapes of Wrath* with "a proportioned and intensified drama," a "vital conflict," or a "continuity of suspense." *The Novels of John Steinbeck*, (Chicago, 1939), pp. 59, 69.

27 For an excellent discussion of this point, see Claude-Edmonde Magny, *L'âge du roman américain* (Paris, 1948), p. 187.

28 Alfred Kazin, *On Native Grounds* (New York, 1942), p. 397.

29 George F. Whicher, "Proletarian Leanings," *The Literature of the American People*, ed. by A. H. Quinn (New York, 1951), p. 960.

30 "Preface," *The Forgotten Village* (New York, May, 1941).

31 *The Philosophy of Literary Form* (Baton Rouge, 1941), p. 91.

32 "John Steinbeck, A Portrait," *Saturday Review of Literature*, 16 (September 25, 1937), p. 18.

33 I cannot resist quoting Harry Slochower's interpretation of this scene: "The reincarnation of Grampa is also suggested by the theme of grapes. Grampa had been looking forward to squashing the grapes of California on his face, 'a-nibblin' off it all the time.' The man in the barn is reduced to such baby acts, 'practicing' them as he drinks Rose of Sharon's milk. The grapes have turned to 'wrath,' indicated by the fact that the first milk of the mother is said to be bitter." *No Voice Is Wholly Lost* (New York, 1945), footnote p. 304.

34 Bernard Bowron persistently ignores this wider frame of reference. He calls *The Grapes of Wrath* "a triumph of literary engineering" because of the great "artfulness—I do not say great art" with which the book utilizes the "romance-formula" of such covered wagon stories as *The Way West*. *The Grapes of Wrath*, says Mr. Bowron, "derives from the 'Westward' novel both the structure and the values that give it its emotional horsepower." See "The Grapes of Wrath: a 'Wagons West' Romance," *Colorado Quarterly*, 3 (Summer, 1954), pp. 84–91.

35 "The Harvest Gypsies," *San Francisco News*, October 6, 1936, p. 3.

36 Further parallels between Casy and Christ have been pointed out recently in Martin Shockley's "Christian Symbolism in *The Grapes of Wrath*," *College English*, 18 (November, 1956), pp. 87–90.

37 Elizabeth N. Monroe, *The Novel and Society* (Chapel Hill, 1941), p. 18.

38 For an excellent contrast of Steinbeck and Dos Passos, see Harry Slochower, "John Dos Passos and John Steinbeck, Contrasting Notions of the Communal Personality," in *Byrdcliffe Afternoons* (Woodstock, New York, January, 1940), pp. 11–27.

39 "American Novels: 1939," *Atlantic Monthly*, 165 (January, 1940), p. 68.

40 For parallels to this scene, see Maupassant's "Idylle"; Byron's *Childe Harold*, Canto IV, Stanzas CXLVIII-CLI; Rubens' painting of old Cimon drawing milk from the breast of Pero; and an eighteenth-century play called *The Grecian's Daughter*, which is discussed in Maurice W. Disher's *Blood and Thunder* (London, 1949), p. 23. See also Celeste T. Wright, "Ancient Analogues of an Incident in John Steinbeck," *Western Folklore*, 14 (January, 1955), pp. 50–51.

41 George Bluestone, *Novels into Film* (Baltimore, 1947) appeared too late to be included in the present discussion. Mr. Bluestone's chapter on *The Grapes of Wrath* illuminates several aspects of that novel, particularly the function of animal imagery.

CHAPTER 10

1 Lewis Gannett, "Introduction," *The Portable Steinbeck* (New York, 1946), p. xxiv.
2 Frank Scully, *Rogues Gallery* (Hollywood, 1943), p. 46.
3 Lawrence Clark Powell, "Toward a Bibliography of John Steinbeck," *Colophon*, 3 (Autumn, 1938), p. 562.
4 John Steinbeck, *The Forgotten Village* (New York, May, 1941). Photographs by Rosa Harvan Kline and Alexander Hackensmid.
5 See Frederick Bracher, "Steinbeck and the Biological View of Man." *The Pacific Spectator*, 2 (Winter, 1948), p. 14.
6 See Stanley Edgar Hyman, "Some Notes on John Steinbeck," *Antioch Review*, 2 (Summer, 1942), p. 196.
7 Gannett, "Introduction," *The Portable Steinbeck*, p. xxv.
8 By far the best examinations of *Sea of Cortez* in relation to Steinbeck's work are in Woodburn Ross, "John Steinbeck: Earth and Stars," *University of Missouri Studies in Honor of A. H. R. Fairchild* (XXI), ed. by Charles T. Prouty (Columbia, 1946), pp. 179–197, and his "John Steinbeck: Naturalism's Priest," *College English*, 10 (May, 1949), pp. 432–437. See also Eugene Freel's unpublished doctoral dissertation, A Comparative Study Between Certain Concepts and Principles of Modern Psychology and the Main Writings of John Steinbeck, New York University, 1946. Mr. Freel's discussion is interesting in that it relates Steinbeck's "Is" thinking to Gestalt psychology. See also Frederick Bracher, "Steinbeck and the Biological View of Man."
9 "The Secret Weapon We Were Afraid to Use," *Collier's*, 131 (January 10, 1953), pp. 9–13.
10 Gannett, "Introduction," *The Portable Steinbeck*, p. xxvi.
11 The reports continue sporadically until early December, but after October these were written in New York from notes he had made in Europe.
12 "Some Philosophers in the Sun," *The New York Times Book Review*, December 31, 1944, pp. 1, 18.
13 The title is from *Macbeth*, Act II, sc. i. Banquo asks of Fleance, "How goes the night, boy?" and Fleance answers, "The moon is down; I have not heard the clock." Although Stanley Edgar Hyman and Lincoln Gibbs both try to give this "moon" symbolic significance by relating it to other uses of the word in Steinbeck's work, it does not seem likely that Steinbeck meant more than the general indication that it is the dark of night, a time like that in which Duncan was murdered. See Lincoln Gibbs, "John Steinbeck: Moralist," *Antioch Review*, 2 (Summer, 1942), pp. 172–184, and Hyman, "Some Notes on John Steinbeck," p. 190.
14 Gannett, "Introduction," *The Portable Steinbeck*, p. xxvi.
15 "Steinbeck's Faith," *Newsweek*, 19 (April 20, 1942), pp. 72–73.
16 "The Moon Is Halfway Down," *The New Republic*, 106 (May 18, 1942), p. 657.
17 "Correspondence," *The New Republic*, 106 (March 30, 1942), p. 431.
18 "Correspondence," *The New Republic*, 106 (May 4, 1942), pp. 495, 607–608.

19 "Correspondence," *The New Republic*, 106 (March 30, 1942), pp. 431–432. See also "Mr. Steinbeck, Friends and Foes," *ibid.*, p. 413.

20 Richard Watts, "The Wayward Steinbeck," *The New Republic*, 116 (March 10, 1947), p. 37. In France it was published as *Nuits Noires* by a Paris underground press called Editions de Minuit at the expense of patriotic intellectuals in February, 1944.

21 Edward Weeks, "California Bus Ride," *Atlantic Monthly*, 179 (March, 1947), p. 126.

22 "My Short Novels," *Wings*, October, 1953, pp. 7–8.

23 "What Price Conquest," *The New Republic*, 106 (March 16, 1942), p. 370.

24 "My Short Novels," *Wings*, October, 1953, pp. 7–8. This was also the main point of the motion picture *Lifeboat*, for which Steinbeck wrote the story (Twentieth Century-Fox, 1944).

25 Harry Slochower, *No Voice Is Wholly Lost* (New York, 1945), p. 305.

26 Compare these words at the end of the play with Madeline's words, also the last of the play, in Maxwell Anderson's *Candle in the Wind*: "In the history of the world, there have been many wars between men and beasts. And the beasts have always lost, and men have won."

27 John Steinbeck in a conversation with me in February, 1954.

28 "My Short Novels," *Wings*, October, 1953, p. 7.

29 For a full discussion of this point, see Claude-Edmonde Magny, *L'âge du roman américain* (Paris, 1948), pp. 189, 191.

CHAPTER 11

1 "Some Philosophers in the Sun," *The New York Times Book Review*, December 31, 1944, p. 1.

2 "John Steinbeck's Newest Novel and James Joyce's First," *The New Yorker*, 20 (January 6, 1945), p. 62.

3 "Storm and Steinbeck," *The New Republic*, 103 (December 9, 1940), p. 787.

4 *In My Opinion* (Indianapolis, 1952), p. 60.

5 Lewis Gannett, "Introduction," *The Portable Steinbeck* (New York, 1946), p. xxvi.

6 "Steinbeck Delivers a Mixture of Farce and Freud," *PM*, Magazine Section, January 14, 1945, p. 15.

7 Toni Jackson Ricketts [Antonia Seixas], "John Steinbeck and the Non-Teleological Bus," *What's Doing on the Monterey Peninsula*, 1 (March, 1947).

8 "My Short Novels," *Wings* (October, 1953), p. 8.

9 In a conversation with me in February, 1954.

10 Gannett, "Introduction," *The Portable Steinbeck*, xiv.

11 "Foreword" to the Modern Library edition of *Tortilla Flat* (New York, 1937).

12 The customers of Madame Tellier, like those of Dora, are not ne'er-do-wells and scamps, but respectable family men. The girls are innocent working girls who look on Madame as on a kind mother. They are devout and go to church regularly, where they set a good example by their weeping. Once, Madame closes up her establishment so that they can attend a holy confirmation as a group. Like the girls at Dora's, the

girls at Madame Tellier's never mix business and pleasure. They do not speak to men on the street or give them any sign of recognition, even though they have have been together a short time previously. Like Dora, Madame Tellier is offended by coarse language and will not tolerate it in her establishment. Also like Dora, she is community-minded and takes an active part in civic affairs. Like Cannery Row, the little French town holds no prejudice against Madame and her girls but accepts them as part of the community.

13 "Critics, Critics Burning Bright," *Saturday Review of Literature*, 33 (November 11, 1950), p. 21.

14 "East of Eden," *Perspectives USA*, 5 (Fall, 1953), pp. 147–148.

15 In one of his war communiqués (*New York Herald Tribune*, October 11, 1943, p. 17), Steinbeck tells how the captain of a PT boat once saw "a dead woman floating on the oily water, face down and with her hair fanned out and floating behind her."

CHAPTER 12

1 "My Short Novels," *Wings*, October, 1953, p. 8.

2 *The Novel and Our Time* (Letchworth, Hertfordshire, England, 1948), p. 59.

3 Steinbeck probably got this name from the eighteenth-century Jesuit, Clavigero, whose writings were consulted in preparation for the expedition to the Gulf of California. Father Clavigero is frequently mentioned in *Sea of Cortez* (pp. 5, 6, 51–53, 209–210, 224, 232–233).

4 For a detailed though, I feel, inaccurate application of the passage from "Acts of Thomas" to *The Pearl, s*ee Thomas Sugrue, "Steinbeck's Mexican Folk-Tale," *New York Herald Tribune Weekly Book Review*, December 7, 1947, p. 4."The biting of the child by the scorpion, or scarab," writes Mr. Sugrue, "signifies the entrance of the divine nature into the mind; the pearl of great price, the knowledge of spiritual growth, must then be found so that eventually the divine nature can be set free. . . . The horseman is easy to identify as the Spaniard who conquered the Indian, though horsemen representing desires of the lower mind normally in folklore pursue the ego in quest of the soul. Kino, refusing the adventure of the spirit, renouncing his opportunity for realization and understanding and identity, returns to the rim of unconsciousness, the primitive state wherein responsibility resides in nature and wherein man nurses, like a tree, at the breast of earth."

5 *No Voice Is Wholly Lost* (New York, 1945), p. 367.

CHAPTER 13

1 "John Steinbeck's Bus Ride into the Hills," *New York Herald Tribune Weekly Book Review*, February 16, 1947, p. 2.

2 In *Sea of Cortez*, while discussing the possibility of subliminal sound and smell symbols, Steinbeck uses as an example something very similar. "One has the experience again and again of suddenly turning and following with one's eyes some particular girl among many girls . . . what are the stimuli if not odors, perhaps above or below the conscious olfactory range?" (SC, 186)

CHAPTER 14

1   Steinbeck's script for *Viva Zapata* was re-worked by an anonymous writer and published as a short story in *Argosy*, February, 1952.
2   "Critics, Critics Burning Bright," *Saturday Review of Literature*, 33 (November 11, 1950), p. 21.
3   *Ibid.*, p. 20.
4   "Hemingway and Steinbeck," *Saturday Review of Literature*, 33 (October 28, 1950), p. 26.
5   "Critics, Critics Burning Bright," p. 20.
6   *Ibid.*, p. 20.
7   Act II, scene ii. James Graham-Lujan and Richard L. O'Connell, trans., *III Tragedies* (New York, 1947).
8   In a conversation with me, February, 1954.
9   This passage is quoted to Steinbeck from his own journal by Pascal Covici in a letter dated June 6, 1952. The last sentence of this passage appears on page 309 of *East of Eden*, where it is among the last words spoken by Samuel Hamilton.

CHAPTER 15

1   Laura Z. Hobson, "Tradewinds," *Saturday Review*, 35 (August 30, 1952), 4. This article appeared one month before the publication of *East of Eden*.
2   *Ibid.*, pp. 4–5.
3   The motion picture which Elia Kazan made from *East of Eden* is based entirely on this last part of the novel.
4   "It Started in a Garden," *Time*, 60 (September 22, 1952), p. 110.
5   "East of Eden," *Perspectives USA*, 5 (Fall, 1953), p. 149.
6   "John Steinbeck's Dramatic Tale of Three Generations," *New York Herald Tribune Weekly Book Review*, September 21, 1952, p. 1.
7   "A Dark and Violent Steinbeck Novel," *The New York Times Book Review*, September 21, 1952, p. 22.
8   In a letter to C. V. Wicker, September 16, 1955.
9   Robert R. Brunn, in a review of *East of Eden, Christian Science Monitor*, September 25, 1952, p. 11.
10 Harvey Curtis Webster, "Out of the New-born Sun," *Saturday Review*, 35 (September 20, 1952), p. 11.
11 In a review of *East of Eden* in *This World, San Francisco Chronicle*, September 21, 1952, p. 20.
12 Arthur Mizener, "In the Land of Nod," *The New Republic*, 127 (October 6, 1952), p. 23.
13 Bernard Kale, "The Author," *Saturday Review*, 35 (September 20, 1952), p. 11.

CHAPTER 16

1   Lewis Nichols, "A Talk With John Steinbeck," *The New York Times Book Review*, September 28, 1952, p. 30.
2   Carlos Baker's review for *The New York Times* was purely noncommittal, confining itself to an outline of the plot. Louis Barron, writing in

Library Journal, 79 (June 1, 1954), p. 1052, saw *Sweet Thursday* as "still further evidence that Steinbeck is no longer an author to be taken seriously." Brendan Gill's review in *The New Yorker,* 30 (July 10, 1954), pp. 63–64, remarked that "the evidence tends to show that while the author is comparatively young and vigorous, his talent diminishes from book to book." Other reviewers called it a "Grade B pot-boiler" and "stuff that has been salvaged from the wastebasket." The most favorable review, oddly enough, appeared in the London *Times,* whose reviewer saw in *Sweet Thursday* "a quality of inspired idiocy, a genuine harebrained charm." (November 26, 1954, p. 753) In America this same view was expressed by Edward Weeks in *Atlantic Monthly,* who thought that "read in the spirit in which it is written it is good fun."

3   *Holiday,* 19 (January, 1956), p. 25.
4   *Time,* 69 (April 15, 1957), p. 126.
5   Quoted by Frank Scully in *Rogues Gallery* (Hollywood, 1943), p. 46.
6   Lawrence Clark Powell, "Toward a Bibliography of John Steinbeck," *Colophon,* 3 (Autumn, 1938), p. 562.
7   "Critics, Critics Burning Bright," *The Saturday Review of Literature,* 33 (November 11, 1950), pp. 20–21.

A WORKING CHECKLIST

of Steinbeck's published work

1. BOOKS

Cup of Gold. New York: Robert M. McBride & Co., 1929.

The Pastures of Heaven. New York: Brewer, Warren & Putnam, 1932.

To a God Unknown. New York: Robert O. Ballou, 1933.

Tortilla Flat. New York: Covici-Friede, 1935.

In Dubious Battle. New York: Covici-Friede, 1936.

Nothing So Monstrous. New York: The Pynson Printers, 1936. Contains the Junius Maltby episode from *The Pastures of Heaven* with special epilogue.

Saint Katy the Virgin. New York: Covici-Friede, 1936. (Collected in *The Long Valley.*)

The Red Pony. New York: Covici-Friede, 1937. Deluxe edition only, 699 copies, numbered and signed by the author. Contains "The Gift," "The Great Mountains," and "The Promise," all previously published. (Collected in *The Long Valley.*)

Of Mice and Men. New York: Covici-Friede, 1937.

Of Mice and Men: A Play in Three Acts. New York: Covici-Friede, 1937.

The Long Valley. New York: The Viking Press, 1938. Contains first publication of "Flight" and "The Leader of the People."

The Grapes of Wrath. New York: The Viking Press, 1939.

The Forgotten Village. New York: The Viking Press, 1941.

Sea of Cortez (in collaboration with Edward F. Ricketts). New York: The Viking Press, 1941.

Bombs Away. New York: The Viking Press, 1942.

The Moon Is Down. New York: The Viking Press, 1942.

The Moon Is Down: A Play in Two Parts. New York: The Viking Press, 1943.

The Red Pony. New York: The Viking Press, 1945. Illustrated edition. Contains "The Leader of the People," as well as "The Gift," "The Great Mountains," and "The Promise," all previously published.

Cannery Row. New York: The Viking Press, 1945.

The Pearl. New York: The Viking Press, 1947.

The Wayward Bus. New York: The Viking Press, 1947.

A Russian Journal. New York: The Viking Press, 1948.

Burning Bright. New York: The Viking Press, 1950.

Burning Bright. New York: Dramatists Play Service Inc., 1951. (Acting edition.)

The Log from the Sea of Cortez. New York: The Viking Press, 1951. (Contains only "Introduction" and "Narrative" from *Sea of Cortez,* to which is added the biographical sketch, "About Ed Ricketts.")

East of Eden. New York: The Viking Press, 1952.

Sweet Thursday. New York: The Viking Press, 1954.

The Short Reign of Pippin IV. New York: The Viking Press, 1957.

2. PERIODICALS AND NEWSPAPERS

For convenience of reference, stories are identified by the symbol S; articles by A; verse by V; letters by L. Those stories collected in *The Long Valley* are so indicated (LV). Because at this time it is impossible to prepare even a fairly accurate listing of Steinbeck's contributions to newspapers, both in America and abroad, only those newspaper items discussed in the present study have been cited.

S Fingers of Cloud: A Satire on College Protervity. *The Stanford Spectator,* 2 (February, 1924), pp. 149, 161–164.

S Adventures in Arcademy: A Journey into the Ridiculous. *The Stanford Spectator,* 2 (June, 1924), pp. 279, 291.

V If Eddie Guest Had Written the Book of Job: HAPPY BIRTHDAY. *Stanford Lit,* 1 (March, 1926), p. 94.

V If John A. Weaver Had Written Keats' Sonnet in the American Language: ON LOOKING AT A NEW BOOK BY HAROLD BELL WRIGHT. *Stanford Lit,* 1 (March, 1926), p. 94.

V Atropos: Study of a Very Feminine Obituary Editor. *Stanford Lit,* 1 (March, 1926), p. 95.

S Red Pony, *North American Review,* 236 (November, 1933), pp. 421–438. (LV, as "The Gift")

S The Great Mountains. *North American Review,* 236 (December, 1933), pp. 492–500. (LV)

S The Murder. *North American Review,* 237 (April, 1934), pp. 305–312. (LV)

S The Raid. *North American Review,* 238 (October, 1934), pp. 299–305. (LV)

V Mammy. *Monterey Beacon,* 1 (January 5, 1935), p. 7.

V Baubles. *Monterey Beacon,* 1 (January 5, 1935), p. 7.

V   To Carmel. *Monterey Beacon,* 1 (January 5, 1935), p. 7.
V   The Visitor. *Monterey Beacon,* 1 (January 5, 1935), p. 7.
V   Four Shades of Navy Blue. *Monterey Beacon,* 1 (January 26, 1935), p. 12.
V   The Genius. *Monterey Beacon,* 1 (January 26, 1935), p. 12.
V   Ivanhoe. *Monterey Beacon,* 1 (January 26, 1935), p, 12.
V   Thoughts on Seeing a Stevedore. *Monterey Beacon,* 1 (January 26, 1935), p. 11.
S   The White Quail. *North American Review,* 239 (March, 1935), pp. 204–211. (LV)
S   The Snake. *Monterey Beacon,* 1 (June 22, 1935), pp. 10–14. (LV)
A   Dubious Battle in California. *The Nation,* 143 (September 12, 1936), pp. 302–304.
A   The Harvest Gypsies. *San Francisco News,* October 5–12, 1936. Chapter I, October 5, 1936, p. 3; Chapter II, October 6, 1936, p. 3; Chapter III, October 7, 1936, p. 6; Chapter IV, October 8, 1936, p. 16; Chapter V, October 9, 1936, p. 14; Chapter VI, October 10, 1936, p. 14; Chapter VII, October 12, 1936, p. 8.
L   The Way It Seems to John Steinbeck. *Occident* (Fall, 1936), p. 5.
S   The Lonesome Vigilante. *Esquire,* 6 (October, 1936), pp. 35, 186A–186B. (LV, as "Vigilante")
S   The Promise. *Harper's Magazine,* 175 (August, 1937), pp. 243–252. (LV)
S   The Ears of Johnny Bear. *Esquire,* 8 (September, 1937), pp. 35, 195–200. (LV, as "Johnny Bear")
S   The Chrysanthemums. *Harper's Magazine,* 175 (October, 1937), pp. 513–519. (LV)
A   . . . the novel might benefit by the discipline, the terseness. . . . *(sic)* *Stage,* 15 (January, 1938), pp. 50–51.
L   Letter to Inmates of Connecticut State Prison. *The Monthly Record* (June,1938).
S   The Harness. *Atlantic Monthly,* 161 (June, 1938), pp. 741–749. (LV)
A   The Stars Point to Shafter. *The Progressive Weekly,* December 24, 1938.
S   Breakfast. *Progressive Weekly,* May 6, 1939. Steinbeck recalls that this sketch was first published in the Lincoln Steffens Memorial Edition of the *Pine Cone* (February 16, 1934), but a staff member could not locate the item in 1955. (LV)
S   How Edith McGillicuddy Met Robert Louis Stevenson. *Harper's Magazine,* 183 (August, 1941), pp. 252–258. (Collected in *The Portable Steinbeck.*)

Dispatches from European War Theater appearing in *New York Herald Tribune,* June 21 through December 10, 1943.

June: 21, p. 1; 22, p. 1; 23, p. 1; 24, p. 1; 25, p. 1; 26, p. 1; 27, p. 1; 28, p. 1; 29, p. 23; 30, p. 23.
July: 1, p. 21; 2, p. 17; 3, p. 13; 4, p. 7; 5, pp. 1, 9; 6, p. 17; 7, p. 23; 8, p. 21; 9, p. 15; 10, p. 7; 11, p. 14; 12, p. 15; 13, p. 21; 14, p. 21; 15, p. 21; 16, p. 13; 17, p. 7; 18, p. 18; 19, p. 13; 25, p. 12; 26, p. 17; 27, p. 17; 28, p. 17; 29, p. 17; 30, p. 13.

August: 3, p. 15; 4, p. 17; 5, p. 17; 6, p. 13; 9, p. 11; 10, p. 21; 12, p. 17; 26, p. 15; 27, p. 13; 28, p. 7; 29, p. 10; 31, p. 17.

September: 1, p. 21; 2, p. 21; 3, p. 17; 5, p. 5; 17, p. 3; 29, p. 21.

October: 1, p. 21; 3, p. 35; 4, p. 13; 6, p. 25; 8, p. 17; 11, p. 17; 12, p. 21; 13, p. 25; 14, p. 25; 15, p. 1; 18, p. 17; 19, p. 21; 20, p. 1; 21, p. 1; 29, p. 17.

November: 1, p. 17; 3, p. 23; 5, p. 15; 8, p. 17; 15, p. 17; 17, p. 25; 19, p. 21; 22, p. 17; 24, p. 17; 26, p. 21.

December: 1, p. 23; 3, p. 21; 6, p. 21; 8, p. 25; 10, p. 25.

A   Over There. *Ladies' Home Journal*, 61 (February, 1944), pp. 20–21.

S   The Pearl of the World. *Woman's Home Companion*, 72 (December, 1945), pp. 17ff. (Subsequently published as *The Pearl*.)

S   "The Time the Wolves Ate the Vice-Principal," *The Magazine of the Year*, 1 (March, 1947), pp. 26–27.

A   The GI's War. . . . *New York Herald Tribune Weekly Book Review*, May 18, 1947, p. 1. A review of *Yank*.

A   Women and Children in the U.S.S.R. *Ladies' Home Journal*, 65 (February, 1948), pp. 44–59.

S   Miracle of Tepayac. *Collier's*, 122 (December 25, 1948), pp. 22–23.

S   His Father. *Reader's Digest*, 55 (September, 1949), pp. 19–21.

A   Critics, Critics Burning Bright. *Saturday Review of Literature*, 33 (November 11, 1950), pp. 20–21.

A   Duel Without Pistols. *Collier's*, 130 (August 23, 1952), pp. 13–15.

A   The Soul and Guts of France. *Collier's*, 130 (August 30, 1952), pp. 26 ff.

A   The Secret Weapon We Were Afraid to Use. *Collier's*, 131 (January 10, 1953), pp. 9–13.

A   I Go Back to Ireland. *Collier's*, 131 (January 31, 1953), pp. 48–50.

A   Making of a New Yorker. *The New York Times Magazine*, February 1, 1953, Part II, pp. 26–27.

A   A Model T Named "It." *Ford Times*, 45 (July, 1953), pp. 34–39.

A   My Short Novels. *Wings*, October, 1953, pp. 1–8.

A   Jalopies I Cursed and Loved. *Holiday*, 16 (July, 1954), pp. 44 ff.

A   How to Fish in French. *Punch*, 22 (August 25, 1954), pp. 248–249.

A   Robert Capa. *Photography*, 35 (September, 1954), pp. 48–53.

A   How to Tell Good Guys from Bad Guys. *The Reporter*, 12 (March 10, 1955), pp. 42–44.

A   The Death of a Racket. *Saturday Review*, 38 (April 2, 1955), p. 26.

A   A Plea to Teachers. *Saturday Review*, 38 (April 30, 1955), p. 24.

A   Some Thoughts on Juvenile Delinquency. *Saturday Review*, 38 (May 28, 1955), p. 22.

A   Always Something to Do in Salinas. *Holiday*, 17 (June, 1955), pp. 58 ff.

A   Critics from a Writer's Point of View. *Saturday Review*, 38 (August 27, 1955), p. 20.

L   A Letter on Criticism. *Colorado Quarterly*, 4 (Autumn, 1955).

A   Random Thoughts on Random Dogs. *Saturday Review*, 38 (October 8, 1955), p. 11.

A   In a Radio Broadcast Beamed. *Saturday Review*, 38 (November 26, 1955), pp. 8–9.

A   More About Aristocracy. *Saturday Review*, 38 (December 10, 1955),
     p. 11.
A   What Is the Real Paris? *Holiday*, 18 (December, 1955), p. 94.
A   Joan in All of Us. *Saturday Review*, 39 (January 14, 1956), p. 17.
A   Yank in Europe. *Holiday*, 19 (January, 1956), p. 25.
A   Miracle Island of Paris. *Holiday*, 19 (February, 1956), p. 43.
S   How Mr. Hogan Robbed a Bank. *Atlantic Monthly*, 197 (March,
     1956), pp. 58–61.
A   Madison Avenue and the Election. *Saturday Review*, 39 (March 31,
     1956), p. 11.
A   Vegetable War. *Saturday Review*, 39 (July 21, 1956), pp. 34–35.
A   Discovering the People of Paris. *Holiday*, 20 (August, 1956), p. 36.
A   Mail I've Seen. *Saturday Review*, 39 (August 4, 1956), p. 16.
A   Trust Your Luck. *Saturday Review*, 40 (January 12, 1957), pp. 42–44.
A   My War with the Ospreys. *Holiday*, 21 (March, 1957), pp. 72–73,
     163–165.

3. MISCELLANEOUS

Letter, in Berton Braley's *Morgan Sails the Caribbean* (New York, 1934),
     giving Mr. Braley permission to use incidents from *Cup of Gold.*
Letter, *Writers Take Sides* ("Letters about the war in Spain"), ed. by Millen
     Brand, Dorothy Brewster, *et al.* Concord, New Hampshire: The League
     of American Writers, 1938. Pp. 56–57.
Their Blood Is Strong. San Francisco: Simon J. Lubin Society of California,
     Inc., 1938. Contains the *San Francisco News* articles on migrant
     labor together with an epilogue. (Pamphlet)
A Letter by John Steinbeck to the Friends of Democracy. Stamford,
     Connecticut: Overbrook Press, September, 1940. "A letter written in
     reply to a request for a statement about his ancestry. Together with
     the letter originally submitted by the Friends of Democracy." (Pam-
     phlet)
The First Watch. Ward Ritchie Press, Christmas, 1947. Steinbeck's hu-
     morous letter of thanks for the gift of a watch. (Pamphlet)
Introduction, *Between Pacific Tides* (rev. ed.) by Edward F. Ricketts and
     Jack Calvin. Stanford: Stanford University Press, 1948.
Un Grand Romancier de Notre Temps. La Nouvelle Revue Française,
     November, 1951 (*Hommage à André Gide 1869–1951*). P. 30.
Introduction, *The World of Li'l Abner* by Al Capp. New York: Farrar,
     Straus and Young, 1953.
A Postscript from Steinbeck. *Steinbeck and His Critics*, ed. by E. W.
     Tedlock, Jr., and C. V. Wicker. Albuquerque: University of New
     Mexico Press, 1957. Pp. 307–309. (Letter)

INDEX

Abnormal: Steinbeck's interest in, 10, 15; Steinbeck's use of, 13, 24, 66–67, 72, 96

Abramson, Ben, 23, 74, 75, 114, 115, 131, 134, 143, 144

Across the River and into the Trees (Hemingway), 292

Acts of the Apostles, 223; excerpt, 42

"Acts of Thomas," apocryphal fragment, 223

Ainsworth, Mrs. E. G., 24

Air Forces Aid Society Trust Fund, 184

An American Exodus: A Record of Human Erosion (Lange and Taylor), 149

American Idealism (Stovall), 11

American thought, and *Grapes of Wrath*, 11, 153–154

Americana, in *Grapes of Wrath*, 165

Anderson, Maxwell, 193

animalism, 6, 7, 8, 17, 18, 49, 62, 89

animals and plants, Steinbeck's interest in, 6, 8, 9, 36, 44, 48, 49, 53–54, 135

Anthony Adverse (Allen), 179

Arabian Nights, 223

Army Air Force, 184

Arnold, General Henry H., 184

Atlantic, 93, 291

Babbitt (Lewis), *Wayward Bus* compared to, 233

Baker, Carlos, 16, 139

Bakersfield, Cal., 144, 168, 171

Ballou, Robert O., 74, 129

"Battle Hymn of the Republic," 148; *Grapes of Wrath* title from, 169

Beach, Joseph Warren, 11, 138

Between Pacific Tides (Ricketts), 180

Bhagavad-Gita, 223

Bible, 23, 41–43, 161, 162, 164, 169, 170, 177, 261–262, 263, 267–269

Big Sur, Cal., 22, 25

biological view, 16, 17, 22, 36, 53, 55, 64, 229, 240, 274, 278–279, 290, 292

"The Birthmark" (Hawthorne), 27

"Black Marigolds," 215, 223; excerpt, 216

Blake, William, 252

Bobbs-Merrill, 113

Book-of-the-Month Club: *Of Mice and Men*, 142; *The Short Reign of Pippin IV*, 288

Boren, Lyle, 151

Bourke-White, Margaret, 149

The Boys in The Back Room (Wilson), 6

Bracher, Frederick, 17, 18

Braley, Berton, 26

Brunn, Robert R., quoted, 274

Bucks County, Pa., 142

Buddhism, references to, 223

bunkhouse talk, 12

Burgum, Edwin B., 14

Burke, Kenneth, 167

Burns, Robert, quoted, 139

Byrne, Don, 51

Cabell, James Branch, 51

Cain and Abel story, in *East of Eden*, 261–262, 267, 268–269, 276

Caldwell, Erskine, 149, 175

California Commonwealth Club, 75

California Institute of Technology, 281

Campbell, Joseph, 291

Candle in the Wind (Anderson), 193

canticles, *Grapes of Wrath* as reference to, 169

Capa, Robert, 248, 250

Capp, Al, 285

Carpenter, Frederick I., 9, 11, 153

Cather, Willa, 51

Catholicism, 49–50, 94, 224

Cavalcade of the American Novel (Wagenknecht), 15

Chamberlain, John, defends *The Moon Is Down*, 187

Champney, Freeman, 8, 14; describes strike, 109–110; on *Tortilla Flat*, 89

Chekhov, Anton, Steinbeck compared with, 95

Chrétien de Troyes, 77

Christ figures: in *Cannery Row*, 213; in *Grapes of Wrath*, 174; in *To a God Unknown*, 46; in *The Wayward Bus*, 243

Classics and Commercials (Wilson), 6

Collier's, 284

Collins, Tom, *Grapes of Wrath* dedicated to, 112

comedy, 231, 276, 278

Comfort, Alex, quoted, 154, 220

Communism, 96–97, 112–114, 121–122, 124–125, 146, 182, 189, 250–251

counterfeit money, as secret weapon, 184

Cousins, Norman, 13, 14; on *Burning Bright*, 253

Covici, Pascal, 74, 75, 126, 146, 148, 179, 198, 208, 223, 251, 259, 262, 263, 268, 277, 290

Covici-Friede, 75, 93, 108, 109, 113, 130

Cowley, Malcolm, 138; on *Cannery Row*, 198

Crime and Punishment (Dostoevski), 23

Cummings, E. E., Steinbeck compared with, 200–201

Curwood, James Oliver, 23

Darkness at Noon (Koestler), 122

Darwinism, 181–182

Death in the Afternoon (Hemingway), 184

de Kruif, Paul, 291

Depression, 3, 10, 155, 294

Deuteronomy, *Grapes of Wrath,* as reference to, 169, 171

De Voto, Bernard: on *Grapes of Wrath,* 176; on *The Wayward Bus,* 232

Dickens, Charles: characters of, compared with those of *In Dubious Battle,* 127; Steinbeck compared with, 15

Divine Comedy (Dante), *The Wayward Bus* parallels, 246

documentary films, 149, 164, 167

Donovan, Colonel William J., 186

Dos Passos, John, compared with Steinbeck, 4, 164, 176

Drama Critics' Circle Award, 143

Eastman, Max, 8

Ecce Homo (Lorentz), 164

"Ecology and Sociology" (Ricketts), 291

Eisinger, Chester E., 11; on *Grapes of Wrath,* 153

Eliot, George, 23

Elsie Venner (Holmes), *East of Eden* and, 268

Emerson, Ralph Waldo, 153

The Enormous Room (Cummings), 200

Esquire, 93

Everyman, 243

Fadiman, Clifton, criticizes *The Moon Is Down,* 186–187

Fairley, Barker, 4, 11

A Farewell to Arms (Hemingway), excerpt, 52

Farm Security Administration, 112

Farrell, James T., 5; and naturalism, 294

Faust theme, in *Cup of Gold,* 27, 28, 31, 33, 34

Fisher King theme, in *To a God Unknown,* 45, 46

folk idiom, 164

Ford Times, Steinbeck articles in, 284

free will: in *East of Eden,* 267; in *Of Mice and Men,* 138

French, Warren G., quoted, 18–19

Fresno, Cal., 112

Frohock, W. M., 12, 20

From Here to Eternity (Jones), acceptance of prostitution, 205

Gabilan Mountains, 21, 22

Gannett, Lewis, 115; on *The Moon Is Down,* 186

Geismar, Maxwell, 8, 10, 11, 14, 15; on *In Dubious Battle,* 19–20

Genesis, 26

Gerould, Gordon Hall, quoted, 5

Gesta Romanorum, 76

Gide, André 95; on *In Dubious Battle,* 113, 117, 118, 127

The Golden Bough (Frazer), 223

Gone With the Wind (Mitchell): discussed, 179; *Grapes of Wrath* outsells, 151

Green Hills of Africa (Hemingway), 183

Gregory, Susan, 73

Grey, Zane, 23

Group-man theory, 53, 97, 105, 106, 118, 119, 120, 121, 126, 129, 133, 190, 286, 291

Gulf of California (Sea of Cortez), 180

Guys and Dolls, 276

Halifax, Lord, 184

Hamilton, Olive, *see* Steinbeck, Olive Hamilton

Hammerstein, Oscar, 277

Hardy, Thomas, 23, 62

Harper's, 93, 291

Harte, Brett, 96

Hawthorne, Nathaniel, 27, 31, 32, 212

Hearst papers, denounce *Grapes of Wrath,* 150

Hemingway, Ernest, 52, 64, 80, 98, 138, 282; Steinbeck compared with, 147–148, 164, 183, 292

Henry, O., *see* Porter, William Sydney

Herald Tribune: on *The Moon Is Down,* 186; Steinbeck a foreign correspondent for, 185

Highway 66, 164–165, 168

Hoffman, Frederick J., 8, 15, 19

Holiday, Steinbeck articles in, 110, 284

Hollywood, 75, 78, 140, 142, 146, 150, 184, 250

Holy Grail quest theme: in *Cup of Gold,* 31; in *Tortilla Flat,* 31, 77–78

Hopkins, Gerard Manley, 103

Hyman, Stanley Edgar, 7, 10, 11; denounces *Grapes of Wrath,* 151

Industrial Valley (McKenney), 149

Isaiah, *Grapes of Wrath* as reference to, 174

Jackson, Joseph Henry, 8, 169; on *East of Eden,* 274

Jefferson, Thomas, 154; agrarianism of, 153

Jeremiah, *Grapes of Wrath* as reference to, 169

Jones, Claude E., 3, 15

Jones, James, 205

Jonson, Ben, 127

Kaufman, George, 142

Kazin, Alfred, quoted, 7, 12, 167

Kennedy, John S., 8, 15, 16, 17

Kidnapped (Stevenson), 23

King City, Cal., 22

Kino, Eusebius, 222

Kronenberger, Louis, 74

Krutch, Joseph Wood, on *East of Eden,* 264, 273, 274

Land of the Free (MacLeish), 149

Lange, Dorothea, 149

language, 12, 81, 91, 110–112, 134, 148, 164, 256, 269–272

La Paz, Mexico, 218, 223

Lawrence, D. H., 6, 95

Lewis, Sinclair, 15, 175, 233

Life, 213; articles on migrants, 146, 150

Li Po, 223

London, Jack, 23

Lorca, Federico García, 253, 257

Lorentz, Pare, 149, 165; influence on Steinbeck, 164

Lubbock, Percy, 155, 165

McIntosh & Otis, 39, 56, 74, 75, 113, 149

McKenney, Ruth, 149

MacLeish, Archibald, 149

Macmillan, 113

Madame Bovary (Flaubert), 23

Magny, Claude-Edmonde, on *East of Eden,* 264

Malraux, André, Steinbeck likened to, 229

Manhattan Transfer (Dos Passos), 176

Mann, Thomas, 142; Steinbeck likened to, 229

marine biology, 53, 55, 119, 208, 209, 215, 280, 282, 295

Marshall, Margaret, feud with Steinbeck, 5

Mathers, E. Powys, 216

Mathiessen, F. O., 185; on *Cannery Row,* 197

Mauldin, William H., Steinbeck compared with, 186

Maupassant, Guy de, 37, 205

migrant camps, 145, 150, 172, 173, 176

"Migrant John," 145

migrant workers, 21, 109, 110, 138, 139, 143, 145, 146, 149, 150, 152, 156, 170–171, 173

Migratory Labor Board, 152

Miller, Henry, 291

Miron, George Thomas, quoted, 150, 151
Mizener, Arthur, on *East of Eden*, 274–275
Monroe, Elizabeth N., 7; quoted, 174
Monterey Bay, 21, 22
Monterey Beacon, 93, 286
Monterey County, 21, 24, 109
"The Moon Is Down" (popular song), 188
Moore, Harry Thornton, 5, 58
Morgan Sails the Caribbean (Braley), 26
Morgenthau, Henry, 184
Morte Darthur (Malory), 23, 24, 77, 78, 79
motion-picture writing, Steinbeck's attitude toward, 250

Nation, 144, 152
naturalism, 7, 8, 16, 17, 54–55, 81–82, 150, 182, 274, 294, 295
Nazis, 186, 187, 193, 195
Nelson, Frank G., defends *The Moon Is Down*, 187
Nevius, Blake, 14
New Republic, on *The Moon Is Down*, 186, 187
"Newsreel" technique, 164
Newsweek, on *The Moon Is Down*, 186
1984 (Orwell), 86
Norris, Frank, 294
North American, 92, 109
"Notes Left Over" (Whitman), 152–153
Numbers (book of), *Grapes of Wrath* as reference to, 169

Occident, 145–146
Odets, Clifford, 133–134, 143
Office of Strategic Services, 186
Oklahoma, denunciation of *Grapes of Wrath*, 150–151
Olav, Hans, on *The Moon Is Down*, 187

Old Testament, *Grapes of Wrath* style compared to, 161, 169; Lorentz's style compared to, 164
O'Neill, Eugene, 253
On Native Grounds (Kazin), 7, 12
Orwell, George, 86

Pacific Biological Laboratories, 213, 292
paisanos, 21, 200, 224, 289; extended treatment of, 69; in *To a God Unknown*, 69; in *Tortilla Flat*, 69, 76, 78, 80, 82, 83, 84, 85, 86, 88, 89, 90, 91, 272, 279
Paradise Lost (Milton), 23, 123
Paramount Studios, 75, 78
The Patterns of English and American Fiction (Gerould), 5
The People, Yes (Sandburg), 164
"phalanx" theory, 5, 118, 122, 291
"The Philosophy of Breaking Through" (Ricketts), 291
Pizarro, Francisco, 182, 188
The Plow That Broke the Plains (Lorentz), 149, 164
Porter, William Sydney, 96
Powell, Lawrence Clark, 4, 145, 179
Prescott, Orville, quoted, 15, 198
primitivism, 8, 14, 18, 81–82, 88–89
prostitution, 37–38, 69–70, 203–207; in *Cup of Gold*, 37, 69; in *The Pastures of Heaven*, 69
Protestantism, 46, 48, 174–175
Punch, 284

"race-memory," 53
Rascoe, Burton, 115
"Rappaccini's Daughter" (Hawthorne), 27
Redman, Ben Ray, 14
Religion, 17–18, 294. *See also* Catholicism, Protestantism
Republic (motion-picture company), 248
The Return of the Native (Hardy), 23
Revelation (book of), 169

Ricketts, Edward, 37, 64, 96, 180, 181, 184, 205, 213, 214, 217, 223, 249, 251, 278–283, 290, 291, 292

Rigveda, quoted, 41, 42

The River (Lorentz), 149; excerpt, 164

Rodgers, Richard, 277

romantic love, 175; in *Sweet Thursday*, 206, 281, 283

Roosevelt, Franklin D., 184

Ross, Woodburn, 8; quoted, 17–18

Russia, 142, 250–251

St. Francis of Assisi, 78, 83, 104

Salinas, Cal., 21, 24, 109, 144

Salinas Index, 249, 262

Salinas River, 21

Salinas Valley, 21, 22, 38, 262; labor problems of, 110

Sandburg, Carl, 164, 170

San Francisco News, 110, 144, 145, 151–153, 154, 171

San Juan de la Cruz, 223, 233, 241, 244, 245

San Luis Obispo, Cal., 21

Santa Lucia Mountains, 21, 22

San Ysidro, Cal., 244

satire, 24, 62, 83, 85, 286

Saturday Evening Post, 93

The Saturday Review, Steinbeck articles in, 129, 284

Schorer, Mark, 81; on *East of Eden*, 264, 265, 273, 274

Schramm, Wilbur L., quoted, 4

Scott, Sir Walter, 23

Scribner's, 93

sentimentality, 12, 13, 14, 15, 108, 142, 176, 198, 264, 284, 292

sex, attitudes toward: in *Burning Bright*, 38, 252, 253; of *Burning Bright* audiences, 253; in *Cannery Row*, 38, 204, 207; in *Cup of Gold*, 37, 38; in *East of Eden*, 38; in "The Flight," 100; in "Johnny Bear," 96; in "The

Other Burgundian," 37–38; in *The Pastures of Heaven*, 38; in *The Short Reign of Pippin IV*, 286

Sex symbolism: in *To a God Unknown*, 51; in *The Wayward Bus*, 234, 236, 238

Shakespeare, William, 34, 127, 206

Shaw, George Bernard, prefaces, 133

Shumlin, Herman, 117

Slochower, Harry, 4, 195, 229

Snell, George D., 15

social consciousness, 3, 4

social criticism, 69, 139, 147, 197, 231

Socialism, 25

Socrates, 192, 196

"The Song of the Pearl," 223

Southern Agrarians, 153

Spellman, Archbishop Francis J., denounces *Grapes of Wrath*, 150

"A Spiritual Morphology of Poetry" (Ricketts), 291

Stage, 132, 133

Stanford Lit., poems and stories in, 24, 92, 286

The Stanford Spectator, stories in, 24, 92, 286

Stanford University, 24, 25, 35; poems written at, 24, 25; short stories written at, 24, 35

Steffens, Lincoln, 289

Steinbeck, John: birthplace, 21, 22; childhood, 22–23; childhood reading, 23; critical reputation, 3–20; decline, 250, 252, 288–289; father, 22, 131; high-school years, 24; influence of Ricketts on, 279; journalism, 284–285, 286, 289–290; mother, 22, 23, 266; national figure, 178; prose styles, 5, 11, 35–36, 38, 51, 82, 98, 116, 117, 122, 160, 162–163, 164, 165, 169, 226, 246, 247, 257, 272, 273, 287, 293, 294; sister, 23–24; Stanford years,

24–25; war and, 185, 187, 199
WRITINGS OF:
"About Ed Ricketts," 204–205, 249, 251, 258, 278, 290
"Adventures in Arcademy: A Journey into the Ridiculous," 24
"Always Something to do in Salinas," 110
"Atropos: Study of a Very Feminine Obituary Editor," 25
"The Bear Flag Restaurant," early title of *Sweet Thursday*, 277
"Big Train Mulligan" (war communiqué), 185
Bombs Away, 184; as Air Force propaganda, 184–185
Burning Bright, 16, 38, 194, 205, 207, 247, 248–260, 261, 275, 281, 282, 286, 290, 292; on Broadway, 252, 253; compared with Blake's poem, 252; language, 256, 269, 270, 272; play novelette, 251, 256, 258; theme of, 252–253, 254; titles, 252
Cannery Row, 13, 14, 16, 21, 38, 74, 104, 197–217, 218, 223, 224, 228, 232, 247, 251, 259, 265, 277, 279, 280, 283, 286, 291–292, 294, 295; as comedy, 232; dedicated to Ed Ricketts, 279, 292; excerpts, 200, 201, 202, 208; humor, 286, 287; interchapters, 208–209, 210–212; as parable, 215, 278; parallels to *Tortilla Flat*, 199–200, 204; structure, 207–208
"The Chrysanthemums," 11, 93, 95, 292
Cup of Gold, 3, 5, 10, 21–38, 51, 52, 53, 56, 69, 71, 92, 109, 154, 188, 190, 206, 232, 273, 292; Darwinian elements, 182; excerpts, 33, 35–36; language, 256; summarized, 26–34; themes, 27, 28, 29, 31, 33, 34
"The Death of a Racket," 285

"Dissonant Symphony," 58
"Dubious Battle in California," 144, 284
"The Ears of Johnny Bear," *see* "Johny Bear"
East of Eden, 8, 9, 21, 22, 38, 41, 42, 206, 247, 248, 249, 258, 260, 261–275, 276, 290; biblical theme, 263; Cain and Abel theme, 261–262, 267, 268–269; characters, 273, 292, 293; excerpt, 271; as family saga, 262–263; language, 269–272; narrator "I," 262, 266–267; titles, 249, 262, 263
"Fingers of Cloud: A Satire on College Protervity," 24
"Flight," 93, 98–100
The Forgotten Village, 81, 182; as book of pictures, 180; excerpt, 167; motion picture, 180, 291; as social protest, 231
"The Gift," in *The Long Valley*, 101, 103
The Grapes of Wrath, 3, 5, 7, 10, 11, 12, 13, 15, 18, 19, 20, 21, 25, 53, 74, 81, 107, 110, 112, 115, 135, 143, 144–177, 178, 182, 183, 184, 188, 190, 194, 196, 199, 206, 207, 228, 229, 249, 259, 265, 279, 287, 289, 291, 294, 295; as American epic, 294; banned and denounced, 150–151; characters, 167–168, 194; excerpts, 160–161, 162, 163, 164, 176–177; facts attacked, 149–150; humor, 287; interchapters, 155–158, 160, 162, 165, 166, 169, 172, 173, 176; language, 271; language problem, 148; last scene, 33, 176; motion picture, 150; outline, 168, 171, 172; as social protest, 147, 231; themes, 171–175, 176, 177; variant titles, 147

Steinbeck, John (*cont.*)
  "The Great Mountains," 101, 102, 222
  "The Green Lady," early version of *To a God Unknown*, 39
  "The Harness," 93, 94
  "The Harvest Gypsies" series, 110, 144, 145, 151–152, 154, 171, 284
  "His Father," 249, 251
  "How to Fish in French," 284, 286
  "How to Tell Good Guys from Bad Guys," 285
  "If Eddie Guest Had Written the Book of Job: HAPPY BIRTHDAY," 24
  "If John A. Weaver Had Written Keats' Sonnet in the American language: ON LOOKING AT A NEW BOOK BY HAROLD BELL WRIGHT," 24–25
  In Dubious Battle, 3, 5, 6, 7, 10, 13, 14, 15, 16, 19, 20, 21, 25, 53, 78, 81, 93, 96, 108–129, 130, 131, 133, 134, 135, 139, 146, 147, 148, 154, 160, 166, 176, 182, 183, 188, 190, 194, 196, 199, 205, 206, 228, 229, 246, 249, 278, 289, 293, 294; character depiction, 126–128, 194; dedicated to Tom Collins, 112; excerpts, 111, 120; individual vs. group-man, 129; language, 110–112; as social protest, 231; as strike novel, 108–109, 123–126, 128
  "In the Forests of the Night," early title of *Burning Bright*, 252
  "Jalopies I Cursed and Loved," 284
  "Johnny Bear," 93, 95, 96, 206
  "A Lady in Infra-Red," 26
  L'Affaire Lettuceberg, first title of *Grapes of Wrath*, 147; letter retracting, 147, 151
  "The Leader of the People," 93,
    97, 100, 104, 105–107, 118, 131, 170, 182, 190
  The Log from the Sea of Cortez, 205, 213, 249, 251, 290; excerpt, 189
  The Long Valley, 6, 7, 21, 92–107, 116, 175, 271, 274, 275; excerpt, 98–99; psychological portraits, 95–96; rural life, 232
  "Madison Avenue and the Election," 285
  "Mail I've Seen," 284
  "A Medal for Benny" (motion picture), 90
  "The Miracle of Tepayac," 249, 251
  "A Model T Named 'It'," 284
  The Moon Is Down, 8, 10, 13, 115, 119, 186–196, 228, 252, 279; characters, 191–195; excerpts, 192, 194; play novelette, 186, 196, 256; play version, 188, 196; screen version, 186; Steinbeck decorated for, 187
  "The Murder," 92, 93, 94
  "My War with the Ospreys," 284
  "Nothing So Monstrous," 68
  Of Mice and Men, 3, 4, 5, 7, 10, 12, 13, 15, 21, 81, 93, 110, 117, 130–143, 144, 146, 153, 154, 159, 178, 179, 190, 191, 193, 194, 196, 199, 206, 252, 255, 271, 274, 279; best seller, 142; Book-of-the-Month Club selection, 142; Broadway première, 132; characters, 191, 194; Drama Critics' Circle Award, 143; language, 134; motifs in, 134–137, 138; as play, 130, 133, 143; play novelette, 132–133, 191, 196, 256; relation to Burns's poem, 139; as social protest, 139, 231; theme of, 134
  "The Other Burgundian," 37, 69
  "The Palace Flophouse," early title of *Sweet Thursday*, 277

The Pastures of Heaven, 5, 10, 14, 21, 22, 23, 38, 39, 40, 56–71, 72, 73, 74, 75, 92, 94, 108, 109, 154, 199, 206, 210, 265, 281, 294; language, 272; rural life in, 232; summarized, 60–71; women in, 207

The Pearl, 8, 14, 15, 16, 104, 135, 194, 218–230, 232, 247, 279, 294; book form, 218, 231; characters, 194; excerpts, 222, 225, 226, 227; language, 271, 272; as motion picture, 218, 250; novelette, 220; as parable, 220, 225; rural life in, 232; story form, 218; summarized, 219–220, 221, 224; titles, 218

"The Pearl of La Paz," early title of *The Pearl*, 218, 231

"The Pearl of the World," early title of *The Pearl*, 218; outline, 219–220

Pipe Dream, musical adaptation of *Sweet Thursday*, 277

The Portable Steinbeck, 185

"The Promise," in *The Long Valley*, 101, 103; in *The Red Pony*, 93

"The Raid," 92, 96, 97, 109, 206

"Random Thoughts on Random Days," 284

The Red Pony, 15, 21, 22, 23, 63, 74, 92, 93, 100, 101, 102, 103, 105, 131, 274, 275, 294; motion-picture script, 248; rural life in, 232

A Russian Journal, 182, 248, 250–251

"Saint Katy the Virgin," 93, 94, 287

"Salinas Valley," early title of *East of Eden*, 249, 262, 263, 274

Sea of Cortez, 17, 53, 55, 103, 118, 140, 180–184, 186, 188, 190, 199, 200–201, 205, 218, 223, 229, 250, 259, 278, 290; excerpts, 103–104, 115, 119, 120–121, 126, 179–180, 191

The Short Novels of John Steinbeck, 258

The Short Reign of Pippin IV, 19, 206, 285–288, 290; Book-of-the-Month Club selection, 288; characters, 287–288; humor in, 288; novelette, 285; subtitle, 285, 286

"The Snake," 92–93, 95–96, 278

"Something That Happened," first title for *Of Mice and Men*, 140

Sweet Thursday, 9, 19, 21, 74, 205, 206, 251, 276–284, 286, 290, 292; characters, 277, 283, 286; excerpt, 281; humor in, 288; interchapters, 278; as musical comedy, 276, 277, 278, 281, 282, 283; as parable, 278; as novel, 281; romantic love in, 206, 281, 283; sequel to *Cannery Row*, 277; titles, 277

"Tiger, Tiger," early title for *Burning Bright*, 252

"The Time the Wolves Ate the Vice-Principal," 212

To a God Unknown, 4, 11, 22, 25, 39–55, 69, 71, 72, 75, 95, 109, 135, 153, 154, 160, 223, 231, 259, 279, 283, 295; excerpt, 52, 54; summarized, 43–51; women in, 207

Tortilla Flat, 4, 7, 8, 11, 13, 69, 72–91, 92, 105, 113, 131, 154, 160, 179, 196, 198, 199, 202, 204, 206, 224, 265, 277, 279, 286, 287, 293–294, 295; banned and denounced, 75; best seller, 75; as comedy, 232; comic spirit of, 90, 91, 108, 109; compared with *Morte Darthur*, 76–78, 79; excerpts, 80, 86, 87–88; gold medal winner, 75; humor, 83, 91, 288; interchapters, function of, 208–209; language, 81, 91, 272; mock-epic tone, 79, 80,

Steinbeck, John (*cont.*)
279; Modern Library edition, 73, 81; as parable, 278; scheme of, 76–77; short stories, 72, 74; sold to Hollywood, 75, 78; tragicomic theme, 79, 91
"Trust Your Luck," 284
"Vegetable War," 284, 286
"Vigilante," 96, 97, 292
Viva Zapata (motion picture), 248, 249, 250, 258
The Wayward Bus, 4, 8, 14, 16, 21, 135, 206, 223, 231–247, 253, 261, 275, 279, 282, 288, 291, 294; affirmations, 247, 248, 259; as allegory, 233, 240, 244, 245; characters, 233–241, 246; epigraph, 243; excerpt, 246; humor of, 287; language, 271; summarized, 233–245
"The White Quail," 92, 95, 292
"Yank in Europe," 284, 285
Also *see* 310–314
WRITINGS ON:
American Fiction, 1920–1940 (Beach), chapters on Steinbeck, 11
"Bankrupt Realism" (Cousins), 14
"The Californians: Storm and Steinbeck" (Wilson), 6
"The Case of John Steinbeck" (Redman), 14
Fifty Years of the American Novel (Kennedy), 8, 15
Grapes of Gladness: California's Refreshing and Inspiring Answer to John Steinbeck's "Grapes of Wrath," 149
"*In Dubious Battle* Revalued" (Baker), 16
In My Opinion (Prescott), 15
"Jeffersonian Agrarianism in *The Grapes of Wrath*" (Eisinger), 11
"John Steinbeck: American Dreamer" (Carpenter), 9
"John Steinbeck and the Coming Literature" (Fairley), 11
"John Steinbeck: Earth and Stars" (Ross), 8
"John Steinbeck: Journeyman Artist" (Beach), 11
"John Steinbeck: Life Affirmed and Dissolved" (Kennedy), 15–16
"John Steinbeck: Naturalism's Priest" (Ross), 17
"John Steinbeck's Men of Wrath" (Frohock), 12
The Modern Novel in America (Hoffman), 8, 15
The Novel and Society (Monroe), 7
The Novel and the World's Dilemma (Burgum), 14
The Novels of John Steinbeck (H. T. Moore), 5
"The Philosophical Joads" (Carpenter), 11 .
The Shape of American Fiction (Snell), 15
"Steinbeck against Steinbeck" (Nevius), 14
"Steinbeck and the Biological View of Man" (Bracher), 17
Steinbeck and His Critics (Tedlock and Wicker), 265
"Steinbeck at the Top of His Form" (Baker), 16
"Steinbeck of California" (Baker), 16
"Steinbeck: One Aspect" (Nevius), 14
The Truth About John Steinbeck and the Migrants, 150, 151
"Who Are the Real People?" (Cousins), 13
Steinbeck, John Ernst, Sr., 22, 131
Steinbeck, Olive Hamilton, 22, 266
sterility: as theme of *Burning Bright,* 252, 257; in *Yerma,* 253, 257

Stevenson, Robert Louis, 23, 68

Stovall, Floyd, 11

Strange Interlude (O'Neill), *Burning Bright* compared with, 253

"A Study of Genius" (Ricketts), 291

The Sun Also Rises (Hemingway), 98

Swift, Jonathan, 247

Swope, John, 184

symbolism: in college stories, 24; in *Cup of Gold*, 5, 22, 28, 29, 30, 31, 33, 35; of Doc, 278–279; in *East of Eden*, 42, 262; in "Flight," 99, 100; in *Grapes of Wrath*, 19, 158–159, 166, 167, 168, 169, 170, 173, 175, 176; in *The Long Valley*, 95, 99, 100, 102, 106, 107; in *Of Mice and Men*, 134–135, 136, 137, 138, 159, 294; in *The Pearl*, 221, 222, 225, 226; in *The Red Pony*, 22; in *Sweet Thursday*, 278, 282, 292, 294; in *To a God Unknown*, 4, 44, 46, 51, 53, 294; in *Tortilla Flat*, 79; in *The Wayward Bus*, 242–243

"A Systematic Study of Sex" (Ricketts), 291

Taylor, Paul S., 149

"Technique as Discovery (Schorer), 81

Thackeray, William Makepeace, 51

These Are Our Lives (WPA), 149

"Thesis and Materials for a Script on Mexico, which shall be motivated oppositely to John's *Forgotten Village*" (Ricketts), 291

Thurber, James, attacks *The Moon Is Down*, 186, 187, 192

Time, 263–264

timshel, interpretation, 42, 262

Tolstoy, Leo, 118, 154, 155

Traubel, Helen, in *Pipe Dream*, 277

Travels with a Donkey (Stevenson), 23

Treasure Island (Stevenson), 23

Twentieth-Century Fox, 248, 249

Uncle Tom's Cabin, reaction to, compared with reaction to *Grapes of Wrath*, 151

"The Undefeated" (Hemingway), 98

U.S.A. (Dos Passos), 176

Vedic hymns, 41, 42, 50, 223

La Vida del San Bartolomeo, 223

Viking Press, 262; published *Grapes of Wrath*, 148

Vinaver, Eugène, 78

violence, 12, 63–64; comment on, 125; in nature, 54; Steinbeck's use of, 62, 63, 64, 95, 97, 101, 103, 116, 117, 210

Virgin of Guadalupe, 243, 247, 251

Virginibus Puerisque (Stevenson), excerpt, 68

"A Voyage to Brobdingnag" (Swift), *The Wayward Bus* compared with, 247

Waiting for Lefty (Odets), 133, 196

War, Steinbeck and, 120–121, 179–180, 183–186, 188–189, 199

War and Peace (Tolstoy), 118, 154–155

The Wasteland (Eliot), 46

Webster, Harvey C., quoted, 8–9, 274

Weeks, Donald, 14

Whicher, George F., quoted, 167

Whipple, T. K., 5; quoted, 101

Whitman, Walt: influence on Steinbeck, 164; on migrant labor, 152–153

Wilson, Edmund, 6, 7, 8, 9, 15, 20, 274; on *Cannery Row*, 198, 288; on *Tortilla Flat*, 89, 198, 288

Woman's Home Companion, 218

women in Steinbeck's work, 206–207

Woollcott, Alexander, 178

The World of Li'l Abner (Capp), 285

WPA case histories, 149

Yerma (Lorca): *Burning Bright* compared with, 253, 257; sterility theme, 253, 257

You Have Seen Their Faces (Caldwell and Bourke-White), 149

Zanuck, Darryl, 150
Zapata, Emilio, 249–250